KYOTO CSEAS SERIES ON ASIAN STUDIES 6
Center for Southeast Asian Studies, Kyoto University

INDUSTRIALIZATION WITH A WEAK STATE

T0351356

KYOTO CSEAS SERIES ON ASIAN STUDIES 6
Center for Southeast Asian Studies, Kyoto University

INDUSTRIALIZATION WITH A WEAK STATE

Thailand's Development in Historical Perspective

SOMBOON SIRIPRACHAI

Edited by

Kaoru Sugihara, Pasuk Phongpaichit, and Chris Baker

NUS PRESS

Singapore

in association with

KYOTO UNIVERSITY PRESS

Japan

The publication of this volume was funded by the Center's International Program of Collaborative Research.

NUS Press
National University of Singapore
AS3-01-02, 3 Arts Link
Singapore 117569
www.nus.edu.sg/nuspress

ISBN 978-9971-69-651-1 (Paper)

Kyoto University Press
Yoshida-South Campus, Kyoto University
69 Yoshida-Konoe-Cho, Sakyo-ku
Kyoto 606-8315
Japan
www.kyoto-up.or.jp

ISBN 978-4-87698-355-1 (Paper)

National Library Board, Singapore Cataloguing-in-Publication Data

Sombūn Siriprachai.
    Industrialization with a weak state: Thailand's development in historical perspective / Somboon Siriprachai; edited by Kaoru Sugihara, Pasuk Phongpaichit, and Chris Baker. – Singapore: NUS Press in association with Kyoto University Press, c2012.
    p. cm. – (Kyoto CSEAS series on Asian studies; 6)
    Includes bibliographical references and index.
    ISBN: 978-9971-69-651-1 (pbk.)

    1. Industrialization – Thailand – History. 2. Industrial policy – Thailand – History. 3. Rent seeking – Thailand – History. 4. Income distribution – Thailand – History. I. Sugihara, Kaoru. II. Pasuk Phongpaichit. III. Baker, Christopher John, 1948–. IV. Title. V. Series: Kyoto CSEAS series on Asian studies; 6.

HC445
338.9593 — dc23   OCN785810774

Printed by: Mainland Press Pte Ltd

CONTENTS

List of Tables   vii

List of Abbreviations   ix

Preface   xi

Introduction: An Appreciation of the Work of Somboon Siriprachai   1

1.   Problems in the Industrialization Process in Thailand   11

2.   Export-oriented Industrialization Strategy with Land Abundance: Some of Thailand's Shortcomings   22

3.   Population Growth, Fertility Decline, Poverty, and Deforestation in Thailand, 1850–1990   52

4.   Inconsistencies and Inequities in Thai Industrialization   70

5.   Mercantilism: Is it a Doctrine or an Economic Policy? Application to the East Asian NIEs   92

6.   Development Economics, Rent Seeking, and the East Asian Miracle   105

7.   Growth, Technological Inertia, and a Weak State   134

Original Publication Details   157

About the Author   158

Bibliography   160

Index   180

LIST OF TABLES

3.1   Total Population, Chinese, and Density (present territory)   54

3.2   Population, Annual Growth Rates, and Density, 1911–86   55

3.3   Trend of Total Fertility Rate   57

3.4   Source–Destination of Migration, 1965–70, 1975–80   65

7.1   Changes of Government, 1932–2001   135

7.2   House of Representatives, February 2005 Elections   136

7.3   Rates of Growth of GDP and GDP per capita, 1951–2003   138

7.4   Main Economic Indicators, 1950–99   138

7.5   Growth Accounting   139

7.6   Sources of Growth by Sectors, 1981–95   140

7.7   Sectoral Growth and Shares   142

7.8   Deficit in Non-budgetary Balance   144

7.9   Labour Force, 2000–4   150

7.10 Poverty Incidence, 1962–2002   152

7.11 Income Distribution, 1975/76–2004   153

7.12 Human Development Index and Human Poverty Index,
       1990, 1999, and 2003   154

LIST OF ABBREVIATIONS

AFTA	ASEAN Free Trade Area
ASEAN	Association of Southeast Asian Nations
BOI	Board of Investment
EOI	export-oriented industrialization
ERP	effective rate of protection
GATT	General Agreement on Tariffs and Trade
GDP	gross domestic product
GNP	gross national product
HYV	high-yielding variety
IMF	International Monetary Fund
ISI	import substitution industrialization
MP	Member of Parliament
NAIC	Newly Agro-Industrialized Country
NESDB	National Economic and Social Development Board
NIE	Newly industrializing economy
OPEC	Organization of Petroleum Exporting Countries
R&D	research and development
SAL	structural adjustment loan
TDRI	Thailand Development Research Institute
TFP	total factor productivity
TRT	Thai Rak Thai (Thai loves Thai) party
UNESCO	United Nations Educational, Scientific and Cultural Organization
UNIDO	United Nations Industrial Development Organization
USAID	United States Agency for International Development
WHO	World Health Organization

PREFACE

The modern economic history of Southeast Asia is surprisingly under-researched, particularly the important phase of industrialization over the past half century. This industrialization differs from the experience of Japan and other East Asian economies, and from the more recent case of China, but why and how is not so clear.

In 2006 I began a three-year project on "The Asian International Economic Order: Past, Present and Future" within the framework of the JSPS-NRCT Core University Project headed by Kyoto University and Thammasat University. I asked Somboon Siriprachai to act as my counterpart. He readily accepted my request, but was unable to join the project as much as he had wished, as he was quite busy with his teaching and other projects. However, we met several times during conferences in Bangkok, and discussed the possible contribution he could make to the project.

I had read his articles published in English and greatly appreciated his clear, intricate, and passionate account of Thailand's experience with industrialization. The articles were particularly relevant to the theme of labour-intensive industrialization in Southeast Asia, one of the main foci of the project. I urged him to publish a book of these articles as part of our project. At first he hesitated. Clearly he was primarily interested in communicating his message to a Thai audience; he had published over 30 academic articles and reports in Thai, and was for a long time the enthusiastic editor of the *Thammasat Economic Journal*. However, he had also been thinking of an English-language collection, and he eventually agreed with my suggestion. In 2007, I sent a book proposal to Paul Kratoska, managing director of NUS Press, who agreed to publish the book after the usual peer review.

There was a series of mail exchanges about the contents of the book in 2007 and 2008, but the outline remained unchanged. On 21–22 December 2008, Somboon attended a workshop on labour-intensive industrialization in South and Southeast Asia, held at the Center for Southeast Asian Studies, Kyoto University, and made a presentation on "Industrialization and Inequality in Thailand", one of the key chapters of this book. On 24 December, we met in my office for about an hour to discuss the publication. Somboon was happy with it, and showed no sign of physical distress.

Somboon Siriprachai died suddenly on 25 December 2008 during the bus journey from his hotel in Kyoto to Kansai International Airport. The cause of his death was diagnosed as ischemic heart disease.

With the help of Dr Patamawadee Pochanukul Suzuki, Dean of the Faculty of Economics, Thammasat University, and Professor Pasuk Phongpaichit, I visited Thammasat on 11 February 2009 to meet Khun Sompit Siriprachai, Somboon's wife, and asked her to allow me to proceed with the publication, with the help of Professor Pasuk Phongpaichit and Dr Chris Baker. She duly accepted my request.

The Publication Committee of the Center for Southeast Asian Studies, Kyoto University agreed to take on the negotiation with Kyoto University Press and NUS Press. We are grateful to the Center's International Program of Collaborative Research for a publication grant.

Although most of the articles have been published earlier, they have been completely re-edited with the aim of making them clearer and more readable, while taking great care not to alter the content, argument, or conclusions. Chapter 6 is compiled from two original articles, one of which was a shorter and slightly amended version of the other. We are grateful to the original publishers, as shown on p. 157, for permission to reproduce the articles. We would like to thank Khun Sompit Siriprachai and Dr Patamawadee Pochanukul Suzuki for their help in locating the original drafts. Chris Baker took on the editorial work, while Pasuk Phongpaichit contributed an introduction with an appreciation of Somboon's work.

In the notes to the original articles, Somboon repeatedly acknowledged the help and support he received from his doctoral supervisor, Professor Christer Gunnarsson, at the University of Lund. He also thanks Johannes D. Schmidt, Benny Carlson, and Jaya Reddy.

The editorial group would like to thank Professor Yoko Hayami and Dr Porphant Ouyyanont for their support throughout the preparation of the articles for publication.

It has taken us too long to complete this project, but I am very pleased that Somboon's work now appears as a joint publication of Kyoto University Press and NUS Press.

Kaoru Sugihara
Kyoto, February 2012

INTRODUCTION

An Appreciation of the Work of Somboon Siriprachai

Books in English on recent Thai economic development are hard to come by, especially those that subject the country's industrialization to critical scrutiny; compare Thailand's experience to other Asian countries; highlight the problems of rising inequality, persistent rent seeking, and destruction of the environment; and relate all these to a worldwide debate on the practice of economics as a craft. Somboon Siriprachai's collected essays are a valuable contribution not only to Thai studies but also to the debates on economic development of late-comer countries in general, and particularly the role of the state in that process.

Out of the wide range of issues in this collection, I want to highlight three themes: industrial policy, rent seeking, and income inequality. These issues are as relevant today as they were when Somboon began writing about them with such passion some two decades ago. Indeed, the prolonged crisis in the western economies has refocused attention on the need for governments to rebalance the economy away from export-led growth, and this has brought the issue of industrial policy back to centre stage. At the same time, the evidence of pervasive deterioration of income inequality across the world in the neo-liberal era has put policies about income distribution back on the agenda, especially in the context of social turmoil and political revolt in so many parts of the world.

The State and Industrial Policy

Recently economists have concluded that Thailand is stuck in a "middle income trap". The country qualified for the World Bank's classification as "middle income" since 1987, but has failed to graduate to the next stage and is now one of the longest occupants of this category. It is being overtaken from below by later-comers which still have cheaper labour, while it has failed to accumulate the technology and skills to compete against the already advanced economies.

Somboon attributes this failure to the lack of any concerted strategy or effective implementation in economic policy making. In the 1950s and 1960s, the government adopted some of the import-substitution policies of the era, namely differentiated tariffs and other import restrictions. In the early 1980s, it went for a "Big Push" based on new supplies of natural gas. In the mid-1980s, it promoted export industries through tax concessions and other favours. But Somboon notes that none of these policies succeeded in achieving the real meaning of industrialization, namely the accumulation of technological capability and industrial skills.

In part, this was because policy makers were not really intent on achieving industrialization but had other goals in mind. The tariff policies of the early phase, for instance, were designed more for raising government revenue than for nurturing industrial development. At no stage did Thai policy makers emphasize policies to acquire technology, develop specific sectors through inter-firm and sectoral linkages, or promote R&D. Only later did government increase its investment in secondary education. Never did it punish a firm that was granted promotional privileges but failed to perform. All this stands in contrast to the pursuit of industrial policies by the more successful industrializers of Asia — Japan, and in particular South Korea and Taiwan.

Somboon totally rejects the view that the success of the latter lies "in any general superiority of export-oriented industrialization strategy over import substitution, or of market-oriented policies over state intervention.... Rather, it lies in the competence of the state to direct the accumulation process within the particular historical context and international economic environment."

He agrees with Laurids Lauridsen (1991) that the four basic characteristics of a developmental state are "stable rule by political and bureaucratic elites; cooperation between public and private sectors under the overall guidance of a pilot planning agency; heavy and continuous investment in education and other policies to ensure equitable distribution of wealth; and an understanding of the need to use and respect methods of intervention based on the price mechanism". He rejects the view that the Southeast Asian states of Indonesia, Malaysia, and Thailand deserve the title of "developmental" just because they have mixed market economies, outward-looking orientation, effective macro economic policies, and efficient infrastructure. Somboon is clear that in the modern, highly competitive world economy, countries can only industrialize successfully if their governments have a correct strategy and pursue it effectively.

Moreover, he points out that the same conditions were true of momentous changes in national economies in the past. He argues that the role of today's developmental states in fostering industrialization is not so different from the way that mercantilist states converted agrarian societies into trading and industrial powers in Europe in the sixteenth and seventeenth centuries. He cuts through the historians' debates on the nature of mercantilism by pointing out that "Mercantilism was a very simple and coherent national economic policy under which the state promoted private production and foreign trade to achieve prosperity and power of the nation-state." Mercantilists were nationalists. They used the machinery of state, including law and regulation, to promote private businesses which achieved what they felt were the proper aims of national policy. Access to enterprise was confined to individuals or groups of merchants who had political connections and who were able to repay the government for the privilege of running a legal business. In other words, mercantilist states used selective policies to pursue their economic goals.

Late-comers in industrialization have followed a similar course. The government in Germany in the nineteenth century protected its infant industries from foreign competition as part of its industrialization efforts. In Japan, from the Meiji era onwards, and in South Korea and Taiwan from the mid-twentieth century, governments used selective policies to nurture their enterprises so that their economies could catch up with the developed industrial economies of the West. Korea and Taiwan in particular began with protectionism, and then moved on to promoting exports through subsidies, domestic content legislation, allocation of credit to selected industries, heavy investment in human capital, skill upgrading, and control on foreign investment to ensure that foreign firms contributed to technological transfer.

Why were the East Asian developmental states able to achieve industrialization so quickly while most other countries in the developing world have lagged behind? This is the question Somboon returns to throughout this book. He presents a clear answer, though it is not a simple one, and Somboon himself suggests it is far from complete. First of all, he warns against seeking any single, universal explanation such as the power of the free market, the importance of getting prices right, or the role of Confucian culture. Instead, he urges us to look at the specifics of each case in its context of time and place, and to allow for multiple factors contributing to the result. In the case of the East Asian developmental sectors, he suggests that at least four factors were of importance.

First, these societies underwent land reform and agricultural modernization before seeking industrialization. In Japan, land reform took place in two stages, first in 1873 and again after the Second World War. Japan in turn replicated the first stage in Korea and Taiwan. Land reform was crucial in many ways. It created an internal market with a demand for the products of industrialization. It removed feudal elites that typically demand privileged treatment. It lessened economic inequality and so contributed to social cohesion.

Second, these states faced external threats (colonial powers, communist neighbours) which created a nationalist desire to seek economic growth and national strength, even at the cost of short-term sacrifices.

Third, these states achieved a degree of independence from lobbying by vested interest groups.

Fourth, they launched into industrialization in periods when the world economy was growing strongly, and when the lead country welcomed the success of other countries. From the Meiji era, Britain welcomed Japan's industrialization in the hope of gaining additional markets for its own financial and service sectors. During the Cold War, the U.S. was keen to see other countries prospering under a capitalist system.

Of course, it is not simple for other countries to replicate this experience. In particular, many of the techniques that the East Asian developmental states used to accelerate industrialization have since been outlawed under World Trade Organization (WTO) rules and other international arrangements. For much of the past generation, the prevailing orthodoxy of economic development has tended to decry the kind of interventionism that Somboon perceives as key to late-comer industrialization. But perhaps now there is a new window of opportunity. The economic turmoil in the western economies, and the political turmoil in many other parts of the world, has taken the shine away from the neo-liberal orthodoxy. There are now many economists contributing to international debate who have advocated a new look at interventionist industrial policy. This can be seen, for example in the works of Dani Rodrik (2004, 2010), Ha-Joon Chang (2002), Yilmaz Akyüz (2005), Jomo Sundaram (2003), Richard Doner (2009) and Irfan ul Haque (2007). Perhaps the spearhead is represented by the work of Joseph Stiglitz's think tank, the Initiatives for Policy Dialogue, which has established an Industrial Policy Task Force to promote dialogue on policies to further industrialization.

The crux of the matter is that productivity growth in industrial enterprises is still the key to determine a country's living standard and its ability to compete in the world market. Somboon's work highlights the need for Thailand and other developing countries to refocus on industrial policy. Of course, many such policies are blocked by WTO rules, and this will take time to change. But there are still many other measures which are compatible with WTO rules. For example, there is scope for government investment projects to encourage technological upgrading and linkage formation. There is a need for appropriate institutional support for skill development, better institutions to assist government in regulating foreign investment, and, as Ajit Singh (2002) has advocated, better regulations to prevent unfair competition from large multinational corporations.

Rent Seeking

A strong state alone is not enough to ensure strategic and effective policy making. Some mechanisms are also needed to keep the state relatively honest. The discretionary power that can channel resources towards industrialization can also be used to channel resources into private pockets. As Somboon notes, it is possible to picture many of the mercantilist states as systematically corrupt. Similarly today, in many states of Latin America and Southeast Asia, including Thailand, the discretionary powers allotted to policy makers seem to have been used more for private than public ends. And yet in East Asian states, while rent seeking was not absent, the socially positive uses of discretionary power seem to have outweighed the socially damaging ones. What made the difference?

Neo-classical economists, or the so-called Washington Consensus, argued that the shift from import substitution towards export orientation in East Asian economies was the critical factor because it exposed the businessmen and policy makers to signals from the world market. By contrast, in Latin America, Thailand, and many African countries, the governments clung to a protective import-substitution strategy for too long, allowing local elites to perfect the art of extracting rents from their privileged position and reinvesting them in obstructing any policy change. Somboon doubts whether this explanation is adequate. The switch to export orientation failed to eliminate rent seeking in Thailand, or even in East Asian states. Somboon also finds the theory that weak states in Latin America and Southeast Asia practised rent seeking in order to raise the funds for buying political support simply a circular and tautological argument. He urges us to focus not on why the social costs of rent seeking in certain countries are so high as to be damaging, but rather on why the social benefits of a strong state in certain other countries are so high that they outweigh the costs.

He again cautions against sweeping general arguments and urges us to look at the historical and contextual influences that shaped the institutional framework in each case. In a nutshell, he argues that the process of industrialization in East Asia brought about institutional changes which not only helped to minimise rent-seeking activities but shaped the state as a social guardian. Again he points to the importance of land reform and agricultural modernization as precursors to industrialization. These policies reduced the roles of the landlords, the most important rentier class, and thereby increased the chance of the state being relatively independent. They also raised rural incomes and boosted wage levels, creating a much more egalitarian society. While land reform may not be so practical or appropriate today, Somboon's point about the importance of reducing the influence of rentier interests still holds. Today, taxation on wealth may be a better route to achieve this end.

As much recent work on inequality has shown, in societies with less social and economic division, people have a stronger sense of belonging and participation, and a much lower tolerance of socially damaging behaviour such as rent seeking. As Somboon shows for Thailand, rent seeking continues at high levels in part because very few people are punished, either by legal process or by social condemnation. The same is not true of East Asian states.

Somboon suggests that greater equality in income distribution was a factor contributing to the difference in levels and consequences of rent seeking between East Asia and other regions. While there is no real theoretical basis to support the claim that better income distribution will always lead to less rent seeking, the argument deserves attention.

Industrialization and Income Distribution

In that case, what lies behind the different degrees of inequality in countries which are pursuing similar strategies? The developmental states of East Asia achieved industrialization along with improved standards of living of both agricultural and urban population. By contrast, Thailand has ostensibly applied policies for industrialization for over half a century, and for most of that time income distribution has tended to worsen.

Wages, living conditions, and social protection have remained poor. The labour skills and technological capability in Thailand are nowhere near as impressive as in South Korea or Taiwan. The rural economy has stagnated and the rural population has increasingly survived on remittances from family members working in the urban economy and overseas.

Somboon argues that Thai industrialization happened in the context of a land abundant economy. This differed greatly from the East Asian cases where the shortage of arable land acted as a constraint that forced the state to be more focused in its pursuit of industrialization. By contrast, for much of the era that Thailand was ostensibly pursuing import-substitution industrialization, growth in the economy was coming from extensive agricultural expansion and increased exports of primary products. The Thai elites, including the bureaucracy that evolved from the old feudal nobility, the military, and emerging Sino-Thai business families, could extract profits from this economy without forcing a more dramatic economic transformation with unknown political consequences. Key to this state of affairs was the fact that the cultivated area continued to expand until the 1980s. The semi-disguised costs of this trajectory lay in the destruction of forests and the suppressed incomes of the rural population. The US tutelage of Thailand in this era was another important factor as it provided financial subsidies, conferred international legitimacy, and helped to repress political discontent.

It is not as if Thai policy makers were unaware of the importance of land reform and agricultural modernization. Indeed, these matters have been repeatedly discussed for over a century. Prince Dilok Nabarath raised them in one of the first treatises on the Thai economy almost exactly a century ago. Pridi Banomyong made them central to his Economic Plan of 1932. Farmers groups agitated over these issues in the early 1970s and again in the 1990s. Somboon argues that these issues have been consistently ignored because the state could always rely on farmers surviving by cutting down more trees to create more farm land, even during the era of rapid population growth from the 1950s to the 1970s. Only when the agricultural frontier reached some kind of limit in the 1980s did this policy face a crisis. But by then the Thai state had discovered another apparently easy solution — foreign investment.

When the second stage of industrialization based on exports of manufacturing and tourism took place from the mid-1970s onwards, the share of agricultural output in GDP declined very rapidly. This export-oriented industrialization was largely based on unskilled and semi-skilled labour, using low and medium technology, with any high technology acquired through foreign investment and foreign technicians. The value-added accruing to the local economy was a rather small proportion because Thailand was at the tail-end of global production chains, and because Thailand had failed to invest adequately in education and skill acquisition. Thus the labour share in GDP was low and the expansion of manufacturing employment was never large enough to absorb the labour leaking away from the stagnant agrarian economy.

The urban economy and industrial sector were built with the surplus from extensive agriculture. But the industrialization process never had any real depth as it was based first on simple agri-processing, and later on foreign investment using imported technologies. While foreign direct investment has been very important to Thai industrialization, the Thai government has done little institutionally to make sure that multinational companies contribute substantially to technological development. As Richard Doner (2010) has recently noted, "Thailand's 'high-tech' exports are a misleading indicator of technological capacity; the country remains an assembler, rather than a manufacturer or designer."

So despite impressive rates of GDP growth for half a century, Thailand has failed to achieve what Somboon calls the "real meaning of economic development". The high economic growth rates have created a society with very deep social and economic divisions. Why did the government do nothing about reversing these trends? Why was there no uprising from the aggrieved?

These two questions are related. The pressure for the government to reverse policies was not there for most of the period because of the existence of the land frontier or what Somboon refers to as the "resource curse". Rural insurgency in the 1960s and 1970s forced the elites in Bangkok to pay more attention to the rural population and distribute some resources through anti-poverty programmes in the 1980s and decentralization to local government in the 1990s. But the Thai state has mainly resisted the pressure to change its development strategy. This resistance is embedded in the nature of the Thai state.

In Somboon's analysis, the Thai state was completely captured by "vested interest groups of exporters, industrialists and bankers", while the mass of people simply lacked the means to bargain effectively with the state. The emergent parliamentary democracy was sabotaged by vote buying and symbiotic relationships between bureaucrats, politicians, and vested interest groups. The policy-making process has been dominated by bureaucrats and ministers who snuggle up to the trade, industrial, and bankers' associations while leaving others in the cold. Somboon characterizes Thailand as a "predatory-cum-soft authoritarian state" with no pretence of acting as a benign "social guardian".

How could Thailand get out of this rut of shallow development and increasing inequity?

The Making of a More Benign State?

Somboon's work is a blend of traditional economics, political economy, and institutional economics. He places great emphasis on the nature of the state and its institutional capacity as the core to understanding the course of economic development in different eras and regions. But he also urges us to look at the specific history and political economy of different countries to understand how states and other institutions evolve.

Somboon's thinking seems to have been strongly affected by his time at the University of Lund and by his contact with European modes of politics and scholarship. His restless, angry, questing analysis of the Thai experience of industrialization, and his illuminating parallel between mercantilism and developmentalism, both seem to stem from his time at Lund.

In the history of several northern European countries, the process of successful industrialization through productivity growth leading to welfare-oriented states did not happen automatically, but with much pressure from organized industrial labour and other social movements, including women and rural workers. In South Korea, the pressure of organized labour on the government to improve social welfare also played a part. In Thailand, the roles of organized labour and other social movements have been weak or absent due to strong state repression and a lack of bargaining power. But that situation may be on the cusp of change.

The political movements that have erupted in Thailand over the last decade excite strong emotions on all sides. Some view the Red Shirt movement as an upsurge from below with the potential to transform the "predatory-cum-soft authoritarian state" and perhaps to overcome the constraints that have locked Thailand into the "middle income trap". Others view Thaksin Shinawatra as a prime example of Somboon's vested interests and believe that the Red Shirt movement is simply his tool. Both views probably have some element of truth. In the last paragraphs of this book, Somboon's brief remarks on Thaksin (up to 2005) convey a glimmer of hope that he represents a political force with the power to effect change along with some due caution about his reputation for corruption and abuse of power.

Somboon argues that Thailand failed to acquire the technological capacity and industrial skills which are the "real meaning" of industrialization because the state was neither strong enough nor truly committed to the task as long as there were always easier options (extensive agricultural expansion, foreign investment) which generated enough growth for an old elite to prosper and stay in power. But this situation is under strain. Massive changes in the world economy are abolishing old certainties and creating new opportunities. New political forces in Thailand over the last decade are gradually overhauling the old "predatory-cum-soft authoritarian state". The recent concern over a "middle-income trap" and the consequences of income inequality are signals of change. Somboon's essays are both a map of the past and a guide for the future.

Pasuk Phongpaichit
Kyoto, February 2012

CHAPTER 1

Problems in the Industrialization Process in Thailand

Thailand is regarded as a newly industrializing economy by the World Bank. This article argues that this description is premature. The main point is that the economic policy reform in the 1980s was too little and too late to solve the problem of increasingly unbalanced growth, or to eradicate poverty in rural areas. The path of development does not give much hope for attaining the goal of poverty eradication through economic growth in the foreseeable future. The World Bank and the International Monetary Fund (IMF) are blind to the real effects of industrialization, and the attempts made by the Thai state to alleviate poverty in rural areas remain open to question.

Historical Background

Thailand was an agriculture-based economy with rice as the main staple. Thai rice farmers were very responsive to world prices. The enormous expansion of production between 1850 and 1900 was predominantly the work of small-scale farmers, especially in the Central Plain, not far from Bangkok, which remained the main outlet to the world market. In addition, a good network of rivers and canals made cheap and efficient transport for bulky commodities possible. Until the 1940s, rice was the major tradable staple.

The 1850s were a very crucial period for the Thai economy. King Mongkut, Rama IV, decided to open up the country. In 1851, trade restrictions imposed by the king were eased, and in 1855, the decisive Bowring Treaty was signed. As a result of this treaty, Thailand became no different from a British colony. By the 1930s, 70 per cent of Thai trade was with Britain and 95 per cent of the modern economic sector was foreign owned, mainly by Britain.

The unexpected revolution in 1932 resulted in substantial political and economic changes in Thailand. The period of 1932 to 1956 was dominated by an ideology of strong-state nationalism that had underlain the revolution. The state conceived that the economy should be in the hands of the Thais instead of being controlled by Chinese and European traders. Hence, up until 1956, the state actively intervened to establish state enterprises.

In the 1940s and 1950s, Thailand was ruled by Field Marshall Phibun Songkhram. Economic growth was promoted through a myriad of state enterprises established under a broad but uncoordinated and incoherent set of policies encouraging industrial investments. The state played a vital role in fostering industrialization through state-controlled enterprises.

Industrialization, 1945–71

Before the Second World War, Thailand developed a very small manufacturing capacity, which was mainly related to agricultural produce, rice, and timber. Other production was in cottage handicrafts. Falling demand for rice and a loss of profits on the rice monopoly caused the government to change its position. The Industrial Promotion Act of 1954 was passed to induce foreign firms to invest in Thailand. Foreign firms were allowed to repatriate capital and profits, and given various tax concessions. Yet the Act was not clear about what types of industries should be promoted. The failure was likely due to the lack of credible commitment from the government. There was uncertainty about competition against state enterprises.

Criticism of state enterprises was used as propaganda to discredit the Phibun regime. There was mounting opposition to Phibun's development strategy from domestic and foreign investors, and in particular from the World Bank. Complaints against corruption came from many domestic business groups, especially from some traders who grew rich as a result of the Korean War boom and then felt disappointed when foreign demand for primary products declined and they were unable to find domestic opportunities under existing government policy. Hence, the Phibun regime was seen as a barrier to the growth of the capitalist economy. In addition, development was seriously hindered by poor infrastructure and a lack of any coordinated planning machinery.

Field Marshall Sarit ousted the Phibun government by coup and became prime minister in 1959. Development strategy was switched to an opposite approach. Sarit committed Thailand to a path of economic growth based on an essentially pro-capitalist economy with private ownership of the means of production and an open trading regime. Policy on state enterprises was revised, and state ownership confined to social overhead facilities. The market mechanism was permitted to function and any intervention was kept at a minimum.

Under the Sarit government, industrial promotion policy was reformed by the Promotion of Industrial Investment Act of 1959. The Board of Investment (BOI) was set up in the same year, along with a Budget Bureau in 1959 and Fiscal Policy Office in 1960.

This period saw a fundamental institutional change. Modern industrial development began in the late 1950s. The era marked by a multiple exchange rate regime and large-scale state enterprises came to an end. In their place came export taxes, a fixed exchange rate, and state investment confined to infrastructure development.

The role of the state was reconceived as a social guardian responsible for providing a stable investment environment for the private sector. Investment incentives were given to selected import-substituting industries. The first and easy stage of import-substitution was completed by the late 1960s and the small domestic market was also easily exhausted. A high rate of tariff protection and a set of investment incentives fostered inefficient promoted manufacturing firms. Sarit's idea of industrialization was based on the Beitzel Report compiled by a US government mission in 1959, resulting in a revision of the investment promotion law in 1962. American advisers played an important role in the policy-making process, in particular, in the first three national economic development plans (1961–76), supported by Thai technocrats. The path of industrialization was centred on laissez-faire policies. The government did not enter directly into production, leaving the field open to private enterprise. The role of the BOI was crucial, not just because of the few incentives it could grant, but because it was a symbol of the state's commitment.

Sarit only stayed in power for a very short period. After his death in 1963, the size of his estate revealed that he had gained many benefits from his political position. But the legacy of Sarit to Thai economic history was an increased role for technocrats in policy-making. To a certain degree the stable macroeconomic performance, significant economic growth, and low inflation rate of this era were the work of competent technocrats.

By 1970, the import of industrial products was still substantial, especially chemicals and machinery. The strategy of import-substitution industrialization (ISI) adopted by the Sarit government and its successors led the economy into structural difficulties in the subsequent period. The strategy did not help the Thai economy to avoid a chronic and growing adverse trade balance and deteriorating balance of payments. The labour absorptive capacity of this strategy was also weak. This adversely affected progress in agricultural modernization and resulted in an expansion of the urban poor.

Industrialization, 1972–93

Import Substitution

Import-substitution industrialization created many problems. While growth of the manufacturing sector had a substantial impact on GDP, it had little effect on total employment. The incentives of the Board of Investment encouraged new investments in what it deemed to be sunrise industries. The structure of tariff rates was quite high, ranging from 30 to 90 per cent during the 1960s and 1970s. The structure of foreign trade changed dramatically after 1960, reflecting the change in the structure of production.

The export of manufactured goods became increasingly important, especially products of light industries and agro-industries, while the relative importance of primary exports declined. In imports, the share of consumer goods declined significantly while the share of producer goods increased over time. The growth of the manufacturing sector, whether for the domestic or export market, brought about increased imports of components, raw materials, and capital goods.

Yet Thailand had a wide range of primary products for export. The abundance of unused land enabled Thailand to have a strong comparative advantage until 1980. Rice production was still increasing. Rapid growth of agriculture during the 1960s and 1970s allowed Thailand to expand primary exports considerably. In fact, economic growth from the 1950s to the 1970s came from the agricultural sector, while the industrial sector also benefited from the abundant cheap labour from rural areas.

From 1955, the price of rice was kept lower than the border price by an export tax known as the rice premium and by other measures. Rice was the main staple and also a wage good for urban labour.

In 1963, the Bank of Thailand warned of the many problems of ISI. However, in terms of economic growth, Thailand performed well during the first two decades after the Second World War. GDP growth averaged

5.2 per cent in the 1950s, and with the adoption of ISI rose to 7.4 per cent during the period from 1960 to 1972. As a World Bank mission stated, ISI began to encounter problems of excess capacity as the market became saturated in the late 1960s.

In reality, ISI became the preferred strategy not because of the rational arguments of the World Bank, but rather because of expeditious policy actions to meet balance-of-payments crises. There was a common interest in ISI on the part of the bureaucratic-authoritarian state, urban manufacturing entrepreneurs, and multinational corporations. But, how much protection was needed and for how long the ISI policy should be continued were open to question. The ISI policy was not targeted according to systematic economic criteria, but was pursued in a chaotic, inefficient manner and for too long. Thai technocrats were aware of these shortcomings by the early 1960s. Nevertheless, strong pressure to retain the apparatus of ISI came from nationalists and populists within the military, from manufacturers, and from powerful new industrial and banking conglomerates. A proposal for outward-oriented trade policies was discussed among Thai technocrats in the National Economic and Social Development Board (NESDB) in the late 1960s. Believing that ISI strategy would eventually be fatal or self-defeating, some supported liberalization of industrial policy and a shift to export competitiveness.

Disturbing Events in the World

In the early 1970s and again in the early 1980s, the world economy was unsettled. The first oil shock of 1973–74 severely affected the Thai economy owing to its heavy reliance on imported oil and industrial materials. However, the shock came almost simultaneously with a world commodity boom. Rising prices of Thailand's major exports, including rice, maize, rubber, and tin helped to prevent a balance-of-payments crisis. The first oil crisis affected Thailand less than other developing countries, yet still gave rise to high inflation in 1973 and 1974, and considerably reduced economic growth in 1974 and 1975. However, all macroeconomic indicators were better than in most other developing countries. The inflation rate was brought down quickly after the petroleum price increase.

The Thai government showed initial signs of moving from ISI to export-oriented industrialization (EOI) with a revision of the Investment Promotion Law in 1972, designed to offset the disincentives inherent in import protection. The Board of Investment offered export incentives aimed at offsetting the cost-increasing effect of protection on domestic prices of intermediate goods. From 1972, exporters were able to claim a refund of all duties and business taxes on imported inputs. But in the 1970s, these duty drawbacks and the Board of Investment's export incentives seem to have been ineffective, largely because of poor administration.

In the late 1970s, Thailand was adversely affected by the second oil shock and the subsequent worldwide recession, partly because the country had become quite open to the world economy. The balance of payments was in deficit for five consecutive years from 1975 to 1979, while the rate of inflation jumped to double digits, and peaked at 19.7 per cent in 1980. However, Thailand, like most developing countries, did not rush into export liberalization immediately. The instruments of import protection existed simultaneously with instruments of export promotion. There was no systematic pursuit of either ISI or EOI.

The middle class began to make its voice heard in politics. After the student-led uprising of 14 October 1973, the business class, and in particular Chinese business, started to assume a more explicit role in policy making. The military never regained the same level of unity or political dominance despite the overthrow of the civilian government in 1976 and the establishment of a new military-backed regime in 1977. Between 1979 and 1981, when the OPEC countries raised oil prices dramatically, the government could not manage its macroeconomic policy in spite of favourable external conditions. The Thai economy entered a period of stagflation experiencing twin deficits. This economic recession partly arose from the fact that the exports of primary products no longer delivered adequate foreign exchange.

Under the fourth five-year plan (1977–81), the export promotion policy was significantly revised to reduce the anti-export bias resulting from ISI. The Board of Investment still had a major role in authorizing and granting exemptions and privileges. Fiscal deficits began to soar, made possible by the newly found access to foreign commercial bank lending. Foreign debt expanded on a large scale from 1976. The Defence Loans Act allowed the government to borrow up to 20 billion baht for defence purposes. Thailand had pursued a conservative monetary policy through the 1950s and the 1960s with the baht linked to the dollar for 26 years (1955–81), the exchange rate remained between 20 and 21 baht per dollar. The Bank of Thailand became famous for keeping the foreign exchange rate stable. However, in the late 1970s the dollar began to appreciate against other major currencies, and a fixed baht/dollar parity became untenable. In July 1981, the government had to devalue the baht by 10 per cent and once again in 1984 by about 15 per cent. The last devaluation was coupled with a change in the exchange rate system. The baht was now tied to a basket of the currencies of major trading partners instead of being solely linked to the US dollar.

Instability and Economic Policy Reform in the 1980s

From the early 1980s, the Thai economy suffered from continuous economic crises. Thailand was not successful in the reform of three important policies: trade, tariffs, and tax policies. Furthermore, most sectoral policies remained in place. Yet Thailand was able to sustain high economic growth and to maintain positive macroeconomic performance. Trade policies were still full of quantitative restrictions. A clear plan to reduce tariffs to relatively low and uniform levels was considered by the Ministry of Finance in the early 1980s. Policy reforms had the effect of raising energy prices and devaluing the baht. The growth of manufactured exports was increasingly a result of exchange rate policy. The two devaluations in 1981 and 1984 helped Thailand to reduce the trade deficit without affecting domestic levels of inflation. The devaluations also reduced the anti-export bias, and increased the competitiveness of tradable goods.

Judged in terms of the conservative policy stance of the Bank of Thailand, these changes counted as major economic policy reforms. Disturbances in the world economy put pressure on Thailand to depart from its traditional exchange rate policy. The volatility of the world financial system in the 1970s and 1980s, in contrast to the stability of the 1960s, also brought about these policy adjustments. But exchange rate policy is not itself a commercial policy. This distinction is relevant in the Thai context with respect to sectoral policy. Commercial policy actually affects import-substituting and export-oriented interests. Chaotic policy making, especially by the Ministry of Commerce, allowed considerable bureaucratic discretion and patronage. In 1982, Thailand became a member of the GATT (General Agreement on Tariffs and Trade). It was widely perceived that a commitment to integrate into the world economy could help a country maintain a sound macroeconomic policy. In essence, the lack of consistency in sectoral policies can be attributed to the rent-seeking society present in Thailand since the 1950s. Individual government departments had wide discretionary powers. The influence that ministers exercised over trade and industrial policies, quotas, licensing and factory promotions was often used to seek economic rents, with some of the rents kicked back to bureaucrats and their political masters.

In the early 1990s, about 150 product categories were governed by export licenses, either automatic or non-automatic. The products included textiles and clothing, certain agricultural commodities, fuels, metals and metal products, wood and wood products, wild animals and their carcasses, pesticides, paper, and sacred statues and images. Export quotas were still in place for sugar, cassava, and textiles. The Import and Export Commodity Act of 1979 empowered the Ministry of Commerce to promulgate regulations imposing quantitative restrictions and other conditions on trade without the approval of the cabinet or parliament. This easily led to corruption and rent-seeking activities.

In addition, an electoral regime and elected coalition government existed from 1975. Politicians spent money as patronage to win support from constituents to ensure re-election and to win support from fellow MPs to gain a ministership. Clientelist politics became pervasive. Trade quotas and factory permits, which were once patronage resources for the military elite, were now wielded by political parties and individual politicians. The allocation of such resources was not based on competition, but used covertly by politicians in power to generate income for themselves or for their party.

As a result, the structural adjustment programmes imposed on Thailand in the early 1980s as conditions of the Structural Adjustment Loans of the World Bank and the standby arrangements of the IMF were ineffective in bringing reform in commercial policy or sectoral policy. These programmes did help the Thai economy to readjust towards greater efficiency, but it was too little and too late. Several studies have shown that the nominal exchange rate of the baht had been overvalued as a result of high import duties to protect promoted firms. In the period from 1961 to 1980, the taxes and restrictions imposed on rice, along with an overvalued exchange rate, discriminated against export producers, especially exporters of commodities. Not surprisingly, the agricultural sector, which was the poorest sector in the country, was left in poverty.

During the readjustment in the 1980s, the Thai government seemed reluctant to implement the structural adjustment programmes fully. Development policy instead aimed at alleviating poverty in the agricultural sector, while government spending and the tax structure were reoriented to create an environment suitable for export-oriented industries in urban areas, especially around Bangkok. The scale of land reform was very limited and ineffective at keeping poor farmers from becoming indebted. The share of total household income commanded by the richest 20 per cent of households increased from 50 per cent in 1975/76 to 55 per cent in 1988/89, while the share of the poorest 20 per cent declined from 8 per cent to 4.5 per cent. Rising income inequality, both between the industrial and agricultural sectors and between regions, partly reflected the nature and orientation of the Thai state. The laissez-faire policy bred rising income inequality and low real wages in the rural areas. Neither import-substituting nor export-oriented industrial sectors concentrated in Bangkok absorbed much labour.

The tariff reforms in the 1980s had little effect. The Thai government needed to rationalize the range of 34 different nominal tariff rates ranging between one and 200 per cent, and reduce the excessive rates of effective protection. In fact, a major tariff reform was attempted in 1982 with some progress made in equalizing rates of protection within individual industries such as textiles, but the results for the industrial sector as a whole were modest. Moreover, some of these gains were reversed when tariff rates were raised once again in 1985. Import taxes were still judged as essential for increasing government revenue when the budget fell into deficit. This left Thailand with the highest average nominal rate of tariff protection (34 per cent) of any of the Pacific Basin developing countries. The Thai government began again to reform tariffs in the early 1990s as a result of a commitment to the Asian Free Trade Area (AFTA) to lower tariffs within the 15 years from 1 January 1993 to 31 December 2008.

Privatization was very limited. The Thai government was unable to deal with problems inherited from the past. In May 1990, Thailand announced plans to dismantle its remaining capital controls and maintain a fully convertible currency under Article VIII of the IMF Articles of Agreement.

Perspective from the Late Twentieth Century (1993)

Thailand has a number of laws which allocate the authority to implement various aspects of national policy, especially on international trade. Exporters form vested interest groups that are able to exert political pressure, while farmers, though many in number are less powerful and are therefore unable to bargain with bureaucrats. The political party system is fragmented and vote buying is rampant. Bureaucrats and ministers consult exporters on various aspects of state intervention.

Not surprisingly, inside information has allowed exporters to obtain large speculative profits through trading. Insecure governments tend to concentrate their resources on urban and industrial sectors in the interest of maintaining their own power and winning international recognition.

However, rural insurgency in the northeast of Thailand in the 1960s and the 1970s compelled the Thai elite in Bangkok to pay more attention to the situation and to distribute some resources.

Data on the standard of living are notoriously difficult to collect, but trends in poverty and labour productivity by the rural sector show that rural people in Thailand, not only in the northeast but also in other regions, are very poor and have little education.

After introducing a Farmers' Aid Fund, the government still depressed the domestic prices of rice through rice reserve requirements imposed by the Ministry of Commerce. This inexorably led to a fall in the cost of living in urban areas, reduced the pressure from urban workers to increase wages, encouraged exports, and enabled export-oriented promoted firms to compete in the world market. Industrialization in Thailand over the last 50 years has seemed to breed corruption and rent-seeking activities.

High growth over more than 30 years has taken place at the expense of the depletion of natural resources and continuing poverty in the rural sector. Low agricultural productivity and rural poverty restrict purchasing power and limit the domestic market for manufactured goods. Since industrialization in urban areas has been unable to bring about modernization in agriculture, it will be impossible for Thailand to become a newly industrializing country. East Asian countries, which have grown at very high rates, have promoted high technological industries through the use of tax incentives under an activist strong state. The nationalist policy in the era of Phibun had some similarities to the insulated development state in South Korea. However, the Thai government switched from bureaucratic capitalism with state enterprises to an import-substitution strategy in which inefficient industries were protected from foreign competition for a long period.

Learn from Thailand?

The emerging consensus that countries following an outward-oriented, market-based development strategy will achieve relatively higher rates of growth and living standards might be premature. The most important factor behind the East Asian Miracle may not be what kind of industrial policy is pursued, but rather what kind of state is in place. The precise determinants of successful industrialization may not be entirely clear, thus the World Bank's use of the word "miracle". Yet the determinants of unsuccessful industrialization are much clearer. Hence, lessons from Thailand are very relevant for developing countries.

There remain serious difficulties and restricting conditions which must be overcome to secure continuous growth in the Thai economy. The immediate bottlenecks are infrastructure and the quality of the labour force. Infrastructure investment needs are enormous. In part because of large government budget deficits in excess of 6 per cent of GDP in the early 1980s, Thailand has saved and invested somewhat less than some East Asian countries. Even though the government has run a surplus since 1988, the share of investment in GDP has risen only to about 26 per cent, somewhat less than it might otherwise have been. A rate of around 30 per cent would be desirable for the long run. Pervasive corruption in government contracting in recent years has reduced the impact of investment in infrastructure.

Additional investment in human capital is urgently needed, including an expansion of secondary education in general, and of technical and vocation education in particular. Science and engineering also need to be strengthened at the university level, and research and development needs to be encouraged. The current budget surplus makes this a propitious time for the Thai government to carry out reform in economic policy and in education.

The Thai government has focused more on economic growth than on income distribution. Even in the absence of debt and balance of payment crises in the early 1980s, the prospects for the poor in Thailand are far from satisfactory. For the period from the 1960s to the 1980s, rapid economic growth existed alongside a declining share of income for the poor. The path of development gives little hope for achieving the goal of eradicating poverty through economic growth in the foreseeable future.

In sum, the Thai economy desperately needs economic, political, and institutional reforms. Rent seeking and corruption should be kept at a minimum by making administrative regulations clear and transparent. Mechanisms are needed to reduce discretionary power. A regime of patron-client relationships acts as a major barrier to any reform. As in other countries with highly developed clientelist governments, economic reform can be both politically costly and irrational.

CHAPTER 2

Export-oriented Industrialization Strategy with Land Abundance: Some of Thailand's Shortcomings[1]

It is widely believed that Thailand will soon be on the verge of joining the ranks of the East Asian newly industrializing economies (World Bank 1993). Over the past two decades, the Thai economy has not merely undergone dramatic structural changes, but also accelerated significantly so that Thailand stands out among developing countries in terms of fast economic growth and stability. The foundations for these changes are partly attributed to the national economic and social development plans started in 1961, and partly to an active private sector or market-oriented economy (Robinson, Byeon, and Teja 1991; World Bank 1988; GATT 1991). An import-substitution strategy was adopted in the first five-year plan in the 1960s. In the early post-war period of development economics, pessimism about the prospects for exports, coupled with enthusiasm for unbalanced growth, led to widespread support for import-substitution. Hence, Thai technocrats, as in most developing countries, started by promoting import-substituting industry through controls and interventions.

[1] I am grateful to Professor Ammar Siamwalla whose insightful article about land abundance in Thailand helped me to formulate the ideas in this article. Professor Christer Gunnarsson gave invaluable comments for improving the article. Jaya Reddy has done a good job of making this paper accurate and readable, but any errors are of course mine. An earlier version was presented at the Nordic Association for Southeast Asian Studies tenth conference on "How Free Are the Southeast Asian Markets?" at Turku, Åbo University, Finland, 10–12 September 1993, and at the European Association of Development Research and Training Institute seventh conference on "Transformation and Development: Eastern Europe and the South" at Berlin, Germany, 15–18 September 1993.

However, from the mid-1970s, industrialization strategy gradually shifted to export orientation. Thailand seems to have pursued "export-driven economic growth" on a pattern similar to the NIEs (Newly Industrialized Economies) (World Bank 1993), and seems to have achieved rapid economic growth through exports from labour-intensive light industries, especially in three subsectors which accounted for three quarters of this export-induced growth: canned and processed food, textile and leather products, and machinery and electrical products (Santikarn Kaosaard 1992). The leading sector of manufactured goods is textiles, which is typically classified as labour-intensive manufacture. Labour-intensive techniques might only be suitable at the beginning of the industrialization process. The next step is of greater importance and requires a competent state to invest in human capital so as to absorb new technology from abroad. Late-comer countries such as Japan and the East Asia NIEs were able to exploit the latest technology at low cost, but how to replicate this success is still an enigma for developing countries. Thailand's success to date hardly counts as economic development. It has achieved short and medium term goals of capital accumulation and GDP growth without attention to welfare.

Neo-liberal economists in Thailand and in international financial institutions such as the World Bank and the IMF argue that remaining problems can be solved by economic liberalism — getting the prices right, letting the market work, privatization, and adopting an export-oriented strategy. Yet Thailand's recent economic performance has already revealed shortcomings in physical and human capital development, as well as created problems like rising income inequality between regions and between agricultural and non-agricultural sectors, shortages of key skilled labour, low secondary enrolment, concentration of industries, resource depletion, environmental degradation, and lack of technological capability.

This paper aims to cast some light on the shortcomings of industrialization in Thailand. Previous studies have emphasized one side of the issue without attempting to look carefully at the course of economic development beyond a neo-classical paradigm. Thailand's success is often attributed to export-led growth without considering the historical context of domestic and international markets. Some economists argue that export-oriented industrialization with abundant land and labour contributed to economic growth. Yet it is prudent to question the likelihood of Thailand joining the club of newly industrialized economies in the coming decade. Attention will be paid to structural change and economic

growth in recent decades. Lessons can be learned from the newly industrializing countries in the late nineteenth century, such as Germany and
Japan, which are classic examples of successful exporters with relatively
skilled and well-paid labour. These countries adopted a cheap labour
policy at the beginning of the industrialization process to assist industrialists, but growth in real wages was essential for industrialization in the
long run, as well as central to the distributional process.

Section 1 is an introduction to recent debates on the possibility of
Thailand becoming a newly industrializing country. Section 2 discusses
trade policies for industrialization in Thailand from the 1960s to the
1980s. It suggests that the Thai elite were influenced by a Lewis surplus
model (Lewis 1954). Section 3 looks at the human capital aspect and the
problems of undertaking import-substitution and export-oriented industrialization with unskilled labour and mass poverty. It argues that the
incentives offered by the Board of Investment, which commits endless
sins of promotion rather than sins of restraint, have allowed foreign firms
to choose labour-saving techniques combined with simple methods of
production (Siamwalla 1991). In this way, they are able to hire fewer
unskilled labourers, reduce their wage bill, and boost their profit. The
result is imbalanced growth in which employment lags behind production
and income inequality increases. Section 4 consists of the concluding
remarks.

It is questionable whether the Thai economy will achieve socially
necessary rates of growth in the long term through export-led industrialization. In addition, chemical, metal and steel industries are generating
increasing volumes of toxic and hazardous waste, and there is some doubt
over whether Thai bureaucrats are capable of coping with the environmental pollution. A better strategy would be selective subsidies or targeting of particular industries coupled with a strong state, as practised in
the past by Japan, Taiwan, and South Korea (Amsden 1989; Gunnarsson
1991; Haggard 1990; Singh 1992; Wade 1990).

A Critical Review of Economic Development

Growth and Structural Change in Production

In line with other developing countries, Thailand has undergone dramatic
economic changes during the late twentieth century. Its economic expansion has many features in common with the East Asian NIEs, in particular the pursuit of growth through manufactured exports, though other

features differ from their patterns. Here I will survey structural changes and economic growth between the 1960s and the early 1990s.

In the post-war period, the Thai economy achieved steady and stable growth with good macroeconomic performance. After 1960, the GDP growth rate neither became negative, nor fell drastically, even in the worldwide recession of the early 1980s. The country has embarked on high and sustained growth without severe inflation except when the oil shocks of the 1970s caused deterioration in the balance of payments, and resulted in increased external debt and domestic inflation. Compared to other developing countries, Thailand has not only ranked very high in terms of the pace of economic development over the three last decades, but also performed very well during the downturns of the world economy (Oshima 1993; Ranis and Mahmood 1992). Real GDP grew at an average of 4 per cent in the 1950s, 8.2 per cent in the 1960s, 7.2 per cent in the 1970s, and around 6 per cent in the 1980s. However, due to poor agricultural performance and the oil price increases, GDP growth dropped sharply from 9.4 per cent in 1973 to 5.4 per cent in 1974. Moreover, facing a second oil price shock in 1979 combined with a weak agricultural performance, the Thai economy slowed down significantly.[2] In the second shock, the rate of growth again dropped sharply from 10.1 per cent in 1978 to 6.5 per cent in 1979. In spite of these two oil price shocks, the average growth rate from 1975 to 1978 was still 8.5 per cent, but declined to 5 per cent between 1980 and 1985.

Thailand's economy has been dynamic[3] and satisfactory compared to Latin American countries or other developing countries adversely affected by the world crisis in the early 1980s, especially some Asian countries such as the Philippines (see Hughes and Singh 1991; Oshima 1993; Ranis and Mahmood 1992; Yoshihara 1995). The growth rate accelerated again over 1987–90, and has averaged around 10 per cent per annum since the late 1980s. At present (1997), Thailand is cited as one of the fastest growing countries.

---

[2] Over 90 per cent of Thailand petroleum products are supplied by imports. This made Thailand vulnerable to the oil price rises in 1973 and 1979. Although Thailand was hurt by the first oil price increase, the additional import cost was offset by increased prices for rice exports in 1973–74.

[3] Some Thai economists working at the Thailand Development Research Institute (TDRI) argue that the composition of manufactured exports since the mid-1980s indicates that the external sector has become more dynamic (Akrasanee and Wattananukit 1990).

The agricultural sector, once the main contributor to GDP, has been steadily declining. Between 1970 and 1990, the growth rate in agriculture was about 4 per cent per annum. In 1987 and 1990, the growth rate in the agricultural sector became unexpectedly negative. By contrast, the growth of the manufacturing sector has been impressive. By 1980, manufacturing by both import-substituting and local sub-sectors had become the largest contributor to the GDP.

This transition from agriculture to industry was achieved by state intervention. The Thai government imposed a heavy tax on the export of rice, the staple primary crop. This tax, known as the rice premium, affected most Thai farmers over a long period (Siamwalla 1975; Thanapornpun 1985). This was in fact negative protection for Thai farmers who provided cheap food and labour for the manufacturing sector — an "urban bias" in the pursuit of import-substitution industrialization. Rice is a wage good as labour spends much of its income on rice.[4] The heavy taxation on rice was first imposed when Britain demanded that Thailand pay her war indemnity in rice. A Thai Rice Office was established to ensure these obligations were fulfilled. The rice premiums remained an important source of government revenue between 1955 and the early 1960s (Ingram 1971).

Between the 1950s and 1990s, a major change in the economic structure took place. The share of agriculture in value added declined from 24.8 per cent in 1975 to only 16.0 per cent in 1989. With impressive growth rates, the manufacturing sector experienced some structural change. Import-substituting industries in food processing (food, beverages, tobacco) did well in the 1960s and early 1970s, but food processing's contribution to value added in manufacturing declined from 34.6 per cent in 1960 to 20.1 per cent in 1978 as several new manufactured products emerged, for instance, tapioca processing, canned food, animal feed, and dairy products, while established sub-sectors such as textiles, paper and paper products, rubber products, and chemical products also became more important. The structure of the manufacturing sector had changed by 1985 when food products still had the largest but no longer dominant

---

[4] The price of rice was kept below the border price or world market price via the rice premium and other quantitative restrictions, such as export bans or quotas. The rice premium not only supplied government with revenue, but worked against the Thai farmer. Government kept the rice price down in order to facilitate low wages (Siamwalla 1975).

share at 15.4 per cent, while textiles contributed 14.9 per cent, wearing apparel 11.4 per cent, beverages 8.1 per cent, transport equipment 7.4 per cent, tobacco 5.6 per cent, non-metallic mineral products 6.0 per cent, and petroleum products 4.1 per cent.[5]

At the same time, Thailand's agricultural sector had performed well compared to other lower middle-income countries. However, this growth was made possible by expanding cultivated areas at the expense of national forest land. This issue will be discussed at length later. Thailand did not participate in the Green Revolution by adopting high-yielding rice varieties such as IR-8 (Setboonsarng and Evenson 1991), but relied upon its abundant supply of land rather than improving productivity. Land productivity (yield per hectare) remained low and stable, while labour productivity (output per farmer) increased significantly (James, Naya, and Meier 1989; Timmer 1991; Watanabe 1992).

Structural Changes in International Trade

The Thai economy was forcibly incorporated into the world system in the 1850s (Ingram 1971). Since then, the country has been a major rice exporter. Rice is not just the main export item, but also a staple good. In the 1950s, rice accounted for around 95 per cent of all cultivated area, and around 50 per cent of the total value of exports. Together, rice, rubber, tin, and teak comprised 83.1 per cent of total exports. The contribution of manufactured goods was negligible (Falkus 1991; Ingram 1971).

Over the 1960s and 1970s, the structure of Thailand's international trade changed. Diversification began in the early 1970s, both within the agricultural sector into a wider range of crops, and beyond agriculture into manufacturing and services. In the first half of the 1970s, Thailand was severely hurt by the first oil shock. Fortunately, being a major exporter of primary commodities whose prices increased steeply between

---

[5] Import-substitution can be divided into two stages. In the first "easy" stage, non-durable goods are produced which have standardized technology, limited economies of scale, substantial demand at low income levels, and low capital requirements, such as textiles, shoes, cement, tires, processed food and beer — labour-intensive manufactured goods. In the second "difficult" stage, durable consumer goods and capital goods are produced. Most developing countries achieve the first stage because they have comparative advantage from abundant labour. The second stage, requiring economies of scale, foreign resources, expertise, and high technological capabilities, is more difficult to achieve (Chen 1989; Pomfret 1991).

1972 and 1974 as a result of worldwide drought, the Thai economy still performed soundly. Thereafter, the economy promptly recovered in the second half of the 1970s through a surge in infrastructure investment and a rapid expansion of manufactured exports. In the early 1970s, Thai bureaucrats started promoting export-oriented industries. Many import-substituting industries were suffering from saturation due to the small domestic market. Meanwhile, the import of inputs, materials, and capital goods showed no sign of declining. Technocrats began to realize that high protective tariffs and other incentives received by import-competing industries had failed to achieve import-substitution.

In the 1970s, manufactured exports began to expand rapidly. Their share of merchandise exports rose from 2.4 per cent in 1961 to 10 per cent in 1971 and 35.8 per cent in 1981. Export growth was remarkably high at the rate of 15.2 per cent per annum. The Thai economy reached a turning point in terms of economic growth and international trade in the mid-1980s when manufactured exports surpassed agricultural exports in value for the first time. Mainstream economists both in Thailand and international institutions such as the World Bank, the Institute of the Developing Economies, and the Overseas Economic Cooperation Fund of Japan noted that Thailand's exports had penetrated strongly into the world market (Sussangkarn 1990, 1992; OECF 1991).

Manufactured exports grew at an average of 35.7 per cent per annum between 1985 and 1990, despite a prolonged recession in the advanced economies (Hughes and Singh 1991; Singh 1992). The main segments of manufactured exports were textiles and garments, canned foods and canned fish, gems and jewellery, and integrated circuits. Two broad categories of goods dominated: natural resource-based and labour-intensive manufactured goods (Jansen 1989; Santikarn Kaosa-ard 1992). These manufactured exports became the new rising stars.[6]

Yet import growth was no less impressive. Over 1960 to 1980, the first stage of import-substituting industrialization in consumer goods seemed to succeed, but progress to a second stage of consumer durable goods, intermediate goods, and capital goods seemed to fail. The major

---

[6] Thai policy makers perceive these as sunrise sectors though they have become sunset in Japan and the East Asian NIEs. Exports of labour-intensive manufactures, especially textile and clothing, are encountering increasing protectionism in industrial markets. The Multi-Fibre Arrangement allows developed countries to reduce textile imports from developing countries (Anderson 1992; Suphachalasai 1992).

categories of imports were raw materials (including petroleum), capital goods, and chemical goods. ISI had not reduced import dependence and had not yet deepened the manufacturing sector (Jansen 1991; Santikarn Kaosa-ard 1992; UNIDO 1992). Since the mid-1980s, the growth rate in imports had even surpassed the high growth rates in exports. This suggests that Thailand might have tried to exploit import-substitute-then-export strategies in manufacturing (Taylor 1993). The current account deficit swelled from 7.9 per cent of GDP in 1989 to 12.4 per cent in 1990.[7] This prolonged deficit was attributed to rapidly rising imports of capital goods, intermediate goods, and raw materials.

Trade Policies for Industrialization

Why the Thai Elite Started with Import-Substitution Strategy

On industrialization, Thailand initially lagged behind other developing countries with similar levels of income, such as the Philippines, but had surpassed the Philippines by the 1980s (Oshima 1987, 1993; Tambun-lertchai 1987; Ranis and Mahmood 1992; Yoshihara 1995). Thailand's industrialization may be divided into four phases: the initial import-substitution period, 1961–71; export promotion, 1972–76; the Big Push, 1976–82; and transformation into manufacturing export-led growth, 1983 to present.[8]

After the Second World War, there were very few manufacturing plants in Bangkok, mostly rice mills and saw mills. The Thai government pursued import-substitution industrialization with three broad objectives, though these were never specified: to reduce dependence on imports of foreign goods; to raise the level of income through increasing value added; and to save foreign exchange. Such a strategy usually includes an overvalued exchange rate, import controls, high tariffs, and quantitative restriction on imports.

It is not clear why the industrialization strategy in Thailand began with import-substitution. It is possible that policy makers were simply following an international trend.

---

[7] The current account deficit was 3.5 per cent of GDP in 1970, and 6.4 per cent in 1980.

[8] On the periodization, see Santikarn Kaosa-ard and Israngkura (1988). This periodization is based on phases in policy, not effectiveness.

The elites in many developing countries, despite a wide range of difference in their historical legacy, culture, natural resources endowment, and size, were attracted to the "inward-looking strategy" of import-substitution. Many Latin American countries and some newly independent nations such as India, Pakistan, the People's Republic of China, Egypt, and Israel consciously adopted an inward-looking strategy. The experience of the great depression in the 1930s probably convinced the governments of many developing countries that international trade and the market mechanism were too unstable and too risky. The labour surplus model of Arthur Lewis (1954)[9] and the unbalanced growth strategy of Albert Hirschmann (1958) might also have influenced Thai elites. In the early 1950s, the Thai rural sector was seen as being very remote and full of underemployed and misapplied labour. Population growth and a plentiful labour supply seemed to confirm this impression. Population had grown at 3.0 per cent over 1947–60 to reach 26.3 million. It then grew further to 36.1 million in 1970, 46.7 million in 1980, and 56.1 million in 1990.[10] Thailand seemed to be suitable for the Lewis and Hirschmann models. Industrialization seemed to offer a route to become rich like the developed countries. Import-substitution seemed to be the right strategy to save foreign exchange, increase employment, and reduce rural poverty.

During the import-substitution period, the Thai government was strongly biased against the agricultural sector, while for promoted industrial firms, mostly big foreign firms located in Bangkok, the government provided protection and incentives. Export taxes were imposed on agricultural products including rice, rubber, and timber. Manufacturing was not subject to taxes and was highly protected by quantitative restrictions. Promoted firms received tax concessions on imported machinery, equipment, raw materials, and other imported intermediate inputs. It made sense for promoted firms to use more capital inputs rather than more labour inputs. Markets were highly distorted. Contrary to expectations, ISI did not lead to efficient allocation of resources by promoted firms (Bhagwati 1988a).

---

[9] Field Marshall Sarit had read one book by Arthur Lewis while he was in the US for an operation in the early 1960s.

[10] Since the early 1970s, fertility rates have fallen steeply, and the population growth rate dropped from 3 per cent per annum in 1960 to a mere 1.7 per cent in 1988.

The import-substitution policy was pursued not only through tariffs and an overvalued exchange rate, but also through quantitative restrictions and grants of specific privileges which gave bureaucrats considerable discretion, and opportunities for rent seeking. As Thailand's pursuit of import-substitution involved high levels of protection but no sense of direction, entrepreneurial energies and real resources were wasted.

Thai policy makers began to be aware of the adverse effects of the import-substitution strategy, particularly the tendency of firms to adopt capital-intensive techniques, and the temptation for bureaucrats to engage in rent-seeking activities and corruption (Tambunlertchai 1987; Bhagwati 1988a; Krueger 1974; Siriprachai 1993a). The import-substitution strategy neither achieved the government's objectives, nor matched the state of factor markets, namely the cheap labour supply. Despite the land abundance which prevailed until the 1970s and labour abundance which prevailed until the late 1980s, the development of industry prioritized the use of the one factor that was in scarce supply, capital. The import-substitution strategy failed to create forward and backward linkages among industrial sectors, and failed to raise labour productivity. Siamwalla and Setboonsarng (1989) commented on the role of the BOI in promoting industrial firms as follows:

> The importance of BOI lies not so much in the granting of promotional privileges ... in the form of tax holidays, exemptions from taxes on imports of machinery and raw materials and the like ... but in its role as a forum where private business can legitimately submit requests to the government for these privileges. The government, in a sense, has become involved in the private sector decisions, and having been involved, it also has become responsible for the survival of the enterprises. BOI's importance for the analyst lies therefore, not so much in the privileges that it grants, but as an indicator of the trust of government policies. As the guiding philosophy of BOI in the 1960s was import-substitution, protection of industry became the norm.... Industries were promoted, but most agro-industries in Thailand (like rice milling and rubber processing which are small and medium-scale) cannot gain access to BOI promotional privileges. Such policies show a clear, albeit implicit, bias against agriculture.

The Failed Shift to Export Orientation

In the early 1970s, in the Third National Economic and Social Development Plan (1972–76), technocrats in the NESDB advocated a shift of

industrial strategy towards the promotion of export-oriented manufacturing. The stated objectives of this plan were to correct balance of payment problems, to increase overall employment, and to adjust the import
structure. Why did the technocrats attempt this shift during a downturn
in the world economy?

High-ranking policy makers in the NESDB were impressed by the
"miracle" of the East Asian NIEs in achieving high economic growth
through outward-looking industrialization (Tambunlertchai 1987). In
addition, the World Bank and IMF routinely put forward to developing
countries, including Thailand, the idea of abandoning ISI and adopting
EOI. In the late 1950s, the World Bank had advocated ISI for Thailand,
but by the early 1970s it condemned ISI because of excessive regulation
of private enterprises leading to resource misallocation, rent seeking, and
corruption.

Yet in the period of this plan (1972–76), export promotion failed.
Tariff policies, quantitative restrictions, and other elements of ISI not only
remained in place but were strengthened by the Ministry of Finance.

Some imports were liberalized in 1974, but protective barriers
were again raised in 1978. In 1972, the investment promotion law was
replaced by the National Executive Council Announcement No. 227,
which provided more incentives for export industries. In another revision
in 1977, the BOI's range of incentives for promoted firms was actually
increased.[11] This amendment gave the BOI power to levy a special import surcharge to help promoted firms. In addition, imported material
inputs and imported products to be re-exported were exempted from import duties and business taxes when the income was derived from export
activities. Promoted firms were permitted a 2 per cent deduction on the
increases of income over the previous year for income tax purposes.

---

[11] The BOI could grant exemptions, or reductions of up to 50 per cent, of import
duties and business taxes on imported machinery, as well as business taxes on domestically produced machinery; reductions of up to 90 per cent of import duties and
business taxes on both imported materials and domestic materials; exemptions from
corporate income taxes for three to eight years, with carry-forward of losses for up to
five years after the period of exemptions; exclusion from taxable income of fees for
goodwill, copyright and other rights for a period of five years after income was derived
from the promoted activity; and exclusion from taxable income of dividends derived
from the promoted activity during the period of tax holiday.

The BOI has considerable discretionary authority to determine which firms got what privileges. The 1972 Investment Act and the 1977 revision of the Industrial Promotion Act empowered the BOI to grant privileges to promoted firms. In the early 1970s, Thai technocrats started to realize the seriousness of the problems being created. Some import-competing industries were highly inefficient as a result of high tariff protection and heavy reliance on imported capital goods and intermediate products. Industry had little employment absorptive capacity. Firms were heavily concentrated around the capital, with over 75 per cent of total value added of the manufacturing sector deriving from Bangkok and the surrounding provinces. In addition, the Third Plan (1972–76) pointed to poverty problems created by rapid industrialization, increasing income disparity between households in different regions and between residents in rural and urban areas, and rising trade and current account deficits as a result of inadequate domestic savings to finance rapidly growing investment. The Fourth Plan (1977–82) reiterated a similar list of problems.

Despite the amendments to the investment promotion law in 1972 and 1977, the structure of incentives still favoured import-substitution industries and was biased against the agricultural sector. The contribution of import-substitution to growth was significant during 1966–72, declined during 1972–75, and became negative during 1975–78. The contribution of export demand rose from 6.5 per cent during 1966–72, to 8.5 per cent during 1972–77, and jumped to 28.2 per cent during 1975–78 (Meesook *et al.* 1988).

The Failed "Big Push"

A large scale industrial development entitled the Eastern Seaboard Development Program was initiated in the early 1980s. The discovery of natural gas in the Gulf of Thailand made this "Big Push" possible. The initial forecast of investment was around US$ 4 billion (in constant 1981 value). The Eastern Seaboard was chosen because of direct access to the Gulf of Thailand through a deep-sea port at Sattahip, and good infrastructure connections to supplies of labour and raw materials from the northeast. Natural gas would be the foundation for a petrochemicals industry, both upstream and downstream, and fertilizer production. NESDB, formerly a planning and monitoring agency, was set to implement the project.

However, the project stalled. Some component ventures were criticized on grounds of economic viability. Financial constraints caused by the oil crisis resulted in sub-projects being delayed, reduced, or deleted from the plan for fear of landing Thailand with the sort of debts saddling Latin American countries. When oil prices declined, enthusiasm for this Big Push project waned.

Export Orientation: The First Attempt Failed, Will the Next Succeed?

In the late 1980s, the Thai economy began to grow rapidly on the basis of rapidly increasing manufactured exports (Akrasanee and Wattanukit 1990; Jansen 1991; Robinson, Byeon, and Teja 1991; Santikarn Kaosa-ard 1992). I shall argue that this impressive growth masked many problems.

The Fifth Plan (1983–86) and Sixth Plan (1987–91) were probably responsible for the impressive growth. The Fifth Plan proposed restructuring of local industries for competitiveness in export production, and highlighted the strategic importance of the machinery industry and agro-industries. The Sixth Plan paid more attention to increasing efficiency in management and utilization of resources as well as enhancing international competitiveness and alleviating poverty in rural areas. The aim seems to have been to become a NAIC (Newly Agro-Industrialized Country) in the short run and a NIE in the medium or long run.

In the 1980s, the world economy was in difficulty. Third World countries were subjected to a series of historically unprecedented external shocks. In the early part of the decade, a slump in industrial countries depressed Third World manufacturing exports, and led to a sharp fall in commodity prices — by some accounts, to their lowest level in the post-war period (Singh 1992). Thailand suffered persistent current account deficits and rapidly increasing foreign debt, eventually obliging the government to go to the IMF and the World Bank for balance-of-payments support and adjustment assistance (Thanapornpun 1990). Unfavourable terms of trade led to the largest trade deficit the country had experienced since the Second World War, rising from 5.8 per cent of GDP in 1978 to 9.8 per cent in 1983. The prices of rice and other traditional crops declined dramatically. The Thai government and public enterprises were still burdened with debts incurred since the 1970s.

This crisis resulted in the destruction of one of the major obstacles facing a successful shift to an export-oriented strategy, namely the over-valued exchange rate.

Thailand had maintained a fixed nominal exchange rate against the dollar for 26 years since 1955. Thai technocrats had become renowned for pursuing conservative monetary policies, particularly the maintenance of this stable rate.[12]

The value of the baht had increased with rise of the US dollar value since 1981, making the baht overvalued compared with other important currencies such as the British pound and German mark, and hindering any strategy of export promotion (Meesook *et al.* 1988). The overvalued exchange rate was biased against export producers, especially primary commodity producers such as rice farmers, and harmful to the export-promoting trade strategy (Bhagwati 1988a). Before May 1981, the Bank of Thailand was reluctant to devalue the baht, despite a significant appreciation of the real exchange rate, because devaluation was considered politically sensitive, and something to be avoided if there was a choice.

But the rise in the value of the US dollar, and the deterioration in Thailand's balance of payments inevitably encouraged speculation that the Thai baht would be devalued. Finally on 15 July 1981, the baht was devalued by 8.7 per cent, and the daily fixing method was abolished. The Thai government had to devalue again on 2 November 1984, setting a new rate at 27 baht per dollar.[13]

Export-oriented industrialization took off from the mid-1980s, in accordance with major changes in the world economic environment. After the Plaza Accord of September 1985, the currencies of the Asian NIEs, except that of Hong Kong, appreciated against the US dollar and other currencies such as the Deutschmark (Shinohara 1989). As the Thai baht was closely tied to the dollar, it was devalued against these other currencies, especially the yen, immensely benefiting the export strategy. The year 1985 was a turning point for the Thai economy. The external environment improved with declines in interest rates and oil prices, while the prices of traditional commodity exports began to recover. Demand for Thai exports had begun to pick up since the two devaluations in 1981 and 1984. The annual increase in export value jumped to 20.7 per cent in 1986, 28.8 per cent in 1987, and 33.9 per cent in 1988. After the currency realignment in 1985, Japanese manufacturers began to relocate their production bases to Thailand.

---

[12] The Bank of Thailand is responsible for foreign exchanges and monetary policy. This conservative stance is a legacy of British advisers in the late nineteenth century.
[13] The rate was set at 21 baht per dollar from 1955 to 12 May 1981, when the Bank of Thailand devalued the baht by 1.1 per cent. After 15 July 1981, the rate was 23 baht per dollar.

By the late 1980s, Thailand had become an attractive investment location in Southeast Asia due to both economic and non-economic factors. The country had high economic growth without high inflation, unstable exchange rates, or political turmoil (Mackie 1988). Furthermore, the private-enterprise economy, positive attitude towards foreigners, and increasingly export-oriented strategy induced foreign investors to relocate industrial plants to Thailand. In particular, Thailand was an attractive country for Japanese firms because of abundant, cheap, and hard-working labour (Ichikawa, Cusumano, and Polenske 1991).

The two devaluations in the 1980s helped to attract a massive influx of foreign direct investment from Japan and the East Asian NIEs, mainly into labour-intensive and resource-based industries. Despite Thailand still having surplus labour in the rural area, this policy again resulted in the import of capital-intensive technology.

In 1985 and 1986 growth decelerated to 3.5 per cent and 4.5 per cent respectively, but then recovered more rapidly with the growth rate reaching 9.5 per cent in 1987, 13.2 per cent in 1988, and 11.6 per cent in 1990. These rates far exceeded the Philippines (Yoshihara 1995), probably because of Thailand's comparative success in maintaining macroeconomic stability with moderate growth during the downturn of 1973–86 (Ranis 1991; Ranis and Mahmood 1992).

Foreign direct investment increased by 67 per cent in 1986, 360 per cent in 1987, and 140 per cent in 1988. In 1987, Japanese investment approved by the BOI exceeded the cumulative investment in Thailand since the 1960s. Taiwan was the next biggest foreign investor. The large inflow of foreign direct investment was the main contributor to the country's economic recovery and decisive turn to export-oriented industrialization (OECF 1991; Yoshida 1990). Japanese foreign firms invested in both natural resource-based and labour-intensive industries, including electrical appliances, electronics, transportation equipment, metal products, textiles, agricultural and fishery products. Taiwanese investments concentrated on labour-intensive light manufacturing such as sports goods, toys, shoes, bags, plastics, and some agro-industries such as frozen shrimp. Three-quarters of the applications to the BOI were in export-oriented industries with export ratios ranging from 80 per cent to 100 per cent.

Industrial relocation from Japan and the East Asian NIEs to Thailand was undertaken for at least two main reasons: the high yen, and changes in comparative advantage. The Asian NIEs began to lose their comparative advantage in labour-intensive manufactured products such as textiles and clothing.

In the 1980s, industry overtook agriculture as the leading sector of GDP, and Thailand was dubbed the "Fifth Tiger" (Falkus 1992; Muscat 1994; Warr 1993). But will Thailand be able to catch up with the East Asian NIEs in the coming decade? What are the lessons of the Thailand case for other developing countries?

Recent studies show that exports of manufactured goods contributed between 40 and 60 per cent of the increase in GNP from 1984 to 1987, but then declined to 28.8 per cent in 1989 and 11 per cent in 1990 (Santikarn Kaosa-ard 1992). This implies that Thai manufactured exports have not matured.

From 1960 to 1970, domestic demand contributed 89.1 per cent to economic growth, export demand 11.4 per cent, and import-substitution a small negative contribution of –0.6 per cent. By contrast over 1985–8, the contribution of export demand had risen to 45.3 per cent, but the contribution of domestic demand was even higher at 78.1 per cent while import-substitution was strongly negative at –23.4 per cent (Jansen 1991). Thai manufactured exports still depend very much on cheap and abundant labour and natural resources rather than technology, capital accumulation, or human capital formation (Dahlman and Brimble 1990; UNIDO 1992). The measurement of high growth fails to take account of resource depletion including severe deforestation, environmental degradation, and pollution (Brander 1992; see Chapter 3). Factoring in these elements would lower the growth rates.

Unless pollution can be controlled, environmental decline will worsen. A recent study by TDRI estimated that the quantity of hazardous waste would rise from 1.1 million tons in 1986 to reach 6 million tons by 2001. Most of this waste is generated by the manufacturing sector. In addition, the numbers of serious industrial accidents suggests that the Thai bureaucracy is not competent enough to cope with problems emerging from the industrialization process.

Export-oriented Industrialization with Land Abundance and a Weak State

Why was Thailand (and most other developing countries) unable to replicate the successful growth of the East Asian NIEs?

Most recent studies argue that increased manufactured exports and foreign direct investment were the main contributors to Thailand's recent high economic growth (OECF 1991; Jansen 1991). The growth rate of Thai exports has far exceeded that of world exports since 1984. Some economists now compare Thailand to the East Asian NIEs, and attribute rapid growth to an export-oriented strategy, laissez-faire policy, private enterprise, and the magic of the market place. I shall contest this view in two interlocking ways. Firstly, I will question whether the high growth of the East Asian economies can be attributed to the export-oriented strategy and the magic of laissez-faire. Secondly, I will question whether Thailand can be classified alongside the East Asian NIEs given its very different historical inheritance, initial conditions, and institutional context.

Mainstream development economists firmly support the superiority of a trade strategy of export promotion over import-substitution. The rapid rate of economic growth in the East Asian NIEs during the last two decades has frequently been cited as a classic example of export-led growth. The World Bank sells this idea to developing countries no matter what their legacy of historical, cultural, or institutional factors is. It is claimed that an export-oriented strategy is powerful enough to increase per capita income, savings ratios, investment ratios, total factor productivity, employment, and real wages. Other claimed benefits include a fairer distribution of income, a decline in the incremental capital-output ratio, and better adjustment to external shocks (Balassa 1980; Bhagwati 1988a; Donges 1976; Little, Scitovsky, and Scott 1970).

However, many recent studies challenge this thesis (Adelman 1985; Evans 1990; Grabowski 1994b; Gunnarsson 1985; Milner 1990; Oshima 1993; Singh 1992). They argue that East Asian states were highly interventionist. They attribute their successful growth to the existence of a hard state. Their argument raises the issue of why such successful interventionist states are not found elsewhere.

High Economic Growth: What Factors Contributed?

Thailand's high growth from the 1950s to the 1980s was based on high population growth and exploitation of environmental resources, especially forests. Until the 1970s, the agricultural sector was promoted to achieve growth and generate a surplus to support industrialization by squeezing the farmers and using up natural resources, rather than through technological progress.

The Thai government depressed the price of rice through taxation in order to reduce the cost of the staple food and hence lower the cost of living of industrial workers and urban dwellers. The tax on rice was removed in 1986. According to one study, the import-substitution strategy associated with high protection through the overvalued exchange rate was notably biased against primary exports, whilst promoted manufacturing firms reaped the economic gains at the expense of the rural poor (Siamwalla and Setboonsarng 1989).

Thailand was probably the only country in Asia where cultivated land per agricultural worker actually increased until 1977 (Siamwalla 1991). Land abundance made it possible for Thai farmers to expand the cultivated area. Agriculture absorbed large amounts of labour, often seasonal labour, resulting in Thailand still having a larger proportion of its labour force in this sector compared to other Asian countries with a similar income level. The availability of land gave Thailand a strong comparative advantage in agriculture.

High economic growth was attained by increasing the area under cultivation at the expense of forest areas, especially in the uplands, to plant cash crops like rice, cassava, maize, jute, kenaf, and sugarcane. The expansion of cultivated areas without a corresponding increase in productivity was irrational, to say the least.

The resulting rapid deforestation has now turned into a major national problem. Between 1960 and 1990, 90 million *rai* of forest were denuded at the average of 3 million *rai* per year (6.25 *rai* = 1 hectare) (Panayoutou and Parasuk 1990; Panayoutou and Sungsuwan 1989). Forest cover declined from 50 per cent of land area in the early 1960s to approximately 20 per cent in the mid-1980s, and 15 per cent in 1986 according to unofficial estimates — one of the highest rates of deforestation anywhere in the world in the post-war era. By 1968, Thailand became a net importer of wood.

One factor underlying deforestation has been the weak policing of property rights in land. Although illegal logging by people with political connections is often blamed for deforestation, the expansion of titled land under cultivation is more significant. Landless and small farmers clear land illegally in the expectation that they will eventually secure a title (Siamwalla 1991; see Chapter 3).

The Thai state has been too weak to enforce the law protecting forest land from encroachment. There is no framework of political and judicial organizations that effectively and impartially enforce contracts. Thailand seems to fit Gunnar Myrdal's model of a "soft state". Property rights in land in Thailand have been very insecure and chaotic. Some scholars believe this has come about because Thailand has never had a genuine land tax, and thus never instituted a proper system of land titling. Weak property rights discouraged investment in agriculture, and thus contributed to technological backwardness and low productivity.

Imbalanced Structure of Employment

A major problem of Thai industrialization lies in the fact that the employment share of the manufacturing industry did not track the production share. In 1990, manufacturing industry contributed 26 per cent of GDP but employed only 10 per cent of the labour force. The weak labour-absorptive capacity of Thai manufacturing industry is a serious obstacle to agricultural modernization, and has resulted in the accumulation of the urban poor. People migrate from rural areas to find jobs in Bangkok but cannot enter the formal sector because they have low levels of skill, and so enter the informal sector as a last resort. One outcome of this dualistic unbalanced growth is over-urbanization. Bangkok has expanded over time and its ratio of the population living in slum areas remains very high among developing countries. The urban informal sector includes street vendors, peddlers, repairmen, shop assistants, domestic servants, and day workers in construction. Low productivity and low wages in the urban informal sector push down the real wage in this primate city. Rural-urban migration in Thailand is crucial for many farmers who seek jobs in the slack season. Over time, this source of earning has become increasingly significant for rural families (Oshima 1993; Siriprachai 1985b), partly because the price of agricultural products has been declining since the 1980s, and Thai governments have been unable to insulate the domestic market from international price fluctuations.

In 1990, the agricultural sector employed 64 per cent of the labour force yet produced less than 13 per cent of GDP, clearly indicating a very low level of productivity in the agricultural sector (Ezaki 1990). Judging from any standard textbook in economic development, Thailand cannot be classified as a newly industrializing economy, nor can it be said that Thailand has achieved economic development. One measurement of industrialization is the proportion of the working population engaged in manufacturing.

Kuznets argued that as industrialization matures, the gap of productivity (and income) between agriculture and industry will narrow, yet in Thailand the gap has been widening. The industrial sector has not been successful in absorbing the labour force migrating out of the agricultural sector. Industrial wages have been artificially depressed by the low food price policy.

The progress made in shifting the labour force out of agriculture into industrial jobs has been very slow. As the evidence of the past has demonstrated, this imbalance might not be remedied by either import-substitution or export-oriented strategy. The root cause partly lies in the fact that Thailand is a land-abundant country (Siamwalla 1991).

Land Abundance and Its Consequences

Two theories might be fruitful in explaining this imbalanced industrialization process. One is known as the resource curse thesis (Auty 1994). The other is about the nature of the state, and what factors make a state either benign and developmental, or predatory (Grabowski 1994b; Gunnarsson and Lundahl 1994; Johnson 1982; Kohli 1994; Lee 1993; Leftwich 1995; Soon 1994; Wade 1990, 1993). Both theories may apply in the Thai context.

A major and often forgotten difference between East Asia and Southeast Asia is that the agricultural sector in the East Asian NIEs underwent a dramatic period of reform and productivity growth prior to import-substitution industrialization (Grabowski 1994b; Gunnarsson 1985; Kohli 1994; Oshima 1993). This reform was driven by resource constraints, and made possible by land reform. It entailed heavy investment in irrigation and drainage facilities, increased use of fertilizer and higher yielding seeds, and dissemination of knowledge by farmers' groups (Grabowski 1994b; Kohli 1994).

By contrast, in Thailand, pressure for higher output resulted in expansion of cultivated area rather than investments in improving productivity.

When Thailand began to pursue industrialization, there was a large amount of unused land and abundant labour due to rapid population growth since the Second World War (Siamwalla 1991; see Chapter 3). This starting point was as different as chalk from cheese when compared to the East Asian NIEs. Abundant natural resources meant that, unlike much of Asia, Thailand was never haunted by the Malthusian ghost of population pressure. In the absence of such pressure, the Thai government could implement a lax regime of import-substitution industrialization, and rely on the agricultural sector to provide cheap food and cheap labour.

The experience of European countries in the eighteenth century offers a telling contrast. A stream of migrants from the rural areas to the cities resulted in a change from a feudal to a capitalist mode of production. The industrial sector was able to absorb this surplus labour, while technological progress in the agricultural sector gave rise to high productivity in land and labour. As a consequence, a modern economy developed quickly. The pattern of growth in the East Asian NIEs since the 1960s has been similar (Oshima 1978, 1993).

Thailand's resource curse was an abundance of land. In David Ricardo's classical study of the eighteenth century, fertile land often resulted in rent-seeking activities as the landlord tried to capture a large share of the resources made available by God. In the Thai context, the ease of generating exports from natural resources resulting in logging and extensive cultivation, and reduced the pressure on the Thai government to develop labour-intensive and knowledge-intensive manufactured exports from the 1950s to the 1980s. In sum, it may be too simple to embark on economic development relying only on resource endowment. But this was only part of the story.

What Makes States Developmental or Predatory?

The superior economic performance of the East Asian NIEs does not in fact lie in any general superiority of export-oriented industrialization strategy over import-substitution or of market-oriented policies over state intervention. Rather, the key factors were a competent state directing the accumulation process and a favourable international environment (Jenkins 1991).

For strong export growth to coexist with protection of imports requires conditions that are quite hard to come across in many countries. Japan was in many ways the model. The Japanese state exercised its power to channel foreign technologies into targeted key industries identified by the Ministry of International Trade and Industry. It also passed a foreign investment law empowering the state to ensure that technology transfer contracts would benefit the economy. As a result, between the 1950s and 1970s, Japanese industries were successful in accumulating and adapting modern technology from imports.

As clearly pointed out by Thomas *et al.* (1991), the state in South Korea controls investment in local production of luxuries and conspicuous consumer goods as well as restricts imports. It also keeps rent seeking and lobbying under control, suppresses unions, and penalizes executives of companies who misuse their privileges. We are unable to find anything similar from the Thai state, except briefly when Sarit Thanarat was prime minister (1957–63). One reason why the East Asian NIEs are able to avoid rent seeking, as argued by Chang (1994) and Evans (1989, 1992, 1995), is because authoritarian leaders can override interest-group demands by fiat (Haggard and Webb 1993). Furthermore, because they are able to stay in power for long periods, they can introduce major reforms such as trade liberalization without obstruction from vested interests.

The success of the NIEs rested on effective intervention by benign and benevolent states to build up the capacity of the nation in terms of both physical and human capital (Dore 1986; Johnson 1982; Vestal 1993). These states had a degree of autonomy from the dominant class or class fractions and hence their interventions were insulated against vested interests. They were able to concentrate on the acquisition and utilization of technological capacity, often from the advanced economies.

By contrast, in Thailand the state seems to have been impotent. Powerful industrialists and bureaucrats concentrated on extracting an economic surplus from the agricultural sector. The abundance of unused land allowed the Thai state to neglect reforms at the grassroots level. The ruling class was not seriously threatened by any social unrest among the lower classes since the mid-nineteenth century. The Thai state did not take on the characteristics of a strong and paternalistic developmental state, but instead evolved into a kind of bureaucratic polity and klepto-cracy without any accountability to civil society (Christensen and Siamwalla 1993; Riggs 1966; Thanapornpun 1990). While government jobs are well paid and carry prestige in East Asia, the Thai bureaucracy is low paid and full of corruption. The initial condition of abundant land seems to have made the Thai state predatory, not developmental (see Chapter 3).

The conditions which gave rise to the benign state in East Asia were special to a particular historical and institutional setting, and hence not simple to replicate elsewhere.

The transformation of the East Asian states was partly due to ex-ternal threats (Grabowski 1994b; Gunnarsson and Lundahl 1994; Kohli 1994). In the Meiji era, Japan faced the possibility of colonization by a western power. In the Cold War era, Taiwan and South Korea felt at risk from threats of communism and powerful neighbours, namely communist China and North Korea. These threats helped to engender nationalism and popular support for state building, not unlike processes under way in the mercantilist era in Europe from the sixteenth to the eighteenth centuries. Nationalist pressure forced states to become agents of moderni-zation, and successful state policies won popular support and cooperation.

Internal changes were also important. Landlord classes had been destroyed during Japanese colonial rule. In South Korea, there was already a state-controlled banking system which provided finance for infant industries very similar to banks which had played a crucial part in Ger-many's catch-up industrialization in the nineteenth century (Berend and Ránki 1982).

Finally, timing was important. In the post-war era, capital, huge foreign aid, and privileged access to the US and Japanese markets helped to make the South Korean and Taiwanese miracles possible.

Thailand did not experience similar international threats, had never been forced to undergo land reform, had no tradition of state banking, and launched into export-led growth at a time when the world economy was much less dynamic than in the immediate post-war era. In other words, the specific historical experiences and international circumstances of the East Asian states significantly contributed to the development of relatively autonomous state and to the potential for success through export-led strategy. Southeast Asian states like Thailand are in a different position (Kohli 1994; Leftwich 1995; McGuire 1994; McVey 1992a).

In sum, the industrial policies of the East Asian NIEs stemmed from an institutional setting characterized by a hard state and strong government discipline over the private sector as Johnson (1982) pointed out in his seminal work on Japan:

> In the plan-rational state, the government will give greatest precedence to industrial policy, that is, to a concern with the structure of domestic industry and with promoting the structure that enhances the nation's international competitiveness. The very existence of an industrial policy implies a strategic or goal-oriented approach to the economy.

The system of incentives in Thailand bred corruption and rent seeking in part because it offered only privileges and no punishments for poor performance (Thomas *et al.* 1991). It fostered capital-intensive growth, not well matched to the country's factor endowment of abundant labour, by encouraging foreign firms to import labour-saving machinery and equipment.

Revisionists maintain that a hard state and strong government discipline are responsible for whatever success Thailand has achieved. Yet that may not be the full answer (Rodrik 1993, 1994). Timing was also important. The quantitative restrictions and export subsidies which fostered the NIEs' export-oriented industrialization would be difficult to replicate now (Kim 1994; Lee 1993; Leftwich 1995; McGuire 1994; Soon 1994; Wade 1993). As a World Bank study observed:

> The East Asian countries were successful in using protective import policies by avoiding exchange rate overvaluation and offsetting the anti export bias of import protection, their approach would be difficult to replicate in today's world economy. South Korea's approach during the 1960s and 1970s included export subsidies, which other countries

would countervail today, and vigorous government intervention to suppress rent seeking activities viewed as incompatible with export growth. (Thomas *et al.* 1991)

Human Capital Development

In Thailand, primary education is almost universal, but secondary enrolment is low. Most of the rural population sees no need to devote time for extensive schooling because there is no prospect of commensurate material reward. Thailand lags behind other countries in the region, and has the worst secondary enrolment ratios in Asia (Sussangkarn 1990, 1992). The lack of skilled labour is a bottleneck no matter what development strategy is pursued. Even if all primary school leavers from now on were to enrol in secondary education, TDRI projects that in 2000, 70 per cent of Thailand's work force would have only primary education or less (6 years). This will leave Thailand without a development path and a comparative advantage only in cheap labour.

Export-oriented industrialization requires active and strong government intervention in human capital development. Those countries which have succeeded in achieving high rates of growth through exports have a large, highly educated labour force (Oshima 1993). It is doubtful whether Thailand is capable of catching up with the East Asian NIEs. A high rate of secondary enrolment is a prerequisite for sustainable development.

The very successful late industrialization in European countries such as Sweden in the late nineteenth century depended on an educated workforce able to exploit the potential of science and technology (Jörberg 1965, 1972, 1991). This "social capacity" in the term of Moses Abramovitz (1989) is necessary for converting technological knowledge into productivity growth.

The role of the state is, of course, essential for investing resources in formal and vocational education. In the modern world, a basic level of scientific and vocational knowledge becomes crucial. Thailand has failed to develop this crucial "social capacity" and hence the technical competence of its people is very weak (Dahlman and Brimble 1990; Siriprachai 1985a; UNIDO 1992). As a general rule, there is a strong positive relationship between the secondary school enrolment rate and the degree of industrialization. In Thailand, the share of the population with training in technical subjects is low, and there is an acute shortage of engineers and other technical manpower.

The East Asian NIEs spent more on education than other developing countries of a similar income level. They also biased the spending towards technical areas such as engineering. A competent bureaucracy was required to carry out this social goal. Some argue that Confucian social values were partly responsible for the success of the East Asian NIEs, while Islamic and Hindu social values are less conducive to modern economic growth (Oshima 1993).

Infrastructure

The surge of economic growth has created a demand for infrastructure of all kinds — electric power, telephones, transportation, ports, airports, waterworks, and so on. While such infrastructure is undoubtedly needed, I want to draw attention to another form of missing infrastructure, namely a legal system for effective implementation of private contracts as well as contracts between the private sector and the state (Stiglitz 1992).

In Thailand, the role of the state is not merely ambiguous, it is also very vague (see Chapter 4). The state can enforce some kinds of law and maintain political stability, but is often too weak to protect private property rights, or even public property. The Thai bureaucracy has failed to prevent destruction of forests, a form of national property, or to prevent severe pollution from toxic chemical waste. A major task for the Thai government is to reform the legal system, especially in ways that will curb corruption and rent seeking (Sathirathai 1987; Siriprachai 1990, 1993; Pecorino 1992).

The weakness of the legal system allows the development of a political culture which is unlikely to result in sound economic policy. Politicians are able to earn money from the allocation of rent-seeking opportunities, and then invest that money in securing election to stay in positions of power and influence. The party system is fragmented by the competition of different rent-seeking groups. Political entrepreneurs compete to gain influence over sectors of the economy which offer opportunities for rent seeking.

Weak administrative law and the prevalence of patron-client relationships combine to hinder economic development. Political entrepreneurs and state bureaucrats manipulate the legal framework for international trade. Lawyers are aware that Thai administrative law lacks transparency and means for enforcement, thereby allowing state officials to wield excessive discretionary power (Sathirathai 1987; Siriprachai 1990; see Chapter 4). Many young Thai lawyers also observe that Thailand's administrative law code is old, short, lacking in details, and makes the bureaucracy autonomous from legal challenges. The lack of administrative courts only consolidates this autonomy. Under these circumstances, ministers have unlimited power over the control, allocation, and management of economic activities such as the allocation of export quotas for products like cassava and textiles (Siriprachai 1988, 1990). Vote buying arose first in the northeast and later became pervasive (Parnwell and Rigg 1993; Samudavanija 1989, 1992; Tamada 1991). Economic policies are now decided by ministers selected through this system. As a result of the country being under an authoritarian regime for a long period after 1947, the Thai parliament has not developed much of a role in scrutinizing the activities of the bureaucracy (Thanapornpun 1990).

The Distribution of Income

The Thai government has been rather concerned with its traditional functions, namely the provision of social and economic infrastructure, the maintenance of a stable economic framework, and the promotion of growth. Social policy has received less attention; the state has put no emphasis on income distribution or the achievement of specific social goals.

Progress has been achieved in the fields of primary education and health care. Life expectancy has risen, while illiteracy has clearly fallen. The quality of life has also improved. However, living standards remain low among agricultural workers and small farmers. Absolute poverty in rural areas declined from the 1950s to the 1970s. However, the general depression in world commodity markets after the 1980s adversely impinged on Thai farmers at large. Rural poverty started to rise again in the early 1980s. Inequality has worsened. As Timmer (1991) observed:

> Thailand did not use similar trade and pricing for key commodities in an effort to protect domestic farmers from the very low prices that occur from time to time in the world market. Although the strong performance of Thailand in terms of rising labour productivity argues that such free-trade policies promote growth, Thailand paid a price in terms of rural poverty.

In the early 1980s, the Thai government seemed reluctant to implement the structural adjustment programmes fully. Reforms in tax policy, government expenditure, and other matters affecting poverty and distribution were neglected in favour of measures to launch export-oriented industrialization.

Although an Agricultural Land Reform Act was enacted in 1975, land reform has been very limited and ineffective at insulating poor farmers from becoming indebted. Attempts to limit private land owner-ship were never successful due to vested interests. In 1995, a government fell because of corruption over a land reform programme.

Monetary and financial policy has focused on maintaining a stable exchange rate and low inflation (Siamwalla and Setboonsarng 1989). No serious measures have been implemented to achieve greater equity in regional and personal income levels. Indeed the priority rating of this matter has even fallen over time.

Some benefits of high growth since the 1960s have of course trickled down to the poor. Absolute poverty declined steadily from 57 per cent in 1962–63 to 24 per cent in 1981. Many recent studies on income dis-tribution emphasize that a decline in the incidence of poverty can take place simultaneously with a worsening of income distribution. Income inequality has worsened in every region, both in rural and urban areas, over three decades (Hutaserani and Jitsuchon 1988; Sussangkarn 1992; Tinakorn 1992).

The income share of the richest 20 per cent of households increased from 50 per cent of total in 1975–76 to 55 per cent in 1988–89, but declined to 43 in 1990–91. The share of the poorest 20 per cent declined from 8 per cent in 1975–76 to 4.5 per cent in 1988–89 but recovered to 8.5 per cent in 1990–91 (Sussangkarn 1992). These data should be interpreted with caution. The gap between rich and poor was once much less in Thailand than in Latin America countries such as Brazil and Mexico, but that difference has been eroded. The Gini coefficient was around 0.45 between the 1960s and 1980s, but rose to 0.52 in 1992.

Rising income inequality both between the industrial and agricul-tural sectors and between regions reflects the nature and competence of the Thai state (see Chapter 4). Neither import-substituting nor export-oriented industries have absorbed much labour (Santikarn Kaosa-ard 1992; UNIDO 1992; Ezaki 1990; Watanabe 1992). Government price-support programmes have not been able to counter the downward trend of commodity prices on the world market. Sussangkarn (1990, 1992) points out that uneven development in productivity between agricultural and industrial sectors is a crucial cause of worsening income distribution. Rising inequality is a function of several factors inherent in a develop-ment strategy, as pointed out by Griffin (1989):

> These factors include the distribution of productive assets (particularly land), the distribution of education opportunities, the employment

intensity of development path and the general policy stance of government.... It is possible to prevent large income disparities emerging and the income structure being wrenched apart by adopting a development strategy that places high priority on an equal distribution of agricultural land, universal access to primary and secondary education, labour-intensive methods of production and a pattern of international trade that reflects the relative availability of resources.

The Thai government, as in most developing countries, has been biased against the agricultural sector and in favour of the industrial sector. Government investment has also been biased towards the urban areas, in particular Bangkok. Despite writing objectives of eradicating rural poverty into national plans, coining slogans such as the "year of the farmer", and launching a programme of land reform in the early 1990s, efforts at alleviating poverty and inequality have been very limited. Thai governments have been inclined to subsidize urban workers by providing food subsidies via a cheap rice policy. Rural migrants seeking jobs in the informal sector in Bangkok in the slack season also benefit directly. But the main beneficiaries are urban workers and consumers in the industrial and the service sectors.

Thai agriculture is characterized by small family farms in the cultivation of rice and upland crops except sugarcane. Not being colonized by western countries during the mid-nineteenth century, Thai farmers have been saved from a plantation economy. But small farmers have difficulty mounting strong collective pressure because of very high transaction costs and a free rider problem (Olson 1965). Cooperatives and other farmer associations have concentrated on buying inputs and selling outputs in order to increase bargaining power with middlemen. They have not been successful at lobbying for assistance from the state in contrast to manufacturers' associations that have successfully sought protection and subsidies.

The development of democracy has not yet resulted in any policies to counter worsening inequality. The collapse of the military oligarchy in 1973 led to a semi-democracy or soft authoritarian regime with a parliamentary system (Samudavanija 1989, 1992). Elected members of parliament are now motivated to assist farmers in their constituencies. However, this results in pork barrel politics, not substantive reform. Politicians compete to gain access to public funds which they can distribute as support payments to their constituents in the hope of being rewarded by re-election (Siamwalla and Setboonsarng 1991).

Concluding Remarks

Thailand began its industrialization process with import-substitution and later shifted to an export-oriented strategy. The main problems are growing inequality in income distribution, an imbalanced structure of employment and production, environmental decline, concentration of manufacturing in Bangkok, and low secondary enrolment. The trends seem to be worsening.

Export-oriented strategy is just a trade policy, not the equivalent of development strategy. The Thai state practises a laissez-faire philosophy, wishing that the magic of the market will reduce income inequality and deliver high economic growth. In fact, the protection provided by the Thai state through the BOI and other institutions allows exporters of manufactures to reap profits while the agricultural sector bears the burden. Foreign investment helps to hasten economic growth and induce the rural poor to migrate to the city. Thailand enjoys high but higgledy-piggledy economic growth (Siamwalla 1993), and lags behind in the real meaning of economic development.

We cannot understand the present without understanding the past. Looking at Europe's industrialization, O'Brien (1994) concluded:

> Structural change refers to the fact that their accumulating stocks of capital, work forces, and technologies became discernibly less and less engaged with producing food and agrarian raw materials, or with servicing agriculture, and more involved with industry, especially manufacturing, and with the trade, transport, finance, and construction related to industry. Structural change which appears in the composition of European nation outputs, in the allocation of labour across sectors of economies, and in relation to the modernity of the machines, tools, and forms of organization utilized to produce goods and services were invariably accompanied by population growth and urbanization, the spread of literacy, the integration of markets, closer involvement in international commerce, the diffusion of advanced technology, institutional and political reforms, and several other familiar features of modern economic growth.

Judging from the above description of structural change in industrialization, Thailand will need to institute a genuine policy reform in the years to come. At the moment (1997), a truly democratic regime is needed to formulate economic and social policies which can bring about a better standard of living, increase economic opportunities, and make income distribution more equal.

Economic development as a historical process is strongly determined by the initial conditions. In Thailand, the striking feature of the initial conditions was land abundance. As a result, Thai elites focused on tapping natural resource rents to such an extent that resources have dwindled to a critical level. There is a need for new technologies which will raise the agricultural and industrial sectors to a high level in order to sustain economic growth. A benevolent state is needed to create key new institutions for achieving economic growth and equity. So far, attempts to create such institutions have not been successful due to Thailand's historical and institutional context which has hindered rather than promoted any positive substantial changes in the last 50 years.

CHAPTER 3

Population Growth, Fertility Decline, Poverty, and Deforestation in Thailand, 1850–1990

The goal of this paper is to tie together a number of ideas on population in Thailand during the period 1850–1990 with a focus on the linkages between economic growth, fertility, poverty, and environment, particularly deforestation. Previous studies have emphasized one or another of these issues without attempting to integrate them. Here, I follow the excellent paper by Malcolm Falkus on Thai economic history during the last 150 years (Falkus 1991), particularly his insights on rapid economic growth during the late 1980s as the culmination of the prior two decades' major transformation of the Thai economy. Until the 1970s, the economy was primarily agricultural with a low level of productivity and relatively poor infrastructure facilities. Agriculture contributed almost twice as much as manufacturing to GDP, while exports relied heavily on a few products such as rice, rubber, tin, maize, and tapioca.[1]

Thailand's relatively rapid economic growth dates from the first half of the 1970s with real GDP expanding at annual rates of about 6 per cent on the basis of an import-substitution strategy led by domestic growth. With the first oil shock in the early 1970s, Thai policy makers began to turn towards export-led growth. Since the mid-1980s, Thailand

---

[1] In the colonial era, Thailand maintained its independence but developed a colonial economy, producing rice for export under high comparative advantage as vent for surplus, mainly to areas where colonial regimes fostered a monoculture of existing export crops (Ingram 1971; Resnick 1970). Thailand developed a rice monoculture in the nineteenth century, and diversified its agriculture after the Second World War (Brown 1963; Silcock 1970).

has been among the fastest growing economies in the world, stimulated by enormous expansion of manufactured exports, tourism, and foreign direct investment. Manufacturing has been dynamic. During the last two decades, Thailand has also succeeded in reducing poverty. According to TDRI, around 25 per cent of the population is estimated to be living below the poverty line of 20,705 baht per year for a rural family of two adults and three children or 31,620 baht for an urban family (Sussang-karn 1992). Economic growth, especially the relatively high growth rates achieved in the recent past and expected in the future, tends to improve living standards. At the same time, rapid growth has created acute problems in Bangkok; these include garbage collection, water shortage, flood prevention, and congested roads.

The first section of this paper traces population trends from 1850 and 1990. The second explains the demographic transition in which fertility rates fell markedly between the 1960s and 1980s. As most population economists believe that this transformation of reproductive behaviour constitutes a special case among Third World countries (Knodel, Havanon, and Pramualratana 1984), this section attempts to identify the factors contributing to the rapidly declining rates of fertility in Thailand. The third section explores the relationship between population growth and deforestation. The fourth presents a bird's eye view of economic growth in Thailand, along with probable bottlenecks.

Population in Thailand, 1850–1990

There are a number of problems concerning the reliability of population estimates for Thailand. Perhaps the best known estimates are those of Skinner (1957). However, Manarungsan (1989) has recently shown that much of that data is not reliable. It seems likely that in the nineteenth century the whole of the kingdom had less than 6 million people.

Historically, the economy has been characterized by expensive labour. The Thai feudal or *sakdina* system primarily aimed at controlling the labour force.[2] During the late nineteenth and early twentieth centuries, an influx of Chinese immigrants played an important role in overcoming

---

[2] The *sakdina* system was a social system based on unequal exchange of goods, services, and prestige within a hierarchy of social rank and patron-client relations (Siamwalla 1980; Eoseewong n.d.).

Table 3.1 Total Population, Chinese, and Density (present territory)

Year	Population ('000)	Index (1860 = 100)	Chinese (%)	Persons (per km²)
1825	4,750	87	4.8	9
1850	5,200	95	5.8	10
1860	5,450	100	6.2	11
1870	5,775	106	6.0	11
1880	6,200	114	7.0	12
1990	6,670	122	7.5	13
1900	7,320	134	8.3	14
1910	8,305	152	9.5	16
1913	8,689	159		
1917	9,232	169	9.8	18
1922	10,202	187	10.5	20
1927	11,419	210	11.7	22
1929	12,058	221		
1932	13,087	240	12.2	25
1937	14,721	270	11.8	28
1938	14,980	275		
1942	16,066	295	11.7	31
1947	18,148	333	12.0	35
1950	19,817	364	11.8	37
1960	26,668	489		51
1970	36,341	667		70
1980	46,474	853		90
1983	49,459	908		95

Sources: 1825–42 – Skinner (1957: 79); 1947–83 – Corsel (1986: 57).

the labour shortage. Chinese immigrants accounted for around half of Bangkok's net population increase, and ethnic Chinese likewise contributed half of its population (Skinner 1957). Following the depression of the 1930s, the inflow of Chinese immigrants decreased, and decreased again after an Immigration Act limited the number of immigrants from each country to 200 per year. After the Second World War, the indigenous population increased rapidly, although prior to the 1950s there had been no sign of a population explosion. Thailand developed from a sparsely settled country with abundant land and expensive labour into a frontier of settlement with cheap labour (Falkus 1991). More significantly, population growth has been unevenly distributed. The northeast region, the poorest and least well endowed area, now contains around a third of the total population.

In any event, population estimates of Thailand have to be interpreted with caution. The transportation network was completed only in 1960s, bringing possibilities of high rural-to-urban and rural-to-rural mobility. Seasonal migration became a regular phenomenon (Fuller, Kamnuansilpa, and Lightfoot 1990; Prothero and Chapman 1985; Goldstein and Goldstein 1986; Sussangkarn 1987). Even the usually reliable population estimates in each region produced by census may be outdated and thus not capture the real figure. Projections by TDRI indicate that Thailand's population might reach 64 million by the year 2000, with an annual growth rate of 1.4 per cent between 1990 and 2000. If this projection is correct, and much of it is based on questionable reading of the evidence, then it would show that the population explosion was not a permanent phenomenon but only a demographic transition.

Table 3.2 Population, Annual Growth Rates, and Density, 1911–86

Year	Population (million)	Annual Growth	Density (pop./km²)
1911	8.3	–	16
1919	9.4	1.4	18
1929	11.5	2.2	22
1937	14.7	2.9	28
1947	17.5	1.9	34
1960	26.3	3.2	51
1970	43.4	2.8	67
1980	44.8	2.7	92
1986	52.6	1.6	98

Source: *Statistical Yearbook of Thailand.*

Population Growth and Fertility Decline

An Overview of Demographic Transition

Thailand experienced no population pressure in the nineteenth and early twentieth centuries. The population almost doubled in the 36 years between 1911 and 1947, largely due to Chinese immigration. It doubled again in the 23 years between 1947 and 1970 due to natural population increase with very little Chinese immigration. The most rapid population growth took place in the 1950s and 1960s. In this era, the Thai government encouraged child bearing. Propaganda in the mass media was complemented by governmental incentives for married couples with children. More important factors behind this baby boom were, however, the disappearance of wartime restraints and medical advances for the prevention of malaria. The end result was that Thailand became a densely populated country with cheap rural labour.

The Fifth National Economic and Social Development Plan (1982–86) stated that rapid population growth had become a major problem, with implications on poverty, the natural environment, and resource base. In essence the problem lay in very high fertility rates (Prasith-rathsing 1987). The Plan aimed to reduce the growth rate per annum to 1.5 per cent by 1986. In the late 1960s, the Thai government received substantial foreign aid from international organizations such as the World Bank, WHO, and USAID to reduce fertility rates.

Many models suggest that lower birth rates mean more savings available for investment, whereas high population growth causes a shortage of production factors such as capital, land, and natural resources in general (Ohlin 1991). International organizations such as the World Bank began to provide funds to developing countries to launch family planning programmes. A flood of World Bank missions came to Thailand and recommended strategies to reduce the fertility rate in rural areas. World Bank economists doubted whether the Fifth Plan would reduce the growth rate to 1.5 per cent by 1986. They believed that further reduction in fertility would be considerably more difficult to achieve than in the past (World Bank 1984).

Seeing rapid population growth as a problem was in part prompted by the reactions of some international organizations, comprising of a majority of members from the West, to a food crisis in India and Asia as a whole during the 1960s. This led to an exaggerated revival of neo-Malthusian ideas. Even though the idea of rapid population growth causing food shortages and famines is quite ancient, it suddenly seemed that the growth rates of Third World populations would outstrip their capacity to feed themselves (Ohlin 1991).

Thailand had never experienced severe food shortage and famines, even with rapid population growth throughout the twentieth century due to in-migration, declining mortality, and continued high fertility (Huta-serani and Roumasset 1991). From the mid-1960s, fertility levelled off as a result of socioeconomic changes and successful national family planning programmes in the early 1970s (Knodel, Havanon, and Pramualratana 1984). This decline was faster than in most Asian countries, and was comparable to the historical experience of most developed countries (Knodel 1977). The decline continued with population growing at an annual rate of 2.7 per cent over 1960–70, and 2.5 per cent over 1970–80 respectively. Total fertility levelled off from 6.3 in the mid-1960s to 5.4 in the early 1970s, 4.9 in the mid-1970s, 3.9 in the early 1980s, and 2.1 in the late 1980s. According to the projections of Fred Arnold and TDRI, the general fertility rate may fall from 174 in 1970 to 70 during 1995–2000. That will give Thailand a population of about 64 to 65 million by the turn of the century.

Table 3.3 Trend of Total Fertility Rate

Year	Survey	Total Fertility Rate
1964–65	SPC1	6.30
1965–67	SOFT	6.25
1968–69	LS1	6.12
1970–74	SOFT	4.85
1974–76	SPC2	4.90
1978	CPS1	4.00
1981	CPS2	3.90
1984	CPS3	3.57
1987	TDHS	2.11

Sources: National Statistical Office, Survey of Population Change (SPC); Institute of Population Studies, Longitudinal Surveys (LS); Thailand Demographic and Health Surveys (TDHS); National Institute of Development Administration, Contraceptive Prevalence Surveys (CPS).

In regard to demographic transition, Thailand has followed a path of development similar to the West. Urban fertility declined rapidly in the early 1960s, whereas rural fertility did not begin to decline until the late 1960s. Fertility still appears to be highest in the northeastern and southern regions and lowest in the central and northern regions.

Why was There a Fertility Transition in Thailand?

Thailand constitutes a special case of demographic transition among developing countries in that the fertility rate is lower than normal at that income level. Why did Thailand's population not increase rapidly like other Third World countries such as those in sub-Saharan Africa? Equally remarkable is the fact that food production has increased even faster than the population growth rate.

A World Bank study of cross-section data from 98 developing countries shows an inverse relationship between fertility rate and per capita national income (World Bank 1984). Thus there appears to be a causal link between income and fertility. In higher-income regions, the fertility rate is lower. A study by Dasgupta using both time-series and cross-section data shows an inverse relationship between fertility rates and per capita national income. He argues that rising income brings more education, improved diet, better health care and sanitation, and ultimately lower birth rates (Dasgupta 1991).

Yet this explanation is not self-evident. Some demographers and economists have tried to understand why the decline happened rapidly in Thailand yet was more sluggish in other societies (Kamnuansilpa, Chamratrithirong, and Knodel 1982; Knodel, Havanon, and Pramualratana 1984; Hutaserani and Roumasset 1991). Among the many possible explanations, I shall consider only institutional factors and the role of children as producer goods.

Institutional Factors

According to Bardhan (1989), "Institutions are the social rules, conventions, and other elements of the structural framework of social interaction." Neo-classical economists have gradually taken more account of institutional factors (Coase 1960). In the case of Thailand, most demographers hold that institutional factors were decisive in the fertility decline (Knodel, Havanon, and Pramualratana 1984). On the basis of prior research and data from group discussions, they argue that there were four major components which interacted to cause the rapid shift in fertility rates. I will consider two — the cultural setting and the role of government.

First, Buddhism as practiced in Thailand does not appear to pose any major barrier to the reduction of family size or the use of contraception. Abortion, however, is prohibited on religious grounds. If I read Knodel's research correctly, he might be overestimating the extent to which the decline in fertility rate was determined by cultural factors unique to Thailand. The Muslim minority in southern Thailand, for example, has not fully participated in the reproductive changes observed in the rest of the country. Hence one ought not to jump to the conclusion that culture and religion are barriers to a slowdown in population growth. Their influence remains very ambiguous.

Second, on the government's role in encouraging married couples to use family planning, most demographers endorse the extended use of national family planning methods, particularly modern contraception. More significantly, they tend to accept uncritically that the prevalence of high contraceptive use indicates success for national family planning programmes. Contraception devices are often supplied by Western organizations, whether or not they are used. Many scholars interested in population problems rely on the government's role to explain the reduction in the fertility rate in the 1970s and 1980s (Kamnuansilpa, Chamratrithirong, and Knodel 1988). Yet few economists believe that family planning programmes satisfactorily reduced fertility just by providing rural households with contraceptives at lower costs. Neo-institutional economics prompts a closer examination of the role of institutions (North 1990).

A more likely explanation centres on the government's indirect contribution in the form of better communications, which leads to fertility decline through changing living conditions. The argument runs as follows. Not until the 1930s was a programme of national road construction begun, but since then, the government has allocated a large budget to creating infrastructure, especially under the anti-communist policy during the Cold War era (Meesook *et al.* 1988). By 1950 there were nearly 4,000 miles of roads. By 1986 over half the state highway network of 7,000 miles was paved, and a substantial network of provincial feeder roads had come into existence. This increasingly effective communication system meant that people had better access to modern, effective means of birth control. Also, the transaction costs of implementing birth control programmes in rural Thailand had become lower than in other developing countries.

By contrast, demographers point to changes in social norms caused by socioeconomic shifts. They argue that rapid and fundamental social and economic changes have been taking place, causing couples to view large numbers of children as a burden with which they are either unable or unwilling to cope (Knodel, Havanon, and Pramualratana 1984). Researchers found that most people of both older and younger generations now perceive that a small family is better than a larger one. The main reason for this changing perception stems from socio-economic changes in the Thai economy within the last two decades.

Every day now they have fewer children (older man, northeast).

Almost everyone wants few children, at most no more than three. When I say this, I mean those my age (younger man, central).

[Having fewer children nowadays] is good because making a living is different than before (older Buddhist man, south).

Few is good. The expense is lower. Money is hard to find now (older woman, northeast). (Knodel, Havanon, and Pramualratana 1984)

The research by Knodel and others used group sessions with a small number of participants to generate a hypothesis which could subsequently be tested by surveys on a broader population base. This method of research can easily confuse the micro and macro aspects. This still leaves us with the question why Thai couples changed their perception about the desirable size of the family.

Children as Producer Goods

In poor countries, children are useful as income earning assets, that is, as producer goods (Dasgupta 1991). This is not a new idea. The innovation lies in viewing children as part of a family partnership. In an agrarian society such as Thailand, virtually all members of a farmer's household except infants contribute to both productive activities and household chores. Children help their parents to plant rice, take care of buffaloes, fetch water, cook food, and perform other tasks crucial to the economic sustenance of the household.

> From about the age of 6 years, children in poor households in poor countries mind their siblings and domestic animals, fetch water, and collect fuelwood, dung and fodder. There are complementary household activities. (Dasgupta 1991)

As an example of the link between high population and children as producer goods, one can point to northeast Thailand, the region with the poorest resource endowment in the country, where the pattern is similar to that of other developing countries. The land is infertile, suitable only for a few drought-resistant field crops. Two decades ago, the northeast was still underdeveloped. Agricultural output was insufficient for adequately feeding the population. Most cultivated land was under rain-fed agriculture with only limited areas under irrigation.[3] Lack of water is the real problem in this region. Children are needed to tap water in the nearby village, thus providing a crucial link between high fertility and an accentuation of hardship among family members.

---

[3] Thai elites in the nineteenth century decided to invest in railway construction and military projects instead of irrigation (Feeny 1979a, 1979b). Paddy output was increased by expanding cultivated land at the expense of forest land.

Hutaserani and Roumasset (1991) found that the fertility decline in rural Thailand was closely related to both the transformation in agricultural production and institutional changes. Thai farmers began to use land-saving methods such as irrigation, land consolidation, and adoption of high-yielding varieties (HYVs). These innovations brought about changes in labour markets. The new methods were complemented by labour-saving innovations such as tractors, wetland broadcasting, herbicides, and threshers. Rising wages in rural areas encouraged farm households to adopt labour-saving and time-saving techniques, rather than employing more labour. Moreover the new technology favours adult labour, not child labour. As employment opportunities in non-farm activities rapidly increased, so did the value of adult household members' time. As a result, rearing children became more costly, and children were shifted from farm work to non-farm activities such as school. The qualitative analysis of Knodel, Havanon, and Pramualratana (1984) supports these findings. Parents' perception of children in Thai families are changing; in the old view, children have an active share in the division of family labour; in the newer view, children are recipients of the family's resources, with the tacit understanding that they will in future repay in some manner the family's support during their formative years.

The main hypothesis is that fertility decline in Thailand since the 1960s has emerged from such economic factors as the transformation of the rural sector accelerated by land-saving technological progress (irrigation, land consolidation, adoption of HYVs, etc.) and labour-saving technologies. It is interesting to note that these changes have been concentrated in the central plain. In the northeast, there remain a sizable number of remote areas that are less fertile and have not yet undergone any transformation. Decline in fertility in this region is predictably sluggish.

From studies in three separate areas, Hutaserani and Roumasset (1991) show that the decline in fertility has taken place simultaneously with a process of rural transformation. Conversely fertility has remained high in areas which are remote or stagnant, such as the northeast which still depends on rain-fed agriculture.

These findings support the hypothesis of neo-institutional economics. Wage rates are increasing, induced by technological progress in rural areas. Most farmers will be content to hire labour from the market instead of using their children. This change is inevitably associated with an increase in the value of the wife's time. The opportunity cost of employing children as capital good is increasing. The case of Thailand's fertility situation seems to fit the hypothesis proposed by Dasgupta:

All this may be expected to relate to high fertility and low literacy rates in rural areas of most poor countries. Poverty, the thinness of markets, and an absence of basic amenities make it essential for households to engage in a number of complementary production activities: cultivation, cattle grazing, fetching water, collecting fodder and fuelwood, cooking food, and producing simple marketable products. Each is time consuming. Labour productivity is low not only because capital is scarce, but also because environmental resources are scarce too. (Dasgupta 1991: 15)

Moreover, Hutaserani and Roumasset (1991) singled out the transformation of the agricultural sector in Thailand. Nevertheless, the conclusion is quite weak since Thailand is basically a land-abundant agricultural economy.[4]

Population Growth and Environmental Degradation

A high rate of fertility and population growth can damage the environmental resource base. The growth of the agricultural sector in Thailand since the Second World War provides evidence to support this hypothesis. Thailand was probably the only country in Asia where cultivated land per agricultural worker actually increased in this era.[5] The abundance of land allowed Thai farmers to expand land ownership for the past three decades without disruption. As a result, agriculture was able to absorb large amounts of labour, and Thailand still has a larger proportion of its labour force in agriculture than other Asian countries with a similar income level. The availability of land gave Thailand a strong comparative advantage in agriculture, but this advantage was rapidly eroded with the closing of the open land frontier and the beginnings of a deforestation problem.

Rapid deforestation over the past two decades has developed into a major national problem. Ninety million *rai* of forest have been denuded between 1960 and 1990 at the average rate of three million *rai* per year (6.25 *rai* = 1 hectare). Less than 28 per cent of the nation (about 90

---

[4] It was rational for Thai farmers to use labour-intensive rather than capital-intensive techniques for cultivation. Wage rates were relatively low, while the rental rate for hiring capital equipment were relatively high owing to scarcity.

[5] This happened because forest land was cleared for cultivation. However, lack of secure ownership rights discouraged capital formation and land improvement.

million *rai*) is now under forest cover, compared to 78 per cent in 1938 (Panayotou and Parasuk 1990; Panayotou and Sungsuwan 1989; Hirsch 1987). One reason often cited as an explanation for deforestation in Thailand is rapid population growth and severe poverty in rural areas.[6] In the 1960–90 period, the agricultural population increased by 14 million.

Deforestation is a complicated issue involving many factors. We cannot blame population growth alone. In legal terms, low-income villagers and landless farmers are often forest encroachers. However, the story is more intricate. Prior to the 1980s, when there was still plenty of new land to be opened up for cultivation, the rural population responded to population pressure and poverty by migrating to other rural areas. New land was found in the northeast and eastern regions of Thailand which were previously forest areas.

Rapid growth of population since the Second World War, ruthless exploitation of natural resources, and inappropriate technology for production have been important factors contributing to the depletion of natural resources and deforestation (Prasith-rathsing 1987). Deforestation has several immediate causes: illegal encroachment by landless farmers, hill tribes, shifting cultivators, illegal logging supported by influential businessmen and corrupt officials (Anderson 1990; Laothamatas 1988; Tamada 1991; Turton 1989); and abuse of forest concessions. The process has been encouraged by relatively high prices for agricultural products in the world market during the 1960s and 1970s. Cultivated area expanded rapidly between 1971 and 1975 against the background of the first oil shock and a boom in commodity prices due to worldwide drought.

Closer examination shows that deforestation is tied up with Thailand's socioeconomic structure. Agriculture still has a very high share of total employment. This share has remained high because farmers were able to escape growing population pressure by migrating to areas which still had available land. With rising crop prices, farmers diversified into new upland crops such as maize, jute, cassava, and sugarcane, especially in the northeastern and western regions where land was still available (Brown 1963; Silcock 1970; Ingram 1971; Feeny 1979b; Rigg 1987). Although crop prices started to decline from the 1980s, Thai farmers failed to adjust in the expected manner (Sussangkarn 1990).

---

[6] Feder and Onchan (1987) found that ownership insecurity causes a substantial number of farmers to encroach on public lands or state lands.

Thai farmers responded well to the incentive of high prices, but not to the disincentive of falling prices. One explanation is that many Thai farmers work a small plot of someone else's land in addition to tending their own. Furthermore, there is no tension between landlords and farmers, as found in most other agrarian societies (Girling 1986). In part this is due to the availability of land and the opportunity for internal labour mobility. Rural-rural migration made Thai society more stable.[7] Landless farmers, low-income villagers, and the rural poor solved their problems by encroaching on reserved forest areas. Most farmers have neither formal title to the land nor even occupation rights. Recent estimates suggest that about 30 per cent of all private land in Thailand has no formal legal documentation (TDRI 1986).

Agricultural production continued to grow because farmers continued to encroach on forest reserves. As long as new land was continuously being brought into cultivation and farmers had access to land, the incidence of poverty was reduced. When government started to protect remaining forest areas from the 1980s onwards, the reduction in poverty became more difficult to achieve (Siamwalla 1989).

But why did the rural poor not migrate to urban areas to find alternative employment? In fact, some did. But the majority of Thai agriculturalists probably perceived that it would be costly and risky to abandon their land and migrate to the urban areas. This perception might well be justified, especially when property rights in land are not well defined. As most rural land has no formal title, it remains the property of the rural poor only as long as they occupy it and cultivate it.[8]

Some economists argue that the land market does not function very well in rural areas (Sussangkarn 1990). However, recent studies of deforestation in Thailand have found the opposite. There are transactions of land even within reserved forest areas. Poor farmers hold onto land in the hope of acquiring a title at some point in the future. Because the government is inconsistent, this hope may be justified.

---

[7] Some anthropologists and sociologists argue that patron-client relations make Thai society more stable and less violent, but this conclusion seems premature. Violence has recently occurred in some rural areas (Anderson 1990; Tamada 1991).

[8] In the past all land in the kingdom of Thailand theoretically belonged to the king. However, legislation on land ownership was introduced in the second half of the nineteenth century. During this era, forest clearing was encouraged by the kings to increase rice output for export to the world market (Ingram 1971).

The latest work dealing with rural poverty was presented at a TDRI year-end conference (Sussangkarn 1992). Researchers found that Thailand is in a vicious cycle of widening income inequality with limited opportunities for upward socio-economic mobility by the poorest groups, meaning farmers in two categories: first, those who have land in poorly endowed areas (the northeast), and second, those who have no land or very little land and therefore have to sell their labour on the market. The limited opportunities for both groups result in considerable pressure to encroach on the forests, sometimes as a last resort.

Table 3.4 Source–Destination of Migration, 1965–70, 1975–80 (per cent)

Source–Destination	1965–70	1975–80
Rural–Rural	63.6	52.0
Rural–Urban	10.5	14.3
Urban–Rural	5.4	9.4
Urban–Urban	8.9	17.2
Unknown	12.6	7.1
Total	100.0	100.0

Sources: 1965–70 – Arnold and Boonpratuang (1976); 1975–80 – Pejaranonda *et al.* (1984).

Hence the pattern of rural-rural migration pattern has continued. The rural poor respond to population pressure and poverty by migrating to other rural areas. Why did this pattern persist over such a long period? First, there was abundant land in remote rural areas. Until the late 1960s, the state not only failed to protect forest land but also passively encouraged encroachment by recognizing illegal forest settlement. The country's principal earnings came from exports of agricultural products. Increasing the total output of the agricultural sector depended on increasing the cultivated area at the expense of forests. Second, the state in Thailand was too weak to enforce the law of the land. The Thai bureaucracy was unable to protect the reserved forest areas. North (1990) explained that only a strong government is able to protect the property rights: "Secure property rights will require political and judicial organizations that effectively and impartially enforce contracts across space and time." The Thai case seems to support this point.

In the past, the absolute state was able to control land and labour. The only threat to the Thai elite was external, coming from the West.

Hence there was little pressure on poor farmers. In addition, "The longer the Thai absolute monarchy stayed in power, the more it lost its flexibility and became more rigid" (Eoseewong n.d.). Even though the Thai polity evolved after 1932 from the *sakdina* system to a constitutional monarchy, enforcement of property rights lagged behind.[9] Under the modern Thai state, property rights in land have become insecure (Feder and Onchan 1986, 1987).[10] There is no taxation on land, and any proposal to introduce such a measure in parliament would probably fail.

According to a TDRI econometric model, higher crop prices or a growing farm population results in a higher demand for land, and the elasticity of demand for land is 1.337 compared to the farm population. This study covered the period of 1961–89 (Panayotou and Parasuk 1990).

In less than 40 years, natural forests declined from 200 million *rai* to less than 90 million. What caused this disaster? Why did Thai bureaucrats fail to protect the natural forests? Four possible causes of deforestation can be listed covering the most important actors.

(1) *Villagers.* Population growth creates demand for more agricultural land, forcing them to encroach on natural forests. In particular migration of farmers from the northeast into the central plain and other regions has resulted in deforestation in those areas.

(2) *Locally influential people.* Influential local people illegally cut trees, and sell land to migrants, mostly from the northeast, or hold it for speculation.

(3) *Government officials.* An inadequate staff of forestry officials, side payments, and personal interests make forest protection ineffective. Often trees are cut and transported without government intervention.

(4) *Government policies.* Policies on logging concessions contribute to the rapid deforestation. The past policy of allocating logging concessions included no incentive to loggers to properly reforest their concessions and to look after reforested areas. In general a cycle of

---

[9] Since 1947, Thai political history has been entirely dominated by the armed forces. Recently, Chinese business leadership has become directly involved in politics by moving from business entrepreneurship to political entrepreneurship. In the past, business leaders financed politicians and the armed forces in exchange for security.

[10] Since 1954, a comprehensive land code has defined procedures for registration of privately owned land under various documents, N.S.4 and N.S.3 or N.S.3K, which demarcate the land boundaries and permit the owner to sell, transfer, and legally mortgage the land.

deforestation runs as follows. First, concessionaires build roads into their areas and cut the large trees; second, villagers follow the roads built by the concessionaires and cut down medium-sized trees for housing and fuel; and finally, villagers and newcomers move into the area where the forest is almost denuded, clear small remaining trees, and start farming.

An important factor here is that Thai agriculture is predominantly rain-fed. Only 26 million out of 148 million *rai* of farm area is irrigated. Rain-fed farming takes place only during the monsoon rains. During the slack period of half a year, poor farmers are reluctant to migrate to the towns, preferring to migrate to other rural areas. This preference may result from their lack of knowledge for seeking urban jobs but also from their reluctance to abandon newly settled land which remains untitled. Some household members have to remain on the land to sustain their claim (Siamwalla 1989).

In this respect, Thailand differs from western countries where governments were able to impose a monopoly on the protection and enforcement of property rights at a lower cost than private groups (North and Thomas 1973). Insecure ownership of land is a fact of life in Thailand. The Thai government cannot protect the forest. Deforestation has allowed Thailand to achieve agricultural growth without technological progress in the agricultural sector (Hayami and Kikuchi 1982).

Path Development in the Thai Economy

Preliminary analysis indicates that there has not yet been any major breakthrough in the path of Thai economic growth.

The strategy of economic development that began in the late 1950s was spurred on by the availability of cheap urban labour. This strategy has been sustained since the 1980s by a flood of migrants from rural to urban areas, especially the Bangkok region. The collapse of worldwide commodity prices since the 1980s plunged Thai farmers into a period of considerable hardship. In particular, the price of rice has declined, provoking more migration.

Rural poverty reflects the growing disparity between regions and occupations. Most manufacturing has been concentrated in Bangkok — about 80 per cent of the total in 1970. The flood of migrants from rural areas contributes to keeping urban wages low. Agricultural growth is repressed by the growing difficulty of encroaching on forest land. The comparative advantage of Thai agriculture growth came primarily from the ability to expand cultivated areas at the expense of the forests. Why did it continue so long? Increasing farmland area is an easy way to increase labour productivity (Fitzpatrick 1989). Thailand's abundance of land meant that the opportunity costs of opening up new land tended to be lower than alternative methods, particularly during the 1950s and 1960s. Hence there was less pressure for a Green Revolution in Thailand, and also no systematic agricultural planning or development of skilled labour required to use and develop the technology. Labour-intensive techniques continued to predominate in almost all regions, except some parts of the central plains where wages rose. Yields, especially of rice, are among the lowest in Asia, at about 1.9 tons per hectare.

The pattern of mechanization has been part of the story (Siamwalla 1989). Tractors have not upgraded per hectare productivity. Instead, they make it easier for a farmer to cultivate a larger plot, and hence became an essential part of the encroachment onto forest land.

Why is urbanization very low in Thailand as compared to other Asian countries? Basically this is another result of the agricultural pattern since the *sakdina* era in the nineteenth century. Opening up new land was the best solution. In the twentieth century, Thai farmers continued to extend their lands.[11] By definition, extensification is not conducive to the growth of towns. In Thailand, there seems to have been no Boserup effect.[12] Another barrier to intensification was the high price of fertilizer in comparison with the price of rice. Rice prices were kept below the world price by government intervention, while fertilizer prices were inflated by infant industry protection (Siamwalla and Setboonsarng 1987; Manarungsan 1978).

In addition, government's policies on manufacturing failed to create jobs in manufacturing. Tariff protection and tax privileges encouraged firms to adopt capital-intensive techniques. Manufacturers absorbed little additional migrant labour. In fact, their main comparative advantage was the existence of cheap urban labour (Santikarn Kaosa-ard and Israngkura 1988).

---

[11] Senghaas (1982) argued that as long as rice could be exported to the world market, and falling prices could be compensated by increasing the exploitation of local labour or by expanding the cultivated area, Thai elites would never be challenged by local labour.

[12] Esther Boserup argued that population increase would drive technical change to ensure enough food.

Another major problem in the near future will be that of education. Much of the population sees little value in extended schooling because it does not seem to bring commensurate material rewards. Rural households see no need for higher education. Thailand already has one of the worst secondary enrolment ratios in Asia (Sussangkarn 1990, 1992). This will create a human resource bottleneck in future decades. TDRI calculated that even if all primary school leavers continued into secondary education from 1992 onwards, 70 per cent of Thailand's workforce in the year 2000 would still have only primary education or less. This will leave Thailand without a development path other than exploiting a comparative advantage in cheap labour. It is difficult, if not impossible, to sustain development in this way. Some economists have warned that successive governments' failure to improve secondary education could close the door to internal migration and job shifts that have helped many escape poverty. A good workforce is a real indicator of economic development.

Population growth is only one of many problems in Thailand. In essence the main problem in Thai economic development is not economics but politics and institutional constraints to sustain development with equity. Thailand is cited by the World Bank as among the most rapidly growing economies in the world. Yet about 25 per cent of the population live below the poverty line (Suphachalasai and Patamasiriwat 1991), showing that there is still much to be done.

CHAPTER 4

Inconsistencies and Inequities in Thai Industrialization[1]

Thailand has been proclaimed an NIE (newly industrializing economy) by international organizations such as the World Bank (1993), but the country faces acute problems that are rarely discussed. Although economic growth has been impressive, areas of human development and income distribution are deteriorating. In fact, this pattern of uneven development can invariably be seen as a trade-off between the agricultural and industrial sectors. For years, the rural poor have been trying to solve their present difficulties by persistent migration to seek work in Bangkok, principally in the so-called informal sectors.

The severe effects and externalities of the industrialization process have been paid less attention. In fact, the production structure is characterized by the hallmarks of an agrarian society. Although manufactured exports have been growing rapidly, at a rate similar to those of the East Asian NIEs in the 1960s and 1970s, population and employment structures are still overwhelmingly rural-based. The share of the agricultural labour force was 70 per cent in 1986, but only declined to 65 per cent in the 1990s. This suggests that a long-term deterioration of rural living standards is quite likely, particularly in terms of a low consumption rate.

The aim of this chapter is to analyze whether the economic policy reforms of the past two decades may have been too few and too late to solve the problem of rising unbalanced growth, and to eradicate poverty. The analysis adopts a neo-institutional economic framework to explore

[1] I am very grateful to Laurids S. Lauridsen, Christer Gunnarsson, and Johannes D. Schmidt for helpful comments and suggestions. Jaya Reddy has done an excellent job in making my language accurate and readable.

the role of the state, and to learn from economic history. It points to major institutional changes that are essential to bring about agricultural modernization and determine how far industrialization can proceed. Continuing to squeeze the agricultural sector will be a significant hindrance to sustainable economic growth. Rapid increases in the productivity of agriculture will be of major importance for increasing domestic demand to absorb manufactured goods. This sector should be subsidized by the state to improve productivity and living standards. These conclusions are reached through a comparison with the experience of the NIEs in economic policy reforms and the role of the state.

A Conceptual Framework

Thailand began its integration into the world economy in the middle of the 1880s and emerged as the major supplier of rice to the rest of the world, in particular the ex-colonies of Great Britain (Ingram 1971). Modern Thai economic growth, however, only began in the late 1950s when many Thai leaders showed serious interest in transforming the country from an agricultural to an industrial society. Yet, the Thai state might be considered inclined to being predatory given the extent that depletion of scarce resources has taken place. Predominant economic strategies created little in terms of public goods. The consequences have been low productivity in agriculture, weak human capital development, and poverty in the rural areas.

There are five reasons for considering the Thai state as predatory and not developmental.

First of all, the outcome of economic development in the last four decades suggests that the state was entirely controlled by a ruling elite including the military, vested interest groups (mostly ethnic Chinese), and bureaucrats who were eager to protect their own interests, and failed to provide adequate education, health care, pure water supply and sanitation.

Second, the state has been rather weak in making any coherent policy effective. The most crucial policies, such as land reform and income distribution, have been implemented, but in a somewhat erratic manner which proved insufficient in the end. This result is a function of the unbounded power of the bureaucracy, which led to arrogance, over-confidence, and an anti-democratic attitude. The East Asian NIEs (except Hong Kong) were very strong and effective as a result of a degree of relative autonomy from vested interests in decision making. The Thai state has been relatively weaker as it has been unable to insulate itself from vested interest groups. The assumption that the state is well intentioned, well informed and competent appears to be wrong. In reality, as in the Thai case, the state might be manipulated and incompetent. Nevertheless, Thailand is fascinating in the sense that, since the 1930s, the armed forces have never held absolute power as in Indonesia, South Korea, or Taiwan. The monarchy, being the absolute source of legitimacy, has been above politics and makes the Thai political economy unique.

Third, the main failure emerges from the fact that the bureaucracy, which evolved from the Thai *sakdina* (feudal) autocracy, has turned out to be a huge and clumsy monster (Riggs 1966, 1993). The rigidity of this hierarchical system has created a klepto-patrimonial bureaucracy, not a meritocratic one (Evans 1995). In fact, there has been no substantial change in the civil service since the reforms of King Rama V. Absolute power was exercised by the king in the past but by technocrats and bureaucrats today. The merit system embedded in the bureaucracy has been gradually deteriorating, to the system's disadvantage, because material incentives are rather low despite a very rapid transformation of the country's economy (Christensen and Siamwalla 1993). The bureaucratic class has dropped in status and the ethics of the organization are weak. But the power structure remains entrenched due to the persistence of authoritarian regimes. The legal authority for administrative measures and the operation of the bureaucracy, as determined by the king in the old days, have been divorced from public liability and accountability (Rosenberg 1958). This is prevalent in the Thai political structure, which has remained unchanged after sixty years of semi-democracy or the so-called "soft-authoritarian regime" (Chamarik 1981; Samudavanija 1992). The military, the technocrats, and their business (Sino-Thai) and academic allies, have repeatedly been appointed to the senate and are instrumental in maintaining a kleptocracy. Hence, discretionary power and arbitrariness have been almost untouched by administrative law. Although rule by royal servants was abolished after the people's coup in 1932, civil servants have taken over and manufactured obedience.

Fourth, it is worth noting that the Thai state has been unable to foster long-term entrepreneurial perspectives among indigenous private elites, thereby lacking one crucial type of state activity mentioned in Gerschenkron's typology: "state entrepreneurial actions to substitute for missing entrepreneurship". In reality, transformation has somehow been impeded rather than promoted by the state, resulting in a relatively limited number of Thai entrepreneurs in commerce and industry. Moreover, commercialization in the countryside is extremely insignificant and dominated by ethnic Chinese middlemen who are seldom autonomous, but subservient to autocrats, aristocrats, and lately the military.

Fifth, the political regime has been (soft) authoritarian despite a very short period of democracy in 1973–76 and again in the 1990s. Agriculture has been heavily squeezed to lend support to the industrial sector. Productivity in the agricultural sector appears to have been stable with increasing output due to the resource endowment of abundant land until the late 1970s (see Chapter 3). Rich natural resources made it possible for the Thai state to extract and dissipate rents when industrialization was initiated. Thai peasants continued to exploit natural resources for longer compared with resource scarce countries like the NIEs. Under different conditions, if the state had generated rapid technological progress, the agricultural sector could have contributed to economic growth without turning forest land into cultivated areas. The "Green Revolution" never had a chance to take root owing to the shortage of irrigation water. Existing dams, drainage and reservoirs are inadequate for success in exploiting the new technologies. In addition, infant industries protected by high tariffs sold products such as fertilizers and agricultural machines to the agricultural sector at high prices. Agricultural growth was extensive rather than intensive. Overall growth was unbalanced and heavily concentrated in Bangkok, often named as the city in the world with the highest level of primacy.

This uneven development with concentration of growth and industrialization in the metropolitan area has in turn led to a wide income gap. The pattern of industrialization suggests that intersectoral conflict will occur and rural-urban antagonism will accumulate (Eoseewong 1993).

The developmental states of the East Asian NIEs cannot simply be emulated by Thailand, because the state and institutional settings are different in their historical and social contexts. How and why these factors matter will be analyzed below.

The Thai state might function relatively well in protecting individual rights and property, and in enforcing voluntarily negotiated private contracts, but it has failed to create a strong domestic market and eradicate poverty in the rural areas. The strategy of the developmental state is quite difficult to implement in Thailand, largely due to the relatively backward agricultural economy. The state has been playing a contradictory role in not closing the productivity gap between agriculture and industry. Thus, a backward dualistic economy continues to exist. Although the state has attempted to industrialize since the late 1950s through import-substituting strategies, this seems unlikely to be successful because of the difficulty in adapting new technological skills and absorbing surplus labour.

This shortcoming is further constrained by the nature of institutions, particularly key institutions. There is no hard state with relative autonomy that can threaten unproductive firms (Amsden 1989; Wade 1990). Moreover, it has been forgotten that the success of the East Asian NIEs came not so much from foreign investment and multinational corporations, but from national capital and indigenous industrialists as well as from rapidly developing an educated population. This requires fostering internal articulation and achieving technological autonomy. In fact, import-substitution industrialization might not have failed in Thailand had it been accompanied by substantial improvements in agricultural productivity and better income distribution that resulted in higher absorption of domestic manufactured goods. Such a process has always been taken for granted by the Thai ruling elite, who were obsessed with the market mechanism as a means of linking import-substitution industries with relatively backward agriculture.

Productivity in the agricultural sector has not been substantially upgraded to the same extent as the industrial sector. In fact, agriculture was dominated by the vestiges of *sakdina*, with cultivation techniques dating back to the previous century. In addition, the bureaucracy is not professionally competent enough to prevent the ruling elite and entrenched interest groups from extracting and distributing unproductive rents. A rent-seeking society is always closely linked to public policy and allocation of scarce resources. Thus, increased social injustice and income inequality not only remain unchanged, but have tended to become more acute and more widespread.

Since the middle of the 1970s, the Thai state has been changing its strategy to one of export-led industrialization, but without solving fundamental problems such as inadequate infrastructure, lack of skilled labour, low secondary school enrolment, low productivity in the agricultural sector, and impoverishment among rural inhabitants who are mostly farmers. Although the new development strategy seemed to keep economic growth high, mainly through the influx of direct foreign investment, the basic failure of the industrialization process, as mentioned above, still prevails today under the same institutional setting. In fact, institutional arrangements appear to have made matters worse in so far as the rise of money politics and vote buying has bred corrupt politicians. In addition, the relative backwardness of agriculture has presented an unintended opportunity not only for the urban bourgeoisie and ex-technocrats, but also for local capitalists and influential persons to run for parliament. Electoral politics have paved the way for them to legitimize their power through money politics. However, to understand the political economy of Thai industrialization, we must turn back to the import-substitution industrialization policy in the late 1950s.

State Promotion of Industrialization

Under the Sarit government, industrial promotion policy was renewed by the Promotion of Industrial Investment Act of 1959. The Board of Investment was set up in the same year. This period saw the second fundamental institutional change since the Chakri kings had undertaken political and economic reforms in the mid-nineteenth century. The multiple exchange rate regime and large-scale state enterprises were supposed to come to an end. The former was replaced by export taxes and a fixed exchange rate, while the state investment was limited to infrastructure development. The role of the Thai state was reconceived as a social guardian or benevolent dictator to provide a stable investment environment for the private sector (Chaloemtiarana 1979).

In this period, the state removed the "invisible foot" and put back the "invisible hand" of the market mechanism in the field of production, permitting private enterprises to develop. The Sarit regime under a Revolutionary Party had a major impact on the power structure of the modern Thai political economy, namely, the monarchy, bureaucracy, and military. In politics, it essentially interrupted and weakened parliament and political parties. From 1932 to 1963, the military was seldom accountable to civil society. Thailand has hardly had the social and economic bases for democratic development. The middle class, which was predominantly Chinese and therefore treated as alien, allied itself to the ruling elites. Very few parliaments completed their four-year terms; they often had to adapt their role to new circumstances (Meesook *et al.* 1988). However, the legacy of Sarit to Thai economic history was an increased role for technocrats.[2] To a certain degree, the stable macroeconomic performance, notably economic growth and low inflation, has been brought about by

---

[2] Academics or experts (*nak wichakan*) are accorded prestige. Thai technocrats include professionals and experts working at NESDB, the Bank of Thailand, and the Ministry of Finance.

a few able and honest technocrats (Thanapornpun 1990). While technocrats concentrate on planning and economic engineering, bureaucrats give approvals and grant rights. They are the patrimonial officials. This is a sharp distinction in modern Thai bureaucracy.

ISI cannot be regarded as successful from the 1950s to the 1960s. Heavy protection was implemented through an ad hoc sectoral policy in the form of high tariffs, import quotas, other quantitative restrictions, and import surcharges. However, it is misleading to assume that the high tariff barriers were part of a strategic industrial policy regime. On the contrary, they were imposed by the Ministry of Finance from time to time as a source of government revenues (Patamasiriwat 1993). ISI should have resulted in the replacement of imported goods by increased production within Thailand to meet the demand of the markets, but resources were instead transferred to industries promoted by the BOI through the provision of relatively cheap machinery and intermediate inputs, mostly from abroad. High tariffs imposed on finished products under ISI inevitably led to the import of more capital and intermediate products for assembly only. Thailand has neither been guided by industrial sectoral planning nor by any industrial targeting strategy as in the East Asian countries.

> The Thai State does not control the markets for credit and foreign exchange, thus depriving policy makers of perhaps the key tools for conducting industrial targeting. Furthermore, there has been little co-ordination or coherence in the use of existing industrial policy instruments, tariffs, investment promotions, capacity controls and local content regulations. (Christensen and Siamwalla 1994: 18)

The BOI, being one of the main authorities for implementing industrial policy, did not establish a coherent import-substitution policy *per se*, nor did it build up a clear-cut framework to oblige targeted firms to meet its requirements. Punishment has never been the case in the Thai context. The one explicit principle of the BOI was to encourage foreign companies to invest, no matter the kind of industry. Later, some criteria such as labour absorption were included. The obvious evidence is that no performance standards and follow-up have been imposed on the recipients of promotion certificates.

There were four prerequisites for making ISI successful in East Asia: the strength of the state, competent bureaucrats, independent technology learning capacity, and increased productivity in agriculture prior to embarking upon export-oriented industrialization. More equitable income distribution led to higher consumption of manufactured goods. This approach raises rather than lowers standards of well-being. The incentives provided by the BOI, namely the granting of eight-year tax holidays, exemption from import duties on machinery, components, and raw materials, and the imposition of bans and surcharges on competing imports, enabled the BOI to seek economic rents rather than enhancing productivity through adapting modern knowledge. Bribery played a significant role in the quest for promotion certificates by industrialists, both foreign and local. However, the BOI is by no means a rent seeker (Meesook *et al.* 1988).

Most incentives (tax breaks) offered by the BOI to firms are opportunity costs to all Thais. Scarce resources distributed to promoted firms are wasted unless these firms succeed in adapting and mastering new technological skills. Linkages were weak, and the expanding manufacturing sector was not able to generate activity throughout the economy. As long as agriculture was left behind, ISI industries were at best foreign enclaves.

The BOI has played an active role in the allocation of the nation's production resources by encouraging specific sectors and discouraging others through the tax system.[3] The BOI is clearly biased against agriculture, contrary to the pattern found in the NIEs. The packages of incentives do not seem to stem from any coherent and strategic industrial policy (Siamwalla 1993). The East Asian NIEs also provided plenty of incentives, but why is the performance of the manufacturing sector in Thailand inadequate by comparison in terms of labour absorption and technological content? A closer look at the contextual and institutional factors is essential for understanding the course of the Thai industrialization process. A high degree of discretion and selectivity in the granting of incentives for a wide range of objectives without any accountability to civil society, accompanied by little monitoring or follow-up of promoted enterprises, made Thailand different from the East Asian NIEs (Christensen and Siamwalla 1994). Technology is more than tools, plants, or machines. It is very complex and embedded in key institutions. The Thai state has not created an indigenous technological capacity to absorb technological transfers from foreign firms.

---

[3] Siamwalla and Setboonsarng (1987) rightly observed that the BOI emphasized the promotion of big industry through tariff protection, exemption from import tariffs on machinery, and income tax holidays. Unfortunately, most agri-processing industries such as rice milling and rubber processing (small- and medium-scale) are entirely denied access to the BOI promotion privileges.

As pointed out by Marzouk (1972), the encouragement of capital-intensive (or labour-saving) techniques with a low contribution to employment led to inefficiencies in the allocation of scarce capital resources. Under ISI, the economy suffered from a constantly increasing trade imbalance and deteriorating balance of payments. Labour absorption was weak under this strategy. This adversely affected progress in agricultural modernization and has resulted in swelling numbers of urban poor. This is entirely contrary to the industrial policy adopted in Japan, South Korea, and Taiwan. One explanation of this difference lies in the relative autonomy of the state and the role of a strong national development ideology in these countries (Siriprachai 1993b). The three East Asian NIEs underwent lengthy periods of agricultural improvement before ISI. They also succeeded in establishing relatively large growing domestic markets for manufactured goods, linking industry to higher productive and dynamic agricultural sectors. An essential contribution is the state's capability to build up a large literate population with limited resources in a short time.

Export Promotion and the Legacy of ISI

Import-substitution industrialization in Thailand left many problems unresolved. By the early 1970s, the leaders had begun to turn away from ISI and adopt EOI. The question is, why did the state decide to make this turnabout?

In 1963, the Bank of Thailand had warned of the many problems of ISI. However, in the first two decades after the Second World War, economic growth had been satisfactory, though not outstanding. GDP growth averaged 5.2 per cent in the 1950s, rising to 7.4 per cent during the period 1960–72. As a World Bank mission stated, ISI began to face problems of excess capacity as the market became saturated in the late 1960s.

In reality, ISI became the preferred strategy in Thailand not because of the rational arguments recommended by the World Bank, but because of expeditious policy actions to meet balance of payment crises. There was a common interest in ISI on the part of the bureaucratic authoritarian state, urban manufacturing entrepreneurs, and transnational corporations. But how much protection and how long ISI should continue were issues for debate.

The infant industry argument was implicitly used. It was widely known that ISI in Thailand was not targeted according to systematic economic criteria as in the East Asian NIEs, but was pursued by the BOI in an incoherent, inefficient manner and for too long (Ingram 1971). In fact Thai technocrats were aware of this shortcoming in the early 1960s. Nevertheless, strong pressure to retain the apparatus of ISI came from nationalist and populist elements within the military, manufacturers, and powerful new industrial and banking conglomerates. The idea of outward-oriented trade policies was being discussed in the National Economic and Social Development Board (NESDB) in the late 1960s. ISI strategy was perceived to be eventually fatal or at best self-defeating without liberalization of industrial policy and conversion to export competitiveness.

The government showed an initial indication of moving from ISI to EOI in 1972. Export incentives provided by the BOI aimed to offset the cost-increasing effect of protection on the domestic prices of intermediate goods. These protection offsets allowed exporters to claim refunds of the full duties and business tax on import inputs since 1972.[4] Duty drawbacks in the 1970s and the BOI's export incentives seem to have been ineffective, largely because of poor administration (Akrasanee 1980). In the late 1970s, Thailand was adversely affected by the second oil shock and the subsequent worldwide recession, partly because the country had become quite open to the world economy. The balance of payments was in deficit for five consecutive years from 1975 to 1979, while the rate of inflation jumped to double-digit figures and peaked at 19.7 per cent in 1980. However, Thailand did not rush into export liberalization immediately, not because the technocrats were wise, but because the red tape within the bureaucracy made it impossible. Thus, the gradual shift to EOI was not the result of good planning. Rather, it was obstructed by the bureaucratic state because its official regulations and procedures were superfluous and cumbersome. The instruments of import protection existed simultaneously with those of export promotion. There was no single set of policy interventions that systematically promoted ISI or EOI. The revision of the Investment Promotion Law in 1972 was designed to offset the disincentive effects of import protection.

Domestically, the middle class began to make its voice heard in politics. The business class, and ethnic Chinese business groups in particular, started to assume a more explicit role in policy making after 14 October 1973.[5] The 1973 student uprising significantly affected the Thai political

---

[4] This system was established in the late 1950s under the control of the Fiscal Policy Office of the Ministry of Finance. The law allows for a partial refund of duties and business tax on inputs.

[5] This was a popular uprising of university students against the military government, resulting in the downfall of the Thanom-Praphat regime, successors to Sarit.

economy as a whole, and the system of patronized capitalism under the authoritarian regime was partly demolished. In other words, the parasitic relationships of clientelism seem to have been weakened with time. An independent private sector was able to run business under the impersonal relationships of market forces. However, patron-client bonds are still present and very powerful. The military never regained the same level of unity or political dominance, despite the overthrow of the civilian government in 1976 and the establishment of a new regime in 1977 (Boonmi 1988; Chamarik 1981).

Between 1979 and 1981, when the OPEC countries raised oil prices dramatically, the government could not carry out its macroeconomic policy. The economy entered a period of stagflation, experiencing twin deficits for the first time. Several austerity measures urgently adopted by the government resulted in slower growth. This economic recession partly came from the fact that the exports of primary products no longer earned growing amounts of foreign exchange. In the third five-year plan (1972–76), policy makers had decided to adjust their strategy and put greater emphasis on promoting manufactured exports. The country shifted to an outward-looking strategy, but again without any coherent industrial policy. The main objective of promoting manufactured exports relied heavily on foreign direct investment and transnational corporations.

In the fourth five-year plan (1977–81), the export promotion policy was significantly revised to reduce the anti-export bias resulting from ISI. The BOI still played a leading role in granting exemptions and privileges. Fiscal deficits began to soar, sustained by the newly found access to foreign commercial banks. Large-scale foreign indebtedness started in 1976. The Defence Loans Act enabled the government to borrow up to 20 billion baht for defence purposes.[6] A conservative Thai monetary policy seemed appropriate in the 1950s and the 1960s, but in the late 1970s the dollar began to appreciate against other major currencies and a fixed baht/dollar parity became untenable.

Economic Policy Reforms, Industrialization and Poverty

By 1970, the Thai government had begun to reassess its commitment to ISI in the light of growing financial difficulties. It was clear that the

---

[6] In 1981, the Act was revised to empower the government to borrow from foreign sources for defence purposes as long as the sum of defence borrowing plus external borrowing for other purposes did not exceed 10 per cent of the budget expenditure each year.

majority of the promoted firms' products were aimed at the urban enclave market rather than the mass rural market (Richter and Edwards 1973). Although the infant industry argument was increasingly invoked to justify the policy (Akrasanee and Atjanant 1986), the industrialization process seems to have acquired little new technology, owing to the lack of skilled labour (UNIDO 1992). Promoted firms were required to export only a certain share of their output to receive promotion support, but the lack of effective monitoring and information gathering to enforce performance criteria made industrial policy less effective. As a result, export-oriented manufactured goods were at best footloose. In addition, the slowdown of the world economy and reduction of American economic and military aid resulted in widening balance of payments and budget deficits. Even though exports had been fairly diversified since the late 1950s, the domestic market was still dominated by primary products. The small domestic market with low effective demand could not absorb the excess capacity of the manufacturing sector. The underdevelopment of the agricultural sector was both a cause and a consequence of this pattern.

By the early 1980s, the economy faced a set of economic crises similar to those that hit other developing countries. Technocrats had to undertake a major change in economic policy, particularly to fulfil conditions for receiving Structural Adjustment Loans (SALs) from the World Bank and standby arrangements supported by the IMF. Under pressure from these institutions, the technocrats agreed to shift emphasis towards EOI. The objective was not only to increase exports but also to reduce balance of payment deficits and scale down the import-competing industries. SALs required major tax reforms to raise more revenues and to make the tax system more efficient. If structural adjustment means the restoration of equilibrium to provide a firm foundation to withstand further shocks and facilitate development (Goldin and Winters 1992), then the SALs in Thailand during the 1980s were hardly successful as packages of economic reform.

Thailand cannot be classified as successful in the implementation of at least three important policies: on trade, tariffs, and tax.[7] Ad hoc sectoral initiatives continued to prevail. Trade policies were still full of

---

[7] The World Bank classifies the conditional content of structural adjustment loans programmes into ten categories: exchange rate, trade policies, fiscal policies, budget/ public spending, public enterprises, financial sector, industrial policy, energy policy, agricultural policy, and other (Greenaway and Morrissey 1993).

quantitative restrictions, though a clear plan for a subsequent reduction of tariffs to quite low and uniform levels was strongly advocated by the Ministry of Finance in the early 1990s (Richupan 1990). In the early 1980s, economic policy reforms of raising energy prices and devaluing the baht appear to have only partly achieved the desired effect. The growth of manufactured exports was increasingly the result of exchange rate policy rather than export subsidies. Two successful devaluations in 1981 and 1986 did substantially help to reduce the trade deficit in 1985 without affecting domestic levels of inflation (Ranis and Mahmood 1992). Devaluations were used to reduce the anti-export bias, and to achieve competitiveness of tradable goods. In the Thai context, the BOI has often followed strictly a one-way route by granting subsidies and privileges for both ISI and EOI. Promoted firms that did not fulfil the conditions were never threatened with sanctions.

Given the conservative financial policy of the Bank of Thailand, the policies were undoubtedly regarded as major economic reforms. Disturbances in the world economy forced Thai monetary managers to depart from the traditional exchange rate regime. Another reason for these adjustments was the volatility of the world financial system in the 1970s and 1980s, in contrast to the stable period of the 1960s. Nevertheless, an exchange rate policy is not a commercial policy *per se*. This distinction is relevant in the Thai context with regard to ad hoc sectoral initiatives. Commercial policy affects import-substituting and export-oriented interests (Rodrik 1992a). Bureaucratic autonomy, discretion and patronage have been shaped or guided by incoherent courses, in particular by the Ministry of Commerce. In 1982, Thailand became a party to GATT (General Agreement on Tariffs and Trade). It was widely perceived that a commitment to integrate into the world economy would encourage a country to maintain sound macroeconomic policy. But this policy change did not make Thailand into a developmental state.

In essence, the lack of consistency in sectoral policy (Grindle and Thomas 1991) can be attributed to the rent seeking prevailing in Thailand since the 1950s. The root of rent seeking lies in the discretionary legal mandates of individual departments. Ministerial discretion over trade and industrial policies, quotas, licensing and factory promotions is often deployed to seek economic rents, some of which is kicked back to bureaucrats and their political masters. The trend has been increasing since the 1990s, and vote-buying politics have contributed as well. The East Asian NIEs may have experienced rent seeking to a considerable extent, but the social benefits of high productivity in agriculture and export-led industrialization exceeded the social costs of rent seeking activities.

About 150 product categories are governed by export licensing, either automatic or non-automatic, including textiles and clothing which have rapidly become the country's highest foreign exchange earning commodity group. Textiles and clothing also contributed substantially to value added in manufacturing, and absorbed approximately three-quarters of manufacturing employment, especially female workers. Other items covered by export licensing include certain agricultural commodities, fuels, metal and metal products, wood and wood products, wild animals and their carcasses, pesticides, paper, and sacred statues and images. Export quotas are still in place for sugar, cassava and textiles. The Import and Export Commodity Act of 1979 give absolute power to the Ministry of Commerce or its permanent under-secretary to promulgate scores of subordinate laws for imposing quantitative restrictions and other regulations on trading without the approval of cabinet or parliament (Siriprachai 1990). Such discretionary powers can easily lead to corruption and rent-seeking activities if bureaucrats do not act as benevolent social guardians. In the Thai context, bureaucrats can restrict supply with very low risk of detection or punishment from above. Clientelism encourages corrupt officials to expand their activities. It is very common for their bosses to share in the ongoing process (Shleifer and Vishny 1993). Low salaries are often cited as the reason for such corruption, but the situation might be more complicated in the sense the institutions cannot retain the most honest and talented people. More importantly, Thailand has never had administrative courts to deter corrupt bureaucrats and curb malfeasance, impropriety and abuse of power on the part of state officers (Klausner 1989). Legal or social deterrence of corruption and rent seeking is very weak.

In addition, under the existing regime of elections and coalition governments since 1975, politicians who wish to be re-elected and desire to be ministers spend a lot of money on patronage to keep themselves in office. Clientelism became pervasive. Trade quotas, capacity controls, and factory permits had been resources for the military elite in the past, but now are wielded by political parties and individual elected politicians in the present. The serious shortage of infrastructure since the mid-1980s has created an opportunity for various ministries headed by elected politicians to carry out big projects. Economic rents in the form of commissions, permits, licences, and so on were repeatedly appropriated by bribery, palm-oiling, or other corrupt means. In many cases the allocation system is not based on competitive bidding, but is used covertly by politicians in power to generate income for themselves or for their party.

Hence, commercial policies, especially ad hoc sectoral policies, were not substantially reformed through the SALs.[8]

It has been argued that the programme of SALs and standby arrangement in the early 1980s rescued the Thai economy by forcing readjustments towards greater efficiency-enhancing measures at the macroeconomic level. In truth, this may have been too little and too late to encourage balanced growth and equal distribution of income and opportunities for the rural poor and unskilled labour. Several studies have shown that the nominal exchange rate of the baht had been overvalued for years due to the imposition of high import duties to protect promoted firms (Siamwalla and Setboonsarng 1987). The agricultural sector was squeezed by the modern sector for a long period, forcing Thai peasants to pay high costs for the products of protected industries. Both ad hoc sectoral policies, such as those concerning rice, and an overvalued exchange rate during the 1961–80 period, conspicuously discriminated against export producers, especially exporters of primary commodities. Not surprisingly, agriculture, which is the poorest sector in the country, has been left in poverty. As rightly observed by Timmer (1991: 138):

> Thailand did not use similar trade and pricing for key commodities in an effort to protect domestic farmers from the very low prices that occur from time to time in the world market. Although the strong performance of Thailand with rising labour productivity argues that such free trade policies promote growth, Thailand paid a price for rural poverty.

During the readjustment in the 1980s, the Thai government seemed reluctant to implement the SALs fully. Development policy aimed instead at alleviating poverty in the agricultural sector, while government expenditures as well as the tax system were oriented towards the creation of an environment suitable for EOI industries, especially around Bangkok. In

---

[8] The main policy recommendations of the World Bank for Thailand were: (1) to raise domestic energy prices to international level; (2) to develop strong deflationary monetary and fiscal policies; (3) to end the import-substitution policy for industry; (4) to emphasize export-oriented industries; (5) to reduce import tariffs and remove all export restriction and taxes; (6) to increase personal taxation and make collection more effective; (7) to end restrictions on the level of domestic interest rates; (8) to undertake a comprehensive review of government organization and expenditure in order to eliminate waste.

the NIEs, development of the domestic market took place before manufactured goods were exported to the world market (Gunnarsson 1991). This fact might not have been discussed among the technocrats in the NESDB.

The scale of land reform was very limited and ineffective in preventing poor farmers from becoming indebted. Until the Agricultural Reform Act of 1975, attempts to limit private ownership were never successful due to vested interests. The revision of land reform in 1993 under the Chuan government is a good example. Scandals over the implementation of land reform, particularly in Phuket in late 1994, suggest that discretionary power resulted in rent seeking from the allocation of scarce resources.

While the state placed priority on maximizing growth, equalization of regional and personal income levels received far lower priority during the 1980s. Of course the impressive growth since the 1960s did, to some extent, trickle down benefits to the poor. Absolute poverty declined steadily from 57 per cent in 1962–63 to 24 per cent in 1981, but income distribution worsened everywhere over three decades (Hutaserini and Jitsuchon 1988; Tinakorn 1992). The share of the richest 20 per cent of households increased from 50 per cent of total household income in 1975–76 to 55 per cent in 1988–89, while the share of the poorest 20 per cent declined from 8 per cent to 4.5 per cent over the same period (Sussangkarn 1992). Recent data show that the share of the richest 20 per cent of households decreased to 42.8 per cent in 1990, while the share of the poorest 20 per cent rose to 8.5 per cent. Rising income inequality, both between the industrial and agricultural sectors and between regions, partly reflects the nature and competence of the state to cope with fundamental problems. Improving income equity and rising real wages in the rural areas cannot be secured through a laissez-faire policy. Both import-substituting and export-oriented industrial sectors, mostly concentrated in Bangkok, have been inadequate for labour absorption (Santikarn Kaosa-ard 1992). The attempted restructuring of the economy in the 1980s gave little stimulus to labour absorption by industry. The output elasticity of employment in the manufacturing sector was very low and declining in the 1980s compared to the 1970s, falling noticeably from 0.74 to 0.39 (Ghose 1993: table 4.11). Employment conditions almost certainly deteriorated regardless of the development strategy adopted.

It has been argued that export-oriented industries are significantly more labour-intensive than import-substituting industries, but this was not the case for Thailand. What factors can explain the very low elasticity of employment in the manufacturing sector in the 1980s?

The monsoon pattern results in seasonal fluctuations in labour demand. In the long slack season, men and women migrate to work in Bangkok, partly because there are not enough jobs in rural industries. Having only low skills and education (due to a weak and predatory state), they mostly find work in the informal sector and live in the slums of the capital. The formal sector, led by transnational and joint venture firms, does not have sufficient capacity to absorb labour. Migration is an essential means of escape from poverty but the migrant workers can only secure jobs in the informal sector with its easy entry and low skills requirements. The low earnings from hard work are needed to support families in their rural homes. The push factor of rural poverty was of greater importance than the pull factor of urbanization; the deficiency of employment opportunities stemming from the collapse of the rural economy forced agricultural workers to migrate to Bangkok. By the mid-1980s, commodity prices on the world market were depressed. The large number of farmers remaining in agriculture received very low incomes. Price-support programmes did not have adequate funds to raise the general level of farm-gate prices for rice (Thanapornpun 1980). In the case of cassava, the quota system was a source of great rent seeking and rent dissipation (Siriprachai 1988). One exception was sugarcane, where the associations of millers and farmers are strong and can cooperate in bargaining with the government. This exception has come about because of the nature of production in the sugar industry.

The Thai economy has undergone rapid economic transformation. The share of agriculture in GDP has been shrinking rapidly and export promotion has replaced import-substitution. Yet the tax system has remained very regressive compared with the NIEs, and has lacked transparency (Tanzi and Shome 1992). The tax structure is rather complex as a result of many special allowances, deductions for different sources of income, granted in particular by the BOI, and a failure to tax fringe benefits. The tax structure has historically depended heavily on domestic consumption taxes and trade levies. In 1992, the Anand government introduced a 7 per cent value added tax in place of a complex and inefficient system of business taxes. The tax system has been subject to constant tinkering over the years without any major reform (Patamasiriwat 1993). Existing tax policy does not promote equitable income distribution. While the state has played a key role in driving economic growth, tax policy has not been used to promote social justice and human rights

(Tinakorn 1992). Government has stimulated exports of manufactures, but any move towards income redistribution or other specific social goals seems remote. Social security or transfer payments have been very limited (Tanzi and Shome 1992). No taxes have ever been proposed to discourage speculation in land which results in higher rents and hence higher living costs for the urban poor.

With advancing commercialization since the 1980s, the numbers of vulnerable agricultural wage earners and unskilled workers near the poverty line have increased, partly because the land frontier has closed (Tinakorn 1992). High land prices have given rise to unproductive expenditures and social waste arising from speculation. Tax incentives granted by the BOI have led to prevalent rent seeking by a public bureaucracy that is a low-paid, poorly trained, dishonourable, but powerful elite (Christensen and Siamwalla 1993). Recently, the BOI began to grant subsidies to luxury hotels and also to urban housing developers, supposedly to provide the urban poor with accommodation. The main objective of establishing the BOI to protect and help infant industry is fading. The social cost of distortions has always been treated as negligible, but is in fact substantial. Incentives will not deliver their beneficial effects if incompetence, corruption, or various forms of rent seeking become the norm. Since the late 1950s, incentive schemes under ad hoc sectoral policies have created discretionary powers which are perfect instruments for enriching a few members of the military elite, bureaucrats, and elected ministers by permitting some investors or traders to evade taxes or to obtain quotas or licences. The loser is, of course, the public interest.

The tariff reforms in the 1980s seem to have had little effect. The Thai government needs to reduce its range of 34 nominal tariff rates ranging between one and 200 per cent, and to lower the excessive rates of effective protection. A major tariff reform was attempted in 1982 but although some progress was made in equalizing rates of protection within individual industries such as textiles, the result for the industrial sector as a whole was modest. In effect, some of these gains were reversed when tariff rates were raised again in 1985. Import duties were still seen as essential for increasing government revenue when the budget fell into deficit. This left Thailand with the highest average nominal rate of tariff protection (34 per cent) of any of the Pacific Basin developing countries (Noland 1990). The government again began to reform tariffs in the early 1990s as a result of a commitment to the ASEAN Free Trade Area (AFTA) to eliminate tariffs within 15 years. Since the 1980s, export duties have become insignificant, but import levies have remained high, delivering 18 per cent of government revenues.

The state has also been incapable of promoting privatization. National or security interests are often cited as reasons to retain loss-making state-owned enterprises. Both civilian and military governments alike have distributed economic patronage by appointing their supporters and friends to manage state-owned enterprises. Clientelist relationships have thus been strengthened and used to seek economic rents to finance political parties and election campaigns.

The early 1980s witnessed a slowdown in infrastructure investment when Thailand faced twin deficits. Most government projects were postponed to keep the economy stable. Nevertheless, after the mid-1980s the economy rapidly recovered. The state invited foreign private enterprises to invest in huge infrastructure projects by granting concessions on a build-operate-transfer basis. This policy was based upon an ideology of privatization, yet the grant of these concessions led to a rent-seeking war among elected politicians, government officials, state enterprises, and private investors, because each mega-project can easily generate a gigantic income for those who have the superior political muscle (Mueller 1989). Privatization was begun without any attempt to draft a standardized legal framework to regulate it. Hence, bribery and "palm oiling" flourished (known commonly as "tea money" or "coffee money").

The Thai State: Between Rent Seeking and Inequality

Thailand has a number of laws and regulations on the implementation of various aspects of national policy, especially in international trade and internal affairs. Political interests and vested interest groups such as exporters, industrialists, and bankers have exerted influence, while workers and peasants are less powerful and unable to bargain with bureaucrats and vested interest groups. The political party system is fragmented and vote buying is evident. Political parties receive financial support from urban vested interest groups, and have no significant bases of support in the countryside. Bureaucrats and ministers regularly consult formal interest groups, such as the associations of trade, industry and banking, on various aspects of state intervention. As pointed out by Laothamatas (1992), these consultations provide these vested interest groups with means of entry into the policy-making process, whereas other social groups have no such access. Some associations are more skilful at lobbying the policy makers than others. Inside information has allowed interest groups such as exporters to obtain large profits through speculative activities. Since 1973, unstable governments have tended to lavish resources on the urban and industrial sectors with the aim of maintaining their own power and winning international recognition. Previously, rural insurgency in the northeast in the 1960s and the 1970s had compelled the elite in Bangkok to pay more attention to the rural poor and distribute some resources.

Reliable and accurate data on the standard of living is notoriously difficult to collect, but trends in poverty and labour productivity within the rural sector reflect an underlying economic environment in which many rural inhabitants, not just in the northeast but also in other regions, remain very poor, with little education beyond the compulsory primary level. In fairness, some infrastructure development by the central government in remote rural areas has helped to improve living conditions. Yet the rural sector has been squeezed for an economic surplus used to subsidize urban industrial development. One example is the rice premium between 1955 and 1986. Even after introducing a Farmers' Aid Fund, the government still kept the domestic prices of rice down through rice reserve requirements enforced by the Ministry of Commerce (Thanapornpun 1985). This inexorably led to a drop in the cost of living in urban areas, reduced the pressure from urban workers for wage increases, and helped export-oriented firms to compete in the world market.

If industrialization in urban areas had been able to bring about modernization in agriculture, Thailand could have become an NIE. This failure is, to a large degree, due to the industrial strategy. The East Asian countries have grown at very high rates by promoting high-technology industries through tax incentives under a strong activist and developmental state. One essential difference is that the Thai state has never threatened to punish promoted firms for not being competitive or efficient. In addition, the technology transfer process, one of the most important linkages of late industrialization, is another missing link in Thai industrial policy. The nationalist governments of the Phibun era were closest to the insulated developmental state in South Korea (Haggard and Moon 1983). But in search of an alternative to bureaucratic capitalism with state-owned enterprises, the government turned to an import-substitution strategy in which inefficient industries were protected from foreign competition for many years.

There is an emerging consensus that countries following an outward-oriented, market-based development strategy achieve relatively higher rates of growth and living standards. It is too early to confirm that this is the case of Thailand. In present conditions, there are still difficulties and restricting conditions that must be remedied to secure continued growth of the Thai economy. One immediate problem is bottlenecks in the provision of infrastructure and another is the quality of the labour force. Infrastructure investment needs are enormous, in part because large government budget deficits in the early 1980s, surpassing 6 per cent of GDP, resulted in Thailand saving and investing somewhat less than some other East Asian countries. Even though the government has run a surplus since 1988, the share of investment in GDP has risen only to about 26 per cent. Additional increases to around 30 per cent would be desirable in the long run (Noland 1990). Since the early 1990s, sustained economic growth has made possible a rate of around 30 per cent. But corruption in government contracting adversely affects the real flow of investment in infrastructure.

Additional investment in human capital is also urgently needed, including an expansion of secondary education in general and of technical and vocational education in particular. Sciences and engineering need to be strengthened at university level. Research and development activities need to be encouraged. A major imperative is to create equal opportunities for the lower classes. A string of surpluses in budgets make it a propitious time for the government to carry out major reforms.

For the period from the 1960s to the 1980s, the trade-off between the speed of economic growth and the share of income of the poor was so bad that the deterioration in the share of income of the poor was quite substantial. The conclusion is that the path of development does not give much hope in the foreseeable future of attaining the goal of poverty eradication through economic growth (Adelman 1992).

Thailand has been able to achieve stabilization in macroeconomic policy, high economic growth, a low inflation rate, and a surplus in government budgets. According to the World Bank (1993) this is due to the outward-looking strategy in which export expansion has been the engine of recent growth. Structural adjustment aimed at correcting imbalances in foreign payments, government budgets, and the money supply in order to control inflation and maintain macroeconomic stability was obviously successful. But progress in economic reform, liberalization, privatization, and institutional overhaul has been questionable. There have been no major institutional and administrative reforms. A recent attempt in late 1994 to amend the constitution on the issue of devolving authority to local government failed entirely. Liberalization through the removal of government interventions under ad hoc sectoral policy such as investment incentives, export quotas, export licensing, and other barriers to entry have not been seriously implemented. Existing policies foster patronage and rent seeking. One example was a corruption scandal in the Commerce Ministry over the allocation of quotas for exporting cassava to the European Union in 1993–94. Privatization through selling government-owned enterprises or contracting out functions formerly undertaken by government has been negligible.[9] There have been few institutional reforms that make it possible for economic reform to work, and little shift away from administered control towards mechanisms that reduce the transaction costs of administration.

In conclusion, the economy needs reform. Rent seeking and corruption should be kept at a minimum by making administrative regulations clear, transparent, and accountable. Thai society needs good governance, particularly sound management of development policy (Leftwich 1995). Accountability, a legal framework for development, better public information, and more transparency are needed to warrant the country's claim to be a democracy. The lack of a mechanism for effectively controlling and countering discretionary power is a serious drawback. Patron-client relationships act as major barriers to reform. As in other countries with well-developed clientelistic governments, economic reform can be both politically costly and irrational.

Most neo-classical economists seem to conceive that export-oriented policies reduce inequality within developing countries, but the Thai case appears not to have confirmed this proposition. Expansion of manufactured exports into the world market does not necessarily lead to reduction of inequality. There are institutional constraints that shape the Thai state as neither strong nor minimally interventionist. An apt description for Thailand might be a predatory-cum-soft authoritarian state.

---

[9] Two state enterprises were sold to private firms during the 1977–91 period, four were closed, two were rented by private enterprises, one received a concession, four became joint-ventures, and four were converted into private businesses. There were 61 state-owned enterprises at the end of January 1993.

CHAPTER 5

Mercantilism: Is it a Doctrine or an Economic Policy? Application to the East Asian NIEs

Mercantilism or the mercantile system has been the subject of a running debate among economic historians for years, in particular in the 1930s. There can be no doubt that mercantilism is still alive in the present day, but in a modified version. There is nothing clear-cut about this term in economic history as rightly pointed out by the distinguished Swedish economic historian, Eli F. Heckscher, who in 1933 wrote a short definition in *Encyclopaedia of Social Science, Vol. 9.* In fact, no school of thought defining itself as mercantilist has ever existed, even though the term has acquired a generally accepted meaning (Screpanti and Zamagni 1993). Mercantilism was important in European economic history roughly between 1500 and 1800. Adam Smith devoted about one fourth of *The Wealth of Nations* (1776) to a criticism of what he termed the "mercantile system", or the commercial system, attacking mercantilist doctrine as a commercial policy, a system of protection (Heckscher 1933). Bullionism has to be distinguished from mercantilism, though the two are interrelated (Roll 1953).

Adam Smith used the terminology of a mercantile system for the economic doctrine that had dominated European political and commercial circles in the sixteenth, seventeenth, and most of the eighteenth centuries. However, there was no theoretical core of mercantilism, and this has led to an endless debate among scholars in the disciplines of history and economic history. Mercantilism was certainly different from the doctrine of the physiocrats, who belittled the role of foreign trade and placed more importance on agricultural production. But mercantilism was also very varied in different national contexts, as shown in the seminal two-volume work of Heckscher (1935). It also had its own historical evolution. As an economic idea, it both contributed to the formulation of policy, as well as stirred intense arguments between bureaucrats and politicians.

Mercantilism came into the language of the English-speaking world in the second half of the nineteenth century. In the 1860s, German writers used the term *Merkantilism* which corresponded to mercantilism in English. The great German writer Gustav Schmoller wrote an essay on *Das Merkantilsimsystem in seiner historischen Beddeutung* (The mercantile system in its historical context) in 1884, published in English in 1896. Schmoller argued that mercantilism was a unified economic system, to a large extent independent of particular economic tenets.

> In its innermost kernel it [mercantilism] is nothing but state-making....
> The essence of the system lies in the total transformation of society and its organization, as well as the state and its institutions, in the replacing of a local and territorial economic policy by that of the nation state. (Schmoller 1884)

He argued that a mercantilist economic policy could aid the establishment of a strong national state. Mercantilism was the economic component of state-building, a component of the processes of national unification as seen in England, France, Germany, Italy, Holland, Spain, and Sweden. Its main ingredient was a commercial policy under which the crown provided private entrepreneurs with protection, subsidies, and other assistance for expansion of their businesses (Allen 1987). In return, the crown acquired the material means for consolidating domestic authority and military strength for foreign colonization. A central tenet of mercantilist thinking proposed that money was equal to wealth, in particular the wealth of nations. Adam Smith disagreed, contending that money was only one form of wealth. Bullionism and mercantilism asserted that treasure was the only type of wealth worth accumulating. Both state and merchants conceived money as the only type of capital that could enhance the nation and increase wealth and power.

Mercantilists tended to be nationalists, as in the case of German writers such as Gustav Schmoller and Friedrich List, who advocated unification of states as a prerequisite for both power abroad and wealth at home — at least for the merchant elite rather than the populace at large. Mercantilists were interested in foreign trade as a means for nations to acquire a stock of precious metals. In *The Growth of English Industry and Commerce* (1882), William Cunningham, a product of the German historical school, wrote on mercantilism as a striving after economic power for political purposes:

The end in view was Power: this was furthered by attention to Treasure, Shipping and Population; these objects could only be obtained by the careful regulation of Industry and Tillage. Such in brief is the rationale of the so-called Mercantile system. (Cunningham 1882)

Heckscher thought that Cunningham confused the ends and means of economic policy. Economic activity had changed fundamentally between the Middle Ages and the Industrial Revolution. Cunningham saw mercantilist economic policy as a means for pursuing national power. Heckscher seemed to conceive of mercantilism as an instrumental concept that enabled us to understand a particular historical period more clearly than we otherwise might. Hecksher believed that the mercantilists' "fear of goods", and their highly singular view of the balance of trade, were based on misunderstandings about the relationship between money and capital. Mercantilists were fixated by the aim of generating a balance-of-payments surplus in order to increase the national stock of specie which was the basis of national power.

Writing on Germany, Cunningham and Schmoller emphasized unification and state-building as the ultimate aims of policy. Heckscher, however, pictured the mercantile system as a form of state regulation in contrast to laissez-faire, which he saw as the best and most expeditious method of bringing about economic development along with social liberty.

Under the mercantilist state, economic agents were subject to specific, detailed regulation. Producers were not allowed to decide what should be produced. Rather, the mercantilist state reserved for itself the right to single out and promote whichever economic activities it rendered desirable and to prohibit those which it considered inappropriate. As pointed out by Charles Wilson (1959), the mercantilist system was equipped with all the devices, legislative, administrative and regulatory, by which societies still predominantly agrarian sought to transform themselves into trading and industrial societies. State regulation was one means of attaining the objective. In contrast, the laissez-faire approach was based on the idea that a nation could grow rich by giving people the freedom to choose and to enrich themselves. Whichever route was chosen, a benevolent state and able politicians were needed.

Heckscher (as well as Adam Smith and Jacob Viner) believed that mercantilist theories were incapable of achieving their aim of enhancing the power, influence, and wealth of the state. He argued that the means would not achieve the ends. He defined mercantilism as that phase of the European economic experience between the *ancien regime* and the coming of laissez-faire, when policy for the first time was differentiated from country to country. He identified five characteristics of mercantilism: desire for unification; pursuit of power as an end; protectionism; a monetary theory linked with the balance of trade; and a conception of society. In fact, the first of these was stressed by Schmoller, the second by Cunningham, and the third and fourth by Adam Smith. But what made Hecksher's work a classic was his ability to bring all five together as a concept of society (Minchinton 1969). However, his work gave rise to a renewed debate on the nature of mercantilism. Viner (1948) argued that wealth was undoubtedly essential to power while power was in turn essential to wealth. Hence, both wealth and power were both proper ends of national policy, without any disharmony between them.

Viner went further by reformulating mercantilism as an economic and political doctrine to serve an essentially new type of organization, the nation-state (Viner 1968). Raison d'état or the national interest still had a key role in the theory, but an added element was the conception of man as a selfish, or at best a self-regarding animal (Viner 1937). An active and powerful government was needed to harness all of this selfish energy for a desirable social end, namely a stable nation-state. This formulation adopted the Hobbesian view that only a strong state with monopoly power could organize human beings for the primary social aim of internal peace.

The mercantilists sought a wide circulation of money within national borders in order to create a broad tax base. To hoard precious metals, they prohibited the export of gold and silver. Countries like Britain, which had no internal mining of precious metals, had to maintain an excess of exports over imports, a surplus balance of trade. To achieve the surplus, exports had to be encouraged and imports discouraged. In Spain, attempts were made to force private companies to pay for imports with goods instead of money.

Viner and Heckscher fell into a polemical debate over wealth and power. According to Heckscher, Schmoller and Cunningham had argued that the goal of mercantilist economic policy was state-making and national power. Viner (1937, 1948) countered that power and plenty, nation-building and wealth, were not antagonistic but inseparable; wealth was not only a means to power, but an end in itself; the mercantilists had sought both power and plenty.

Mercantilism never died but survived over the passage of time. Of late, the successful East Asia countries, especially Japan, Korea and

Taiwan, have used part of mercantilist ideology to achieve economic miracles (Hettne 1993; Gunnarsson 1993).

Mercantilism was a very simple and coherent national economic policy under which the state promoted private production and foreign trade to achieve the prosperity and power of the nation-state. The problem confronting us is to try and understand mercantilism in the context of European economic history and in terms of economic doctrine or economic policy.

Exactly what role did economic doctrine play in the formulation of state policy, both in the mercantilism of the sixteenth to nineteenth centuries, and of more recent times? In this short paper, I would like to draw some conclusions from recent empirical studies on developmental states and industrial policy in the newly industrialized countries of the twentieth century. Both countries in the western world, such as Germany, as well as developing countries such as Japan before the Second World War, grew and industrialized in part by following mercantilist ideology. It is fruitful to study mercantilism not only for its own sake, but to learn from past experience.

Mercantilist Commercial Theories and Policies

This section will centre on the doctrine of mercantilism. Viner pointed out that there were wide differences within the doctrine of mercantilism. The lesson we can learn from the past is that a mercantilist commercial policy is not just about accumulating wealth, treasure, or specie, as often cited. The most famous mercantilist writers such as Gerald de Malynes (1586–1641?), Edward Misselden (1608–54), or Thomas Mun (1571–1641) concentrated on avoidance of a trade deficit (Roll 1953; Blaug 1991). The exchange rate was important in determining the terms of trade. The state's role was to support private entrepreneurs by, for example, granting exclusive privileges to foreign ventures. The Statute of Apprentices (1563) was also a product of the mercantile system (Heckscher 1935).

Recent research by economists of the public choice school has suggested that mercantilism was a kind of rent-seeking activity (Ekelund and Tollison 1981). Mercantilists advocated permanent restrictions on various kinds of foreign trade, without specifying that any particular conditions needed to be present to justify the restriction (Viner 1937). Such government regulation might be unjustified on analytical and practical grounds. Merchants who were well connected to government could accrue monopoly rents, while others were excluded. For instance, the Stuarts granted monopoly franchises and patents to raise revenue without the necessity of resorting to parliament. Ekelund and Tollison (1981) argued that competition among merchants to secure the shelter of the state, reap the rewards, and fend off rivals, resulted in rent dissipation and social waste.

Access to enterprise was actually limited to individuals or groups of merchants who had political connections and who were able to repay the crown or government for the privilege of running a legal business. Patronage was crucial in both politics and society. Private entrepreneurs were milch cows who had to supply the government with the funds needed to fulfil its objective of power. At times, the mercantilist state itself became a rent seeker by engaging in manufacture under protected conditions, such as in Spain in the eighteenth century and France in the Colbertist era in the seventeenth century. Royal factories manufactured only unproductive goods for national defence, such as artillery pieces, or luxury goods such as tapestries, glassware, and porcelain. Most were inefficient and loss-making businesses.

De Soto (1989) argues that the European mercantilist economy was very costly due to the support of so many unproductive bureaucrats and lawyers who served only to wrap, unwrap, and rewrap its country's subjects in laws. He further claimed that mercantilism gradually declined because of its inefficiency, leading to mass migration of the peasantry into the cities, eventually undermining the authority and legitimacy of the mercantilist state.

In the *Wealth of Nations*, Adam Smith claimed that some Elizabethan laws supporting monopoly had effectively been written in blood as the penalties for transgression were mutilation and death. He also criticized the mercantile system for two main mistakes. First, he alleged that the mercantilists confused money with wealth and were irrationally biased in favour of a positive balance of trade. Second, he argued that mercantilism was a conspiracy of merchants and manufactures who were not concerned with the public good but with their own narrow advantage (Minchinton 1969).

Mercantilism was also closely related to colonization. Lawrence A. Harper (1942) argued that English mercantilism provided justification for exploitation and the imposition of power in many forms: capturing booty in war, piracy, monopolizing trade routes, capturing and selling slaves, and monopolizing markets or sources of imports by force. The

Dutch East Indies Company and the British East India Company were monopolistic cartels. Colonies were exploited as sources of demand for mother-country exports, providers of tax revenues, sites for military bases, sources of raw materials and gold, markets for unused products, sources of manpower, and outlets for excess or otherwise unattractive people (Allen 1987). Maurice Dobb argued that the mercantilist state brought results, not by improving the terms of trade, but by creating market imperfections and inelasticities of demand through the colonial system.

By contrast, Thomas Mun's doctrine on the balance of trade proposed that Britain should sell cloth cheaply owing to the elasticity of foreign demand, and should grant more rights to merchants in the East India and Baltic trades to export specie under licence. He argued that the price of goods had to be cheap so as to make exportable goods more competitive in the world market (Mun 1928).

According to the UNESCO *Dictionary of the Social Sciences*, mercantilism is "the belief that the economic welfare of the state can only be secured by government regulation of a nationalist character". This concept is rather vague and meaningless for economic historians as it lacks any historical context. During the sixteenth, seventeenth, and eighteenth centuries, both Britain and many continental European countries were emerging as strong national states anxious to expand their power by all the means at their disposal. To foster economic growth and prevent invasion by enemies, they needed to raise revenue. Colbert, the chief finance minister under Louis XIV, passed tariff acts in 1664 as a means to unify the country by using customs. Under mercantilism, the goal of unification, the pursuit of foreign trade, and colonization were inseparable.

Both Hettne (1993) and Gunnarsson (1993) suggest that mercantilism (or neo-mercantilism) is a general definition for a state having an active role in the economy. The early mercantilist states were obsessed with the balance of trade and with protectionist measures for fostering economic growth. In the twentieth century, these two obsessions have become linked with industrialization. Allen (1987) noted that the focus on management of foreign trade as a device to stimulate the domestic economy has become relevant again in the present day.

Economic historians view the Statute of Apprentices of 1563 as an attempt to counter the depression in Britain's trade in the Antwerp market, the major outlet for British exports at the time. The English parliament passed many pieces of legislation to control or promote economic activities. Heckscher pictured the Navigation Act, Iron Act, Hat Act, and other laws as elements of a coherent mercantilist policy. Other historians such as Heaton (1937) and Judges (1939) argued that the Statute was merely a desperate ad hoc measure. Heaton suggested mercantilism should be seen as simply a system of public finance. Judges (1939) objected to the use of the suffix "-ism".

Heckscher's seminal work (1935) made the pursuit of a favourable balance of trade the defining facet of mercantilism. Certainly mercantilist statesmen were intent on strengthening the powers of the state in its competition with other states, and believed that a favourable balance of trade was needed to finance a strong navy and other means of power. National prosperity stemmed from spending less (on imports), and earning more (from exports). One result was that mercantilist states were forever trying to curb inflation.

But the balance of trade was not the whole mercantilist story. Thomas Mun, who was a director of the English East India Company for many years, was classified as a "real" mercantilist (Roll 1953). He argued that it was permissible to run a trade deficit with some countries which were sources of raw materials or of exotic items for re-export, as this promoted the national production of industrial goods. In a famous metaphor, he noted that a husbandman appeared mad when casting seed corn on the ground but the harvest proved the wisdom of his invest-ment. Through its superiority in technology, Britain was capable of selling goods aboard at high prices (as long as they were not machinery which could help commercial competitors or armaments which could strengthen military opponents).

In sum, the mercantilist notion was focused on the excess of sales over purchases which account for profits. The colonial company operating in foreign trade, like the English East India or Bombay Burma compa-nies, were legalized forms of monopoly power. The prevailing belief was that such exercise of monopoly power shifted the burden onto foreigners. Despite scepticism among English classical economists, there was no anti-monopoly legislation in nineteenth-century England.

Developmental States and Industrial policy

In recent years, the term "developmental state" has become popular among development economists (Adams and Davis 1994; Amsden 1989; Clark and Chan 1994; Evans 1995; Islam 1992; Kohli 1994; Lam and Clark 1994; Leftwich 1994; Moon and Prasad 1994; Wade 1990; White

1988). It has been applied to the fast-growing economies of East Asia, namely, Japan, South Korea, and Taiwan. The speed of their catch-up has become known as a miracle. The simple question is: how did this happen in these countries but not in other less developed countries? Mercantilism might be the key to understanding this success.

Heckscher (1935) claimed that the mercantile system was a theoretical and practical political instrument for increasing the economic wealth of nations, strengthening the position of a country, and preparing the ground for a rapid development of productive forces. The role of the state in fostering industrialization has a long and colourful history in the German historical school. In the nineteenth century, Friedrich List argued that the protection of infant industries from competition was absolutely essential for the economic development of late-comer countries. Mercantilist statesmen saw the subjects of the state as means to an end, and the end was the power of the state itself. Heckscher (1935) pointed out that if power was the object of economic policy and if the total fund of economic power was considered to be static, then the only method of benefiting one country was to take something away from another country.

In the mid-twentieth century, Japan, South Korea, and Taiwan transformed their economies from agriculture-based to industrial within less than four decades. This performance was treated as a miracle by such international organizations as the World Bank (1993). The roots of their achievement need to be traced back to the period prior to the Second World War. Some economic historians have applied the term neo-mercantilism (Hettne 1993; Gunnarsson 1993, Gunnarsson and Lundahl 1994).

The key to this complex story lies in the nature of institutions, especially the relatively autonomous and strong state. The "strong" states or autonomous states in these three countries were unique. They emerged because of external threats. This situation is hard to replicate in other countries. During the 1950s and 1960s, authoritarian governments dominated in South Korea and Taiwan. They took a dirigiste approach to the promotion and protection of infant domestic industry using such means as subsidies, quotas, domestic content legislation, and the allocation of credit to favoured industries. External factors also helped both South Korea and Taiwan to limit the role of the vested interest groups, namely, the landlord class. After land reform took place, the agricultural sector had very high productivity with flexible multi-cropping and off-farm employment in the long slack season (Oshima 1993). Agricultural modernization and rising standards of living for rural people laid the foundations for industrialization as well-to-do farmers were able to afford industrial goods (Grabowski 1994a, 1994b). This pattern of domestic-led growth was very similar to the experience of Britain in the eighteenth century to the extent that domestic markets had already matured before the country's integration into the world market.

Commercial policy was protectionist. Export duties were abolished or kept at a minimum while import duties were raised to protect infant industries and exploit opportunities in the world market. These late-comers were able to acquire and adapt new technology at low cost instead of creating new technology of their own. By achieving economies of scale and absorbing new learning, the protected domestic industries became mature and strong enough to export successfully (Lall 1994). Investment in human capital and physical capital paved the way to successful absorption of new technology from abroad, as pointed out by David Landes (1969) and Nathan Rosenberg (1976). The quality of human capital development was essential, both in terms of education level and good work ethics influenced by Confucian social values. All three countries improved their human capital in a short period of time. As a result, an import-substitution strategy with protectionist measures resulted in a successful industrialization process.

Clearly, promoting exports while banning or restricting imports was key to their success. In this sense, the East Asian countries were emulating the French customs tariffs instituted by Colbert in 1664 in the new context of industrial policy. Japan was the pioneer, but Britain in the eighteenth century was a forerunner of the model. As shown in the classic study by Landes (1969), Britain allowed the import of raw materials essential for national industries, but banned the export of important raw materials such as wool, and even prevented engineers from working abroad.

Mercantilist commercial policy favoured national shipping, and many measures were aimed at strengthening the merchant navy, for example the Navigation Act of 1651 which prohibited the importation of goods in non-British ships. Japan followed a similar path. The Ministry of International Trade and Industry, set up in 1942, played a major role in encouraging Japanese firms to use only Japanese ships (Johnson 1982; Vestal 1993). The distribution system in Japan induced Japanese firms to use only products made in Japan. Japanese nationalistic sentiment effectively prevented domestic industries from using foreign ships and many foreign products.

Mercantilist states often prohibited specific exports, granted subsidies to favoured industries, fostered shipping and fisheries, acquired colonies, and passed laws to ensure the consumption of goods produced by monopolies. For instance, in 1571, all citizens were required to wear an English woollen cap on Sundays. A law of 1662 laid down that corpses had to be buried in English woollen textiles, and this provision was elaborated through further laws in 1662, 1678, and 1680 (Heckscher 1935). In France, Colbert and his successors issued 2,200 pages of commercial laws between 1660 and 1730.

The weakness of a mercantile system is the opportunities created for rent seeking (Ekelund and Tollison 1981). The policy of granting privileges and monopoly rights to large national commercial companies was criticized as a social waste of resources rather than social benefit. Adam Smith observed that some merchants used resources to petition or to bribe the state in order to obtain monopolies that were to the disadvantage of others. The East India Company, as restructured after 1757, became a target of Smith's attack on the mercantile system as inferior to laissez-faire.

Mercantilist industrial policy, which aimed at encouraging productivity activity within the national territory by granting monopolistic privileges, remains relevant to the present day. The East Asian countries were successful in pursuing industrial policy which encompassed protection, subsidies, import of advanced technology, development of skilled labour to enable technology transfer, and punishment of firms that failed to perform (Amsden 1989; Grabowski 1994a, 1994b; Kohli 1994; Vestal 1993; Wade 1990). All of this policy rests on the existence of a strong state that behaves like a social guardian, in contrast to the predatory states found in Latin America and Africa (Evans 1989, 1992, 1995; Gunnarsson and Lundahl 1994; Killick 1993). The mercantilist inspiration of power and plenty came to play a crucial role in East Asia. Some time ago, Viner (1968) concluded that mercantilism was a doctrine of state intervention in economic life, but state intervention of a special pattern and with some special objectives. The East Asian countries seem to have followed this pattern. They were not interested in the accumulation of precious metals, nor a favourable balance of trade, but in the accumulation of skilled labour and modern technology.

Demographic Theories and Policy

It might be misleading to consider mercantilism only from the aspect of economic policy. Demography is also important. An abundant labour supply is needed for industrial expansion. In the mercantilist era, governments played a role in fostering population increase. For instance, in Germany, the prohibition on certain types of marriage was lifted, and rewards were offered for large families. Governments encouraged immigration, restricted emigration, and promoted early marriage in the belief that a growth of population would serve the general mercantilist objectives by increasing labour supply, military power, and the means to generate a large aggregate output.

Mercantilists worried about scarce population. Frequent wars to expand territories or protect borders resulted in a demand for soldiers. The mercantilists believed that wages needed to be kept low (Screpanti and Zamagni 1993). Governments took measures to control wages and interest rates in order to enhance the national competition position in foreign trade. They argued that workers should work 13 or 14 hours a day for subsistence wages, and that higher returns would encourage depravity and laziness, result in rising demands for leisure and perhaps for alcohol, and would ultimately reduce the labour supply. Although these views were justified in terms of Christian morality, the real beneficiary was the merchant class. Mercantilist states also wished to prevent the rural population from migrating to the cities on grounds that the agricultural sector needed to be capable of producing sufficient food to feed the entire population.

Concluding Remarks

Mercantilism or the mercantile system is defined in a few sentences, as follows:

> The term mercantilism denoted the principles of the mercantile system, sometimes understood as the identification of wealth with money, but more generally, the belief that the economic welfare of the state can be only be secured by government regulation of a nationalist character.

Mercantilism can only be studied in specific historical contexts when the use of mercantilist policies appeared under specific conditions. Charles Wilson (1959) argued that mercantilism cannot be studied in the narrow sense of economic policy, but should be extended to cover social policy. Mercantilist states pursued the power and plenty of the nation. One lesson that can be drawn is that state intervention played a role in pre-industrial society. No matter what mercantilism means, the notion is still attractive for economists and economic historians (for example,

Magnusson 1995). The word has gained new life owing to stagflation in industrial countries since the 1970s. Neo-mercantilism proposes the use of non-tariff barriers to protect domestic industries from the cheap exports of the East Asian countries. Mercantilist doctrine, which underlay economic policy in many parts of Europe over three to four centuries, is undergoing a revival to protect the market rather than to foster industrialization (Bhagwati 1988b; Chichilnisky and Heal 1986).

CHAPTER 6

Development Economics, Rent Seeking, and the East Asian Miracle[1]

Some time ago, one looked only at the West as the prototype of successful industrialization which less developed countries desired to emulate, but that might not be true today. The rapid industrialization and sustained high economic growth in East Asian countries — Japan, South Korea, Taiwan, Hong Kong, and Singapore — has been remarkable. Surprisingly, these newly industrializing economies (NIEs) did not adopt the dominant economic development strategies, neo-classical, neo-Marxist, or structuralist, but chose their own courses of development now known as the East Asian Model (Adams and Davis 1994; Islam 1992; Killick 1994; Rodrik 1994, 1995; Singh 1994b; Wade 1994; World Bank 1993). Japan was the first, followed by the four tigers or dragons. This model is now being discussed extensively by development economists. Despite its success, the model still has a large number of shortcomings that will be discussed in this paper. Although economic and social development in the NIEs, especially high economic growth with equity, has been satisfactory by any standards, many scholars question whether they are a robust model of economic policies and strategies for other developing countries (Rodrik 1992b, 1992c, 1993, 1994, 1995; Wade 1994). How were the NIEs so successful in fostering industrialization in a very short period, while most developing countries in Latin America and Africa struggled to avoid economic stagnation? This is largely because their elites made use of development economics as a useful tool for choosing an appropriate industrial strategy.

[1] I would like to thank Professor Christer Gunnarsson and Associate Professor Benny Carlson for useful comments on an earlier draft. Any errors that remain are mine.

Development economics became popular after the Second World War, rejecting neo-classical economics and Keynesian economics. The core of neo-classical economics fits developed countries rather than less developed countries in which markets and other key institutions are either absent or ill-functioning. Since the mid-1970s, both Keynesian and development economics have been assaulted by the new neo-classical or neo-liberal economic theory, with accusations that economists have been incapable of curing macroeconomic ills such as debt crises, stagflation (high inflation and high unemployment rate), increased poverty, persistent deficits in budget, balance of trade and balance of payments, and the like (Hirschman 1981; Lal 1983).

The new neo-classical economics came to the fore when the former centrally planned economies, once part of the Soviet Union and Eastern European bloc, collapsed in the 1980s. Since then, the World Bank and the International Monetary Fund have been busy advising these countries to dismantle state interventions, get the prices and institutions right, and establish private property rights. The story is, however, not as simple as one might expect. The former centrally planned economies have been seeking appropriate paths of development that seem very difficult to find in the available textbooks on development economics. The serious problems that confront these countries are hardly mentioned in these textbooks.

Moreover, the emergence of the East Asian NIEs challenges the new neo-classical advocates since these countries developed capitalism through socialist means such as state-owned enterprises, state-controlled banking sector, and direct state intrusion in private enterprise. These methods were used in Japan, South Korea, Taiwan, Singapore, and even in a nearly purely capitalist market economy like Hong Kong (Amsden 1989; Chang 1993, 1994; Chowdhury and Islam 1993; Clark and Chan 1994; Evans 1989, 1992, 1995; Gunnarsson 1991; Haggard 1990; Wade 1990). From the 1950s to the 1970s, even the Hong Kong government intervened in food and housing to keep wage rates low.

The development economics that emerged after the Second World War faces a dilemma. What advice should be offered to former centrally planned economies on how to overcome their deceleration or stagnation? How can one explain why and how the East Asian NIEs were able to industrialize in such a short period, to the envy of most developing countries? Governments failed in most socialist countries as well as in most capitalist developing economies, but not in the case of the East Asian NIEs, all of which had a substantial degree of state intervention.

The first section of this paper discusses the hard core of development economics, and the rise and fall of its contribution to industrialization. The second section examines the nature and role of the state versus the market in the East Asian NIEs, Latin America, and African countries. The coexistence of plans and markets in the East Asian NIEs resulted in an economic system that is neither a pure capitalist free market nor a socialist economy. The third section examines whether Southeast Asian countries can emulate the East Asian countries. The concluding remarks focus on institutional factors and the role of social norms such as Confucian, Islamic, and Hindu social ethics.

The Hard Core of Development Economics

As a branch of the discipline, development economics is rather new compared to public finance or international trade. The subject was established after the Second World War. The main tools of development economics were borrowed or extended from neo-classical economics insofar as they still embrace bounded rational expectations and methodological individualism. The bounded rationality follows Herbert Simon with a description of human beings who make the best choice from information confronting them. However, while neo-classical economics claimed to be applicable everywhere, regardless of time and space, development economics made a key departure by asserting that Third World countries are different from developed countries in their stage of economic development. Mainstream economics had been touted as a scientific discipline that could be used to explain everything — from marriage to murder.

The methodological presumption of bounded rational choice and individualism might be appropriate for developed countries that have been transformed into so-called post-industrial consumer societies, but seems irrelevant for most developing countries facing a scarcity of clean water, food, and housing (Brunner and Meckling 1977; Brunner 1987). Furthermore, there is ample evidence that people in developing countries make decisions in ways that may seem "irrational" compared to people in developed countries. The term "rationality" is unclear and problematic in development economics because Third World peasants choose their production processes and techniques according to the prevailing circumstances. They are as rational as a Western consumer but the rationality differs in line with the degree of economic development and market institutions. The economies of developing countries are still dominantly agriculture-based with a large number of people in rural areas and low technological capability in all sectors. In many cases the market institutions are imperfect or missing (Elkan 1988; Killick 1993; Stein 1992, 1994a, 1994b).

Clearly there is really no hard core theory in development economics as such. Its theory is an extension of neo-classical economics that has developed to become independent to some extent. Development economics has been elaborated to address the typical characteristics of the economies and societies of the Third World, although it still misses many political aspects. This is a major drawback. Yet development economics has evolved many concrete tools for policy makers. In particular, it has embraced economic planning as a result of the innovation of the late Jan Tinbergen. His famous objectives, constraints, and policy instruments formed the first concrete approach to planning for most policy makers in developing countries. The rapid acceptance of development economics after the Second World War indicates a decline of neo-classical economics among Third World policy makers (Hirschman 1981; Lal 1983). Development economics did not replace Keynesian economics, but offered supplements to Keynesian demand management. In the 1950s, economic growth became the main focus of the discipline, along with the study of comparative economic development, using strict quantification rather than value judgements, as in the work of the late Simon Kuznets.

The birth of development economics coincided with decolonization, the transfer of sovereignty, and the emergence of new nation-states. For these new states, one Keynesian principle that was pertinent concerned the role of the state in bringing about economic growth. The neo-classical view of a self-propelling market mechanism had little appeal. The invisible hand of the market mechanism was overtaken by the invisible foot, invented by Stephen Magee (1984), the idea that the state might actively foster industrialization (Amsden 1989; Cotton 1994; Datta-Chaudhuri 1990; Wade 1990).

Keynesian economics attributed high involuntary unemployment and disequilibrium in goods and factors markets to wage rigidity. The neo-classical economists viewed such disequilibrium as impossible due to the market-clearing mechanism of Say's Law and the absence of money illusion. Factor markets must adjust to a new equilibrium, and the supply and demand for goods are brought into line by the price mechanism.

The neo-classical emphasis on the supply side better approximated the actual conditions in developing countries compared to the Keynesian emphasis on demand, although the neo-classical approach was designed for developed societies where the largest section of the workforce was in manufacturing and key institutions such as private property rights and market institutions functioned well. In predominantly rural developing countries, some crucial markets, such as rural credit, are imperfect or missing. Information is imperfect. Contracts may not work (Hayami and Otsuka 1993).

Development economics became popular among Third World elites because it seemed more relevant. In the hard core theory of neo-classical economics, Pareto optimality cannot be reached if the market is imperfect and transaction costs are positive. Therefore, the governments of Third World countries had a tendency to prefer development economics because it was conceived to supply effective tools of growth. Third World countries also had a tendency to prefer development economics, not necessarily because it was an effective tool, but because it served their nationalistic sentiments of being independent from the West. Leading development economists in the 1940s and 1950s such as Raul Prebisch and Hans Singer proposed strategies for de-linking from the capitalist economy. They argued that the export of raw materials or simple processed export goods, as took place under colonial rule as a vent for surplus, devastated the domestic economy. Due to their low elasticity of demand, export of such primary products could not be an engine of economic growth (Johnson 1991; Timmer 1991, 1992). In fear of being heavily dependent on developed markets, elites in developing countries favoured an inward-looking strategy through import-substituting industrialization.

The Lewis surplus model which appeared in the mid-1950s seemed to offer one means for avoiding this dependence. Since most under-developed and less developed countries had large reserves of surplus labour in the agricultural sector, the model seemed quite appropriate. In fact, the dualistic model of Lewis was structuralist in approach rather than strictly in line with neo-classical development economics (Lewis 1954).

In this period, Gunnar Myrdal (1957, 1968), Ragnar Nurkse (1967), Paul Rosenstein-Rodan (1943), and other leading development econo-mists supported an inward-looking strategy. The disastrous experience of the global depression of the 1930s, consequences of the Second World War, chaotic international trade, collapse of the international financial system, and pursuit of competitive devaluation induced Third World countries to distance their own countries from the capitalist economies. In the historical context, this could be seen as a rational choice.

The Soviet Union implemented its first five-year plan to transform its relatively backward agricultural economy into an industrial state by squeezing an economic surplus from the peasantry to feed a state-owned heavy industrial sector (Gregory 1994; Griffin 1989). Most scholars in this period pictured developing countries as dualistic economies in which agriculture was dominated by vestiges of feudalism with cultivation techniques dating back to the previous century. The Lewis model assumed that there was a large number of surplus rural labourers with zero marginal productivity. The model reflected the experience of European countries, especially Britain, in the eighteenth century, when a stream of rural migrants swelled the cities. The cheap labour supply facilitated industrialization, and industrialization absorbed the army of surplus labour. Industrialists reinvested their large profits. Productivity in the agricultural sector increased to compensate for the drain of labour. In his original 1954 essay, Lewis failed to make a clear-cut distinction between disguised employment and underemployment in the rural areas, leading to a long-term confusion.

The dualistic model (later known as the Lewis-Fei-Ranis model) assumes that marginal productivity in agriculture is low due to underemployment and disguised unemployment, and that marginal productivity in the urban sector is higher, so a transfer of labour from agriculture to urban is always a gain. But the model collapses if rural wage rates rise when labour is withdrawn. If some of the surplus labour is underemployed rather than fully unemployed, this rural wage rise may happen.

In the late 1950s, Albert Hirschman's unbalanced growth model had a substantial impact on Third World policy makers because it described forward and backward linkages which made import-substituting industrialization attractive.

Development economics was still obsessed with the constraints faced by Third World countries due to the lack of domestic savings, lack of domestic demand for industrial goods, a severe shortage of physical and human capital resources, lack of infrastructure, lack of credit and financial institutions, lack of entrepreneurship, and so on. To overcome these constraints, economic planners in Third World countries looked to the record of economic growth in the Western countries. Some analysts argued that the Protestant ethic of working hard and saving for the future was responsible for high economic growth in the West, while Confucian or Islamic thought had no equivalent impact (Bérend and Ranki 1982; Landes 1969; Pollard 1990; Rosenberg and Birdzell 1986). But this approach was challenged, and faded away.

The 1950s was the golden era of development economics with a dominant package of five-year plans, an import-substitution strategy, Big Push projects, a mix of heavy and light industries, and the use of modern machinery (Auty 1994; Dutt 1992; Singh 1992, 1994a). This paradigm was deeply rooted in some concepts like economies of scale and scope, forward and backward linkages, externalities, and so on (Hirschman 1958). Planners in developing countries trusted in the capability and autonomy of the state to bring about industrialization through the invisible foot, rather than relying on the invisible hand of the market through private enterprises. The state was supposed to work hand in hand with the market, but from a clearly superior position. The inward-looking strategy of import-substituting industrialization required regulation of the market through controls on prices, production, credit, and domestic and foreign trade. Private property rights prevailed in the production process, except in the socialist version of the approach. In most non-socialist Third World countries, the means of production did not entirely belong to the state, but state-owned enterprises were of great importance.

The elites of the newly independent nations feared the domination of the rich capitalist economies, partly because the business cycle over the last century had had such an adverse impact on the peripheries. Socialist rhetoric also endorsed import-substituting policy as a means to rescue hundreds of thousands of peasants from the idiocy of rural life. From the 1950s to 1970s, most socialist states pursued an import-substituting strategy.

Newly independent countries viewed import-substituting industrialization as a way to ease the constraints of domestic demand and foreign exchange. Instability in export markets and pessimism about the future of the capitalist economy induced their elites to prefer inward-looking to outward-looking strategy. This mattered when the survival of a nation as an independent economic and political entity was taken into account. The political implications of import-substitution policy were inseparable from the economic rationale.

By fostering industrialization, development economics would consolidate independence and the nation-state. An immediate target was to get rid of the colonial mode of production which had adversely transformed their economies, siphoning natural resources away to the mother countries, and neglecting the development of human resources. In Latin America, this issue had been addressed since the 1940s by the "dependency school" including Raul Prebisch, F.H. Cardoso, O. Sunkel, Theotonio Dos Santos, André Gunder Frank, A. Emmanuel, and Samir Amin. Their principal aim was to overcome an "unequal exchange" between the developed capitalist countries at the centre, and Third World countries at the periphery. They saw import-substituting industrialization as a means to self-reliance, and believed that any supposed constraints of the strategy were illusory and easy to overcome.

In the late 1940s, Paul Rosenstein-Rodan's theory of a Big Push and Ragnar Nurkse's idea of balanced growth offered supplementary support for the import-substitution strategy. Walt Rostow's model of a take-off also lent support to the self-reliant strategy by arguing that investment was essential to reach self-sustained economic growth. Development theorists such as Gunnar Myrdal and Dudley Seers argued that the mainstream theory of comparative advantage should be rejected in favour of more positive economic planning to nurture infant industries, drawing inspiration from nineteenth-century experience when Friedrich List in Germany and Alexander Hamilton in America urged government to nurture infant industries in defiance of British domination of export markets.

At the time, both the World Bank and the IMF viewed inward-looking strategy, with support for heavy and light industries under the infant industry hypothesis, as the right approach for Third World countries to eradicate poverty in rural areas.

In Latin American, sub-Saharan Africa, and some countries in Southeast Asia, an unbalanced or "urban biased" strategy prevailed, featuring overvalued exchange rates and low-priced food for wage earners in the urban areas. The state was seen as a benevolent institution, capable of playing a dominant role in the economy through comprehensive planning implemented by honest and competent technocrats. Many poor countries followed this model (Srinivasan 1994: 21). Export-oriented industrialization was seen as a trap because of the risk of disturbance, as succinctly put by Ragnar Nurkse,

> Industrialization for export is liable to encounter obstacles on the side of external demand. This pattern of industrialization depends for its success on a lenient commercial policy in the older industrial countries. From general considerations, it would seem that such lenience can hardly be relied upon with certainty.... [For the older industrial countries, it is] natural that, for their own immediate comfort, they should wish to avoid or to cushion such adjustments at some cost in terms of their income growth. They feel they can afford to pay the cost. (Nurkse 1967: 199, 221)

Gunnar Myrdal, who did not totally agree with Ragnar Nurkse, supported import-substituting policy on grounds it could overcome the so-called vicious cycle of poverty and underdevelopment, whereas an outward-looking strategy would allow the advanced industrial countries to continue exploiting Third World countries through the international trade mechanism (Myrdal 1957: 275–9).

One common drawback of the Third World countries was a severe shortage of savings for investment. A large number of people were very poor and living at subsistence level so that it was unlikely for these poor countries to have adequate savings for investment. Being poor was also a vicious cycle. Poverty meant that people lacked opportunity to study in formal or informal educational institutions. They might also suffer from malnutrition and both physical and mental debilitation which in turn prevented them from getting good jobs. High earnings required high skills.

The rapid recovery of European countries under the Marshall Plan led to the idea that injections of capital through foreign aid were needed to break this vicious cycle. In Third World countries, the self-reinforcing cycle of low income levels, limited education, poor health, and low levels of saving could not be broken from the inside because of the difficulty of a non-socialist state in squeezing a surplus out of the poor peasantry, and the difficulty of earning foreign exchange in a world with highly unstable trade (Lucas 1988). The Harrod-Domar growth model, which appeared in the late 1950s, lent support to the proposition that the injection of external capital could overcome these constraints. Many poor countries seized on a path of development through import-substituting industrialization made possible by using foreign aid and new sources of "external capital" that could be borrowed from international organizations such as the World Bank and IMF.

The Soviet Union had developed heavy industries under the influence of Rosenstein-Rodan's notion of a Big Push and Alexander Gerschenkron's emphasis on the role of the state in overcoming backwardness for late industrialization. Gerschenkron argued that three strategies were needed: first, constitutional changes to provide appropriate property rights and incentives for economic development; second, monetary and fiscal actions to create an appropriate financial climate for economic development; and third, state entrepreneurialism to substitute for missing entrepreneurship. In the Gerschenkron model, the state was assumed to play the role of an ersatz entrepreneur. Already in the 1920s, E. Preobrazhensky had shown that this strategy could only succeed by depressing rural living standards through moving the terms of trade against agriculture (Gregory 1994). The Russian state under Stalin was only able to achieve heavy industrialization by forcibly and ruthlessly extracting a marketed surplus from agriculture through collectivization (Gunnarsson 1985).

In the thinking of the late 1950s, most Third World countries could not follow the Stalinist model of forced collectivization. Any attempt to raise a surplus from the peasantry under market conditions would fail because the terms of trade would turn against agriculture during the process of industrialization. This proposition was later disproved by extensive empirical research. But at the time, this thinking left no other route for raising capital than introducing it from the outside. International organizations such as the World Bank and IMF embraced this thinking.

Foreign aid and external debt might have enhanced industrialization through import-substituting strategy in a few countries, but foreign aid in most Third World countries hindered economic growth. Relying on foreign aid and external borrowing may have disrupted the potential for local people to solve their own problems. The real question is why the poor countries could not accumulate savings by themselves, partly because a relatively backward economy seemed to prevent them from generating enough income to both spend and save. Foreign aid enabled them at best to solve very short-term problems, but not medium or long-term ones. Furthermore, foreign aid was often wasted on "white elephants" and unproductive projects. Some writers argued that foreign aid retarded rather than hastened economic development (Bauer 1971).

From Inward-oriented and Interventionist to Outward-oriented and Market-based

In the late 1960s, development economics was declining in professional prestige among policy makers, according to Hirschman (1981). In fact the decline began only in the early 1970s when the first oil shock took place. Many countries were still struggling to eradicate poverty and to avoid zero or even negative economic growth. Some countries of Latin America and Africa were able to sustain low or moderate economic growth, but suffered from worsening income distribution. The "trickle-down" effect failed to reduce the big gap between the agricultural and the industrial sectors as well as between rural and urban areas. A lion's share of the pie went to vested interests in the city and some entrenched groups who were closely connected to incumbent elites. Both income inequality and uneven access to non-economic goods such as education tended to rise. As argued by Woo (1990), the failure of the trickle-down hypothesis probably played a more crucial role than increased inequality in income in undermining the prestige of development economics as a useful tool for policy makers.

The turning point towards a new development economics came in the early 1970s with discussion of the effective rate of protection (ERP) by Max Corden (1971). This new technique showed that the poor performance of less developed countries was strongly correlated to the distortion of factor and product markets by urban-biased and import-substituting development strategy. Empirical research by new neo-classical economists such as Bela Balassa (in six countries), Jagdish Bhagwati and Anne Krueger (in nine countries), and Ian Little, Maurice Scott, and Tibor Scitovsky (in six countries) confirmed that economic growth and other economic variables were more positive in countries with fewer policy-induced distortions. These findings undermined the perception of the state as a benevolent social guardian. Market failure, often cited as a key constraint in the 1950s, was supplanted by government failure. Some writers went further, saying that government failures were worse than market failures. The new neo-classical development economists were in favour of the invisible hand of the market, and strongly opposed to the invisible foot of state policy intervention. They supported laissez-faire, minimalist government, and privatization.

In this new orthodoxy, faith in the state was undermined. Indeed, the state was often portrayed as ill-intentioned, ill-informed, incompetent, craven, or manipulated by vested interests. The new role of the state was "getting the prices right", partly by improving market institutions and expanding private sector activity through many measures, in particular providing the physical and legal infrastructure to enable private enterprises to run smoothly and efficiently.

Yet some economists, including Stern, argued that state intervention was still needed in five ways: to overcome market failure that might arise from many possible sources including externalities, missing markets, increasing returns, public goods, and imperfect information; to reduce poverty and improve income distribution; to enforce rights to certain facilities or goods such as education, health and housing; to play a paternal role with respect to such matters as education, pensions, and drugs; and to protect the rights of future generations, including concerns over the environment (Stern 1991: 250–1).

Most of the new neo-classical development economists had been working with the World Bank and the IMF, sometimes since the 1950s. They opposed direct state intervention in the production of ordinary producer and consumer goods. They argued that high levels of state intervention had been responsible for the high degrees of distortion found in some economies of Latin America and sub-Saharan Africa (Felix 1994;

Fishlow 1989, 1994). They claimed that the economically successful countries of East Asian, especially South Korea and Taiwan, had the fewest policy-induced distortions. These arguments were the starting point for a new and intense controversy among development economists since the early 1980s.

Markets and Governments in the Industrialization Process

There is no clear-cut assertion of what is an appropriate balance between the invisible hand and the invisible foot. No theory has authority to say what government should or should not do in the economy. The matter is complex and cannot be generalized to fit all countries. In fact, this debate might even be fruitless if we do not discuss the matter with a specific period or a certain historical context of each country in mind. Here I concentrate on the industrialization process during the post-war era, and in particular on the issue of strategic choices. Jan Tinbergen (1958) was one of the first economists to put forward the view that the role of the state can be crucial in economic affairs. He argued that the responsibilities of the state included achieving sustained economic development with the ultimate goal of human development in all aspects — physical, social, emotional, and intellectual. In fact, development economics has concentrated on the first aspect and neglected the rest. Tinbergen suggested that the instruments of economic policy in the hands of the government must be properly used to achieve desired targets. To this day, the main point of the debate still lies in the nature of the state, its instrumental settings, political environment, and social institutions.

As discussed in the first section above, development economics was at a crossroads in the 1970s. Economic conditions had changed, and the discipline could offer no advice to Third World countries. What was really needed was a deep understanding of their economies and politics that could cause structural changes.

To fulfil Tinbergen's agenda, the state has to behave like a Platonic guardian rather than a predator. What are the conditions which nurture such an institution?

The states in the East Asian NIEs were to some extent authoritarian, yet they worked in the interests of the governed. It is misleading to assume that state intervention will inevitably result in distortion. This conclusion was often embraced by some scholars when they found themselves confused with messy evidence about strong interventions, distortions, and getting the price wrong. But this conclusion is at best insufficient and misleading. Neo-classical and orthodox development economics tend to be over-confident about their methodologies which they claimed are scientific and applicable to every country regardless of time. The real world is more complicated. Neo-classical theory using advanced models and sophisticated computer techniques may fall short. The first requirement is to understand the real problems of development. The structures of markets and institutions in developing countries differ from those in the developed countries so development economics has to be sufficiently flexible and dynamic to take this into account (Stern 1991: 242).

It would be a mistake to examine the issue of the role of the state without linking it to the market. A large number of activities and institutions have public and private aspects that are hard to separate from each other. In the 1950s, states were called upon to overcome market failures, achieve externalities, substitute for missing markets, increase returns, provide public goods, lessen social costs, overcome imperfect information, reduce poverty, facilitate public goods such as education, health, housing, and keep the country peaceful and non-violent (De Jasay 1985; Evans, Rueschmeyer, and Skocpol 1989). These expectations carried the implicit assumption that the government is well intentioned, well behaved, well informed, and competent as a social guardian (Stern 1991; Krueger 1990a, 1990b, 1993a, 1993b). In short, a benevolent state.

A lot of less developed countries, including the East Asian NIEs, started their strategies with import-substitution and then shifted to export-oriented industrialization. The East Asian NIEs were rather successful in fostering industrialization and have become newly industrializing countries since the 1980s, while most Latin American and sub-Saharan African countries are still very poor and underdeveloped. In Latin America, only Columbia has not defaulted on its external debts. Most countries in the two continents have faced serious balance of payment constraints due to limited import capacity that has hampered their ability to make use of new technology from abroad in the form of intangible or tangible knowledge.

What factors, strategies, policies or institutions made the difference between these regions?

At the outset of import-substituting industrialization in the 1950s, many of these countries shared the characteristic of being newly independent countries, but they were quite different in terms of natural resources. After three decades of development, Latin America and sub-Saharan Africa still lag behind the East Asian NIEs. One possible explanation is that the social costs of state intervention outweighed the social benefits as a consequence of rent-seeking activities carried out in a discretionary and non-transparent manner (Evans 1990, 1991, 1992; Grabowski 1994a,

1994b; Gunnarsson 1993), and that scarce resources were diverted away from productive to unproductive activities (Bhagwati 1980; Buchanan 1978, 1980; Krueger 1974; Siriprachai 1993b; Tullock 1967). State intervention hampered competition which is the heartbeat of a capitalist economy. Autocratic governments with absolute power turned out to be absolutely corrupt, resulting in the dissipation of resources on a massive scale (Ampoto-Tuffuor, Delorme, and Kamaerschen 1991; Brooks and Heijdra 1988, 1989; Colander 1984; Mohammad and Whalley 1984; Rowley and Tollison 1986; Rowley, Tollison, and Tullock 1988; Shleifer and Vishny 1993).

The competing explanations about success and failure have concentrated on institutional settings and development strategies.

Neo-classical development economics, in particular the so-called Washington Consensus, claims that the East Asian NIEs, because they shifted to an outward-oriented strategy in the 1960s, increased efficiency and decreased rent-seeking activities, while Latin America and sub-Saharan Africa persisted with import-substitution strategy, failing to read signals from the world market. Even the larger of these countries ran out of steam with import-substitution industrialization.

A prolonged import-substitution policy in conjunction with little contribution to positive externalities and economies of scale resulted in a basis too weak for sustained industrialization. For Washington Consensus economists, the outward-oriented strategy was the decisive step for success for South Korea and Taiwan. "Outward-oriented" was Bela Balassa's term whereas Jagdish Bhagwati called it an export-promoting strategy and Deepak Lal termed it a free trade strategy. The three terms can be grouped into the concept of "neutral incentive strategy".

Historically there had been scepticism about export-led strategy because of vulnerability to instabilities in the world market. During European industrialization during the nineteenth century, exports were often seen as an engine of growth (Pollard 1990). However, the collapse of world trade during and between the two world wars bred mistrust of the export-led growth strategy. Countries that relied heavily on primary exports, based on their abundance of mineral and agricultural resources, were hard hit and struggled to boost agricultural and mineral prices in the world market by several means such as marketing boards in sub-Saharan Africa. Low returns to exports reduced the inflow of foreign exchange to capitalize import-competing industries. Yet by the 1990s, export-led strategy had regained its popularity (Greenaway and Morrissey 1993; Meier 1991; Michaely, Papageorgiou, and Chokski 1991; Milner 1990).

An export-promoting policy is supposed to have no overall policy bias towards the production of any particular product within the tradable sector. The actual situation in the NIEs was a lot more complex. On the one hand, these East Asian states imposed a mass of quantitative restrictions both in the import and export sectors. On the other hand, they provided subsidies to exporters which brought gains outweighing the social costs of import-substitution policy. This is a difficult task for other developing countries to replicate, partly because they need competent bureaucrats to implement such a targeted industrial policy.

It is also too simple to attribute the success of the East Asian NIEs to their outward-looking policy stance, and attribute the failure of the Latin America economies to their persistence with import-substitution. The East Asian NIEs succeeded in the world market because they were able to upgrade their export products — from simple to very sophisticated. This required an effective industrial policy, and a state apparatus able to manage the transition from one policy regime to another. The failure of Latin America countries was not in the choice of policy direction, but in the implementation. They embarked on a second stage of import-substitution policy which required a skilled and educated labour supply to develop and master sophisticated know-how. Because there was no parallel policy to generate such a labour force, the result was disastrous (Felix 1994; Adams and Davis 1994).

The East Asian NIEs initially adopted import-substitution policy because it suited their factor endowment of limited natural resources but abundant cheap labour. However, once the policy had run its course, and once the quality of the labour force had begun to rise, policy makers in the East Asian NIEs were able to make the switch to outward orientation. By contrast, Latin American and sub-Saharan African countries persisted with import-substitution long after efficiency had begun to decline because the strategy still benefited powerful entrenched groups.

Some have argued that the success obtained through trade strategy and industrial policy by the East Asian NIEs has invalidated both old and new dependency schools of thought by showing that peripheral Third World countries can industrialize as long as the right strategy is chosen and consistently implemented with suitable microeconomic policies of tariffs and export subsidies along with sound macroeconomic policies, in particular avoiding an overvalued exchange rate and keeping the inflation rate low.

There is little doubt that competent bureaucrats are essential in keeping the exchange rate appropriate through monetary, fiscal and exchange rate policies. Some large Latin American countries such as Brazil, Mexico, or Argentina faced severe problems of controlling hyper-inflation during the 1970s to 1990s. Many Latin American countries ran an overvalued exchange rate to protect import-substituting industries (ERP of importables higher than ERP of exportable goods). The role of the central bank is critical. The bank governor needs some autonomy to control monetary and exchange rate policy. Unfortunately, most central banks in Latin American countries were not insulated from the political elites. They were not able to monitor the money supply and reduce government deficits.

Some scholars have argued that the failures of Latin American indus-trialization were attributable to bad luck and mismanagement rather than bad strategy. From the Great Depression through the Second World, Latin American countries experienced a sharp reduction in demand for their primary exports of food and minerals. Their states tried to boost agricul-tural and mineral prices in the world market by various means. After they adopted import-substitution policies, continued low prices for their pri-mary exports hindered their ability to earn foreign exchange for financing import-competing industries. The oil shocks of the 1970s brought low growth, high inflation, and chronic balance of payment problems. The import-substituting strategy had failed to spur industrial competitiveness. Industries had not grown from infants to adults, but turned out instead to become infants with long teeth.

The first oil shock substantially affected a large number of oil-importing countries including the East Asian NIEs so this factor cannot serve as a discriminating explanation. Mismanagement of economic policy might have a tragic end result, but this assessment is not easy to prove or disprove.

There are a few key questions. Why did these mismanaged macro-economic policies appear repeatedly in Latin America rather than in the East Asian NIEs? Why did rent-seeking activities or social costs seem to be lower in East Asia than in Latin America and sub-Saharan Africa? Many attempts have been made to explain the different performances, but most of them are still tentative and lack a robust theoretical frame-work (Evans 1992; Rodrik 1993).

An Institutional Approach

One possible explanation for the contrasting experience of Latin America and East Asia can be found in the new institutional economics which provides a framework for understanding the institutional settings which shaped Latin American and sub-Saharan African societies to be different from the East Asian NIEs.

From this perspective, the reasons behind the adoption of different strategies, and the success or failure of implementation, lie in the nature of institutions and in the rules of the game. Findlay (1989a, 1989b) argued that the Latin American countries adopted import-substitution because their rather weak ruling elites could distribute opportunities for rent seeking to buy political support. By contrast, the more authoritarian states of East Asia were insulated from vested interests and appeared as benign Confucian states that imposed policies conducive to economic growth with minimal rent-seeking demands. This explanation is at best tautological, yet has been widely accepted among such revisionists as Alice Amsden, Robert Wade, Stephen Haggard, and Gordon White, even though it is purely based on value judgement without any concrete empirical evidence to support it.

The story of why rent seeking was low in some countries and high in other must be understood from both a wide and a deep angle, namely from both historical and institutional contexts. Economics, sociology, politics, and history have to be blended into a single explanation, using a holistic approach rather than the one-dimensional analysis of new neo-classical economics.

Findlay (1989b) claimed that the East Asian NIEs produced hard (but good) Confucian authoritarian states with key institutions including close government-business relations that were able to reduce or prevent rampant rent seeking. Some have argued that in South Korea the state heavily distorted the economy and society, but rent seeking was kept to a minimum because the state was able to effectively reduce transaction costs, especially those relating to information (Chang 1993, 1994, 1995; Evans 1995).

Both the Latin America countries and the East Asian NIEs adopted a similar import-substitution strategy, using discretionary power, quantitative restrictions, and other measures to nurture both heavy and infant industries. Yet the outcomes were very different. Some writers claim that the success of the East Asian NIEs arose from their uniqueness but this seems exaggerated. Many dimensions and specific conditions combined to make the state and the market work together very well.

In common with most developing countries, South Korea and Taiwan had high surplus labour in the agricultural sector, but scarce natural resources. Under the colonial rule of the Japanese empire, their agriculture was forcibly improved to supply food to Japan. Prior to the 1950s, the productivity of labour and land had increased many times, partly because landlord classes were suppressed by forced land reform. Of course, this process was very painful for the local people, but the benefits were substantial. When South Korea and Taiwan adopted import-substitution in the 1950s and forcibly transferred surplus labour to the industrial sector, the agricultural sector was already strong and able to absorb the products of industry. This process was not new, but resembled the earlier industrialization in Europe, especially Britain. The difference was that the East Asian NIEs were able to avoid the Kuznets curve — an initial worsening of income inequality before a subsequent improvement — and achieve sustained economic growth with equity, as had occurred in Japan. This can be called an intensive-growth pattern, relying on dynamic comparative advantage to foster industrialization because of the limited supply of natural resources. By contrast, Latin America had a traditional and static comparative advantage of having abundant natural resources. As a result their states pursued an extensive-growth pattern, relying on the rents raised from exploiting these abundant natural resources. The main difference between intensive and extensive growth lies in the role of the state and other social institutions.

However, attempts to explain the role of the state can be very subjective. For instance, claims about the role of Confucian social values are misleading. Some key elements have to be taken into account.

The second Industrial Revolution of the twentieth century in electronics and computers helped to shorten the process of industrialization. East Asian countries acquired their technological capabilities by importing and buying know-how from the West instead of doing basic research and development that would have required a high investment cost (Lall 1993a, 1993b, 1993c). But arguing that it was a lack of natural resources that forced Japan, South Korea, and Taiwan to make use of technology from the West is not a sufficient explanation on its own as many countries started with similar constraints.

Critical to the process is the nature and disposition of the state, whether it is benignly committed to the common interest, or whether it is predatory. Some have attempted to explain the benign nature of East Asian states with reference to Confucian ethics, and especially the importance of education in societies governed by Confucian social values. But such social values alone do not provide an adequate explanation. Other societies with similar values did not have such successful economies. The place of such values must be understood within the context of a particular social and political economy.

Some argue that East Asian states were both strong and accountable to their people because they faced severe external threats. But again this characteristic was shared by many other states that were much less successful. Nevertheless, external threats appear to have made the East Asian states strong and accountable to their governed as their legitimacy was insecure or threatened. More importantly, these states could adopt sound macroeconomic policies with few difficulties because they were not manipulated by landlords or other vested interests. Land reform and agricultural modernization, undertaken prior to industrialization, made possible a transfer of labour and marketed surplus from the rural areas to the cities. Agricultural transformation is the key factor in generating a marketed surplus to feed industry. But this process is effective only when the real wage in agriculture rises, creating incentives to invest in both industry and agriculture. This was the case in South Korea and Taiwan. If other countries had achieved more equal distribution of income, they would have fared better.

Successful land reform schemes in South Korea and Taiwan were not exogenous factors, but absolutely endogenous to an industrialization process achieved by intersectoral transfer of labour and marketed surplus from the rural areas to the modern industrial sectors in the cities. The other key condition of the success is related to the world economy led by the United States after the Second World War (Haggard 1990; Jenkins 1991). Export-led industrialization worked because the exports found a market in the United States during the Cold War era. Moreover, a large amount of foreign aid to these two countries might have played some role during the 1950s and up to the mid-1960s.

These conditions have faded since the 1970s as the Unites States changed her role from free-trading to a fair-trading country where protectionist sentiment has revived.

The Lewis model assumed there was an unlimited supply of labour at a given real wage and that therefore the transfer of labour from agriculture to industry would not hamper agricultural production. Empirically this was not borne out. In the countries of Latin America and sub-Saharan Africa, prices of agricultural produce rose because output failed to adjust to the demand from industry. Heavy state interventions in trade, natural disasters such as prolonged droughts or sudden floods, and a shift in the terms of trade in favour of agriculture added to the problem, cutting industrial profits and hence retarding growth. High prices of agricultural products also spurred inflation that made these countries' tradable products less competitive in the world market. The influence of the Lewis model contributed to both successes and failures in different regions of the world.

Agricultural transformation was key to generating a marketed surplus to support industry. Rising real wages in agriculture acted as an incentive to invest in both industry and agriculture. The Lewis model of the agricultural marketed surplus, and the Harrod-Domar model on the limited capacity of a domestic capital goods sector for transforming savings into investment, are both characteristics of a closed economy. The East Asian NIEs broke through these constraints by shifting to export-promoting industrialization after the 1960s. The dynamism and unpredictability of the world economy forced South Korean and Taiwanese entrepreneurs to become flexible and efficient. Along with peasants, urban workers bore the costs of industrialization through depressed real wages, but the period was very short compared to other developing countries. Japan, South Korea, and Taiwan all now have highly subsidized agricultural sectors (Anderson and Hayami 1986; Johnson 1991).

In sub-Saharan Africa, both agriculture and industry have low productivity, employment, and output. Many countries fail to produce enough food for their population. Tony Killick (1993) identified six serious shortcomings: (1) A heavy dependence on imported raw materials, equipment and skills severely limits linkages with the rest of the economy and the potential contribution of manufacturing to the balance of payments. (2) Capacity levels in industry are too high given the size of the domestic market and the availability of necessary imported inputs. (3) Industry is biased towards final-stage processing of consumer goods, especially in inefficient assembly plants for vehicles and electronic goods, rather than processing of local raw materials and the production of intermediate and capital goods. (4) In a dualistic structure, there are very few transactions between a large number of informal and small scale enterprises on the one hand and a small number of relatively large-scale modern plants on the other. (5) There is still a very small base of individual skills and supporting services, and thus an absence of "agglomeration economies", and much inappropriate low-productivity technology. (6) Heavy investment in state-owned enterprises, often with the worst of the above characteristics, and also heavily subsidized by government, adds to already acute budgetary difficulties.

The Japanese model of the state's role in the economy, emulated by South Korea and Taiwan, has been labelled "sponsored capitalism". On the one hand, the economy works by capitalist means, namely on profit-making stimulus under private-enterprise competition. On the other hand, Japanese, South Korean and Taiwanese states have not permitted the free play of market forces without a clear direction (Dore 1986; Johnson 1982; Vestal 1993). States set national priorities. Competent bureaucrats use the carrot and the stick to ensure targets are fulfilled. However, there are still failures. Some firms could not reach the targets. In South Korea and Taiwan, punishment has always been applied (Amsden 1989; Chang 1993, 1994).

The case of the East Asian NIEs led to a hot debate in development economics because their success rests on a mix of conflicting policies. Rodrik (1993: 25) summarized the mix as follows: (1) There has been a lot of government intervention and an active trade and industrial policy. (2) Intervention has taken place in a context of stable macroeconomic policies with small budget deficits and realistic exchange rate management. (3) The governments' commitment to exports has helped minimize the resource costs and incentive problems that would have otherwise arisen from heavy intervention. (4) A "hard" state has imposed on the private sector. Most of this mix is lacking in most other developing countries.

The "East Asian model" is a mix of neo-classical development economics and other schools of thought. A discretionary and regulatory framework of allocating resources by controlling private decisions, as practised by many socialist countries, is also found in South Korea and Taiwan. These countries often used quantitative restrictions rather than price-based measures mediated through the markets. It is not true that hard interventionist states prevent rent seeking (Rodrik 1995). In July 1995, a crowded department store in South Korea collapsed, resulting in great loss of life. Those responsible for the construction were given life sentences. The case suggests that South Korean bureaucrats are as corrupt as elsewhere.

Interventions made in NIEs, such as quantitative restrictions, have often been similar in kind to interventions which, when practiced in socialist states or other developing countries of Latin America and sub-Saharan Africa, have led to rampant rent seeking. This contradicts the rent-seeking theory of analysts such as Buchanan, Tullock, and Krueger, and suggests there is some qualitative difference in the nature of the state and state institutions.

Some Tentative Learnings

It is too early to make any concrete conclusion about the factors explaining the success of the East Asian NIEs and the contrasting failure in Latin America and sub-Saharan Africa, but some lessons can be drawn in a tentative way.

First and foremost, institutional settings do matter, but how they matter is difficult to say. The hard, authoritarian and strong governments in South Korea and Taiwan created incentive systems to ensure firms or industries that enjoyed protection were nurtured to succeed. This differed from the one-way command processes of socialist countries which created severe free-rider problems. In both South Korea and Taiwan, private firms risked losing the benefits of import restriction or other subsidies such as credit if they failed to perform. With this strict monitoring, domestic prices could be kept close to border or world market prices. As a result, neo-classical economists could claim that the NIEs were practising a free-market strategy. Others have used the term "developmental state", with the clear implication that government is leading the market, rather than leaving it alone. One key role of the developmental state is to reduce the transaction costs of acquiring new technology. In Japan, South Korea, and Taiwan, governments played a key role of managing the transfer of technology from foreign sources, while simultaneously controlling the penetration of foreign capital into the domestic economy. This point is often ignored.

Second, by shifting to an outward-oriented strategy in the 1960s, these states exposed their entrepreneurs to the world market, forcing them to upgrade the efficiency of their firms, and hence further develop the country's dynamic comparative advantage. The infant industries were forced to grow up. Even when protectionist sentiment appeared in the developed markets such as the United States and European Union in the 1980s, South Korea and Taiwan were still able to expand their exports of manufactures to these markets.

The export-promotion policy reduced the negative effects of import-substitution. Yet an import-substituting policy was needed at the initial stage of economic development in order to build up basic and heavy industries and to create backward and forward linkages. Nurturing infant industries does not necessarily lead to bad results. It depends on the institutional setting.

Import-substitution strategy can only work if the agricultural sector is able to produce a rising marketed surplus with less labour through improving the productivity of labour and land. It helps also if the terms of trade are moving in favour of agriculture so that the peasantry has improved well-being and growing capacity to consume the products of industry. The East Asian NIEs of Japan, South Korea, and Taiwan had already enhanced their productivity in agriculture before they adopted import-substituting strategy.

Third, states in the East Asian countries were well disciplined in the sense of maintaining a sound macroeconomic policy, at the same time providing various incentives under sectoral policies. It is still not entirely clear how they were able to keep rent-seeking costs low even though they have had strong state intervention. Some argue that the state's major contribution was the creation of a large stock of skilled labour (Rodrik 1994, 1995). Some attribute this success to Confucian social values but such explanations are personal value judgements (Oshima 1978, 1993). The most difficult element to understand and explain is the underlying relationship between the state and the market. This was both complex and dynamic. In the literature of development economics, there is no consensual explanation.

New neo-classical development economists (including those in the World Bank) have argued that the East Asian NIEs states are "market friendly", in that they work hand in hand with the private sector (World Bank 1993; Rodrik 1994). In both South Korea and Taiwan, states created a network for two-way exchange of information between firms, governments, and other social institutions, in particular regarding markets and technology (Evans 1992: 85). These economic and social networks worked well because those countries are socially homogeneous. State interventions were transparent, rule-based rather than discretionary, and restrictions were price-based rather than quantitative, hence rent-seeking opportunities were kept to a minimum (Srinivasan 1994: 27).

But the term "market friendly" is misleading. The systems of incentives set out by these states were interventionist and discretionary, in conflict with market principles. Rent seeking did arise, but the social gains from adapting and mastering new technology from the West outweighed the social costs stemming from rent-seeking activities.

Some have attributed the East Asian NIEs' success to cultural homogeneity and Confucian values which in particular promoted education and facilitated the very rapid acquisition of knowledge (Adams 1993). They argue that other cultural settings, including Islamic and Hindu, are not similarly conducive to modern economic growth. This argument is a little surprising given that Max Weber once claimed that Confucianism was one reason for Asian backwardness in contrast to the Protestant ethic of the capitalist West. Perhaps such arguments need to be treated with care.

Fourth, it has been argued that non-economic factors played a vital role in shaping the East Asian states as developmental in contrast to the predatory states that work for the benefit of autocrats, elites, or bureaucrats as found in Latin America and sub-Saharan Africa.

The external threats to South Korea and Taiwan gave rise to powerful autocratic states. The achievement of high growth became a major way in which these states established their legitimacy (Haggard 1990, 1994; Jenkins 1991; Rodrik 1992a, 1992b, 1992c, 1994, 1995). Rodrik (1992a) argues that business communities offered no resistance to the carrot-and-stick interventions by government. Kohli (1994) argues that the hard states of South Korea and Taiwan were inherited from the secret police systems developed under the Japanese empire.

Fifth, it has been argued that the homogenous populations in South Korea and Taiwan were fertile ground for nationalistic sentiments, which not only supported state-making but also acted as a restraint on the abuse of power by state elites.

Sixth, sub-Saharan Africa suffered from a severe shortage of agricultural produce from the 1970s to the 1980s. This shortage may have compounded the difficulties facing a weak state in the early stages of development. States were easily manipulated by vested interests. The people were unable to organize to restrain the influence of powerful interest groups or political cliques. Policies nominally designed to promote growth or assist the poor in fact benefited the affluent. Governments are not omniscient, selfless, or social guardians (Krueger 1990a).

One lesson is that it is hard to distinguish between market and government failures in less developed countries. As put by Krueger (1990a):

> One must ask why economists were ever comfortable with the simultaneous belief that individuals in the private sector act in their self-interest and that individuals in the public sector are motivated by a Benthamite vision of social justice. In addition, one must ask why collective decisions are likely to be the result of the same utility calculus as individual decisions.

Can Southeast Asian Countries Imitate East Asian Countries?

In the academic world, a new idea always emerges to challenge or invalidate existing knowledge. Recently, Schmidt (1993) proposed that Southeast Asian states can be characterized as developmental states like the

East Asian NIEs. I shall argue that the East Asian developmental states achieved their miracles under special conditions which cannot be emulated by other developing countries.

The East Asian success story — the fast growth rates achieved by Japan, South Korea, Taiwan, and the two islands states of Singapore and Hong Kong — raises the issue of how this experience might be copied in other countries. There have been two competing paradigms explaining why the East Asian NIEs so successfully expanded manufactured exports since the 1960s. A well entrenched view, rooted in neo-classical economics, claims that the East Asian success provides a clear demonstration of market competition. Some economists prescribe openness and price liberalization as key to replicating the East Asian experience. The alternative interpretation contends that the state was the "engine of growth", and government intervention was pervasive (except in Hong Kong).

There is now strong empirical support for the view that state intervention was substantial in the East Asian NIEs. The point is not that state intervention *per se* played a crucial role in their successful industrialization, but that state intervention was effective within a capitalist economy. Some economists prefer to characterize this as state-led capitalism, in which the government uses its strong arm for the purpose of achieving economic development. The state was able to maintain stable macroeconomic policies, and to formulate and implement coherent economic strategies.

A prerequisite for adopting a consistent strategy is a degree of state autonomy from the dominant class or class fractions, making it possible for the state to pursue goals without being interrupted by vested interests. By autonomy here, I mean a capacity to act independent of social forces, namely economic forces. East Asian NIEs achieved their miracles through a hard state with efficient and cohesive bureaucratic machinery able to design and implement a coherent economic strategy. A crucial common feature of the East Asian NIEs is the autonomy of the state from classes and class fractions.

Recently some scholars have argued that Southeast Asian states can be placed in the same category of strong, paternalistic states able to manage both domestic and international environments for competitive growth (Yuen, Sudo, and Crone 1992; Schmidt, 1993). They argue that South Korea and Singapore became developmental states in the mid-1960s, Malaysia since the mid-1970s, and Thailand and Indonesia in the early 1980s. What criteria do they use? Yuen, Sudo and Crone (1992) suggest that there are five main common factors which characterize

Malaysia, Indonesia, and Thailand as developmental states, namely, state capacity, mixed-market economies, outward-looking orientation, effective macroeconomic policies, and efficient infrastructure.

The developmental states of East Asia were a complex mix of authoritarianism and capitalism. Lauridsen (1991) proposes four fundamental characteristics: stable rule by a political and bureaucratic elite; cooperation between public and private sectors under the overall guidance of a pilot planning agency; heavy and continuous investment in education and other policies to ensure equitable distribution of wealth; and an understanding of the need to use and respect methods of intervention based on the price mechanism. In comparison to Lauridsen's definition, the factors suggested by Yuen, Sudo and Crone (1992) are descriptive of developing countries in general.

Can Southeast Asian States Copy the East Asian NIEs?

Some have argued that the key difference between the successful East Asian NIEs and the less successful developing countries of other regions is outward-orientation versus continued inward-looking attachment to import-substitution industrialization. I argue that the story is more complicated than just trade strategy. The superior economic performance of the East Asian NIEs does not in fact lie in any general superiority of export-oriented industrialization strategy over import-substitution, or of market-oriented policies over state intervention (Jenkins 1991). Rather, it lies in the competence of the state to direct the accumulation process within the particular historical context and international economic environment.

The relative autonomy of the state in the East Asian NIEs was rooted in some specific historical factors. Landlords had been destroyed in the colonial period. External threats fostered state building, nationalism, and autocracy. Other developing countries do not face the same circumstances. In other words the specific historical experiences and international circumstances of East Asia states have given the state more relative autonomy than is found elsewhere. The Southeast Asian states do not have the same relative autonomy, nor do they have the qualities which Rodrik lists for a developmental state (Rodrik 1993: 25; McVey 1992b; Yoshihara 1988).

It is not clear whether other countries are able to emulate the East Asian NIEs. In particular, a strategy of strong export growth coexisting with import protection requires conditions that are hard to achieve in many countries. In South Korea, the hard state limits spending on luxury products and other consumer goods through restrictions on imports. The state controls rent seeking and lobbying, suppresses labour unions, and penalizes executives of companies that misuse their privileges (Thomas *et al.* 1991). Such actions are not found in Southeast Asian states. East Asian NIEs can avoid rent seeking, and undertake reforms such as trade liberalization, because authoritarian leaders can override the demands of interest groups and stay in power for longer time (Haggard and Webb 1993).

The revisionist school attributes East Asian success to industrial policy, but this conclusion may be too simple. As pointed out above, having the right policy is not enough; the main thing is the effectiveness of the implementation. Moreover, today it would be hard to replicate the mass of restrictions and subsidies of that industrial policy. As noted by a World Bank document, the East Asian countries were successful in using protective import policies by avoiding exchange rate overvaluation and offsetting the anti-export bias of import protection. Their approach would be difficult to replicate in today's world economy. South Korea's approach during the 1960s and 1970s included export subsidies, which other countries would countervail today, and vigorous government intervention to suppress rent-seeking activities viewed as incompatible with export growth (Thomas *et al.* 1991).

Yoshihara (1988) argues that Southeast Asian countries are plagued with rent seekers, crony capitalists, and bureaucratic capitalists closely associated with political power, especially in the Philippines and Thailand which have a historical background of dictatorship. There are no effective checks on the use of political power, no accountability in politics. The government is able to dispose of economic resources with impunity. Such Southeast Asian states should not be regarded as developmental states.

Concluding Remarks

Development economics as a discipline is criticized for being unable to guide policy makers in less developed countries. This limitation in fact comes from its inherent methodology. Development economics borrowed its hard core theory from neo-classical economics, and made some adaptations to the general characteristics of the less developed countries regardless of time and space. A main drawback is that it cannot incorporate institutions (organizations and rules of the game) as endogenous variables, but treats them as exogenous and frictionless.

The debate on the role of institutions in development economics is still quite limited (Eggertsson 1990; North 1990; Van Arkadie 1989). Since the collapse of the Soviet bloc in the 1980s, a new institutional economics has acquired some momentum, in particular in the appreciation of transaction costs and property rights. This bodes well for conventional economic analysis. As pointed out by North (1993), one serious shortcoming of new neo-classical economics, including development economics, is that transaction costs are assumed to be zero, which is unlikely to be the case in the real world. In a market economy, there are transaction costs, shaped by existing institutions, which might hamper economic development. Institutions can hinder as much as enhance economic growth.

Among new neo-classical economists, there has been an intense debate on the role of the state in agricultural development. What is needed, however, is more attention to the complex systems of institutions, including household behaviour, credit, marketing and distribution networks, risk, uncertainty, supply response, and asymmetric information. Economists are looking beyond the market principle and paying more attention to institutional settings within local societies. Nobel Laureate Joseph Stiglitz puts it as follows:

> Simple prescriptions have one obvious advantage: they enable economists to make policy judgements with virtually no knowledge of the country in question. But the flaws in the simplistic approach make it all the more important to accumulate detailed information on most of the developing world. The first step in any systematic analysis of agricultural policies is therefore to describe as accurately as possible the consequences of each policy. This requires a model of the economy concerned and a model appropriate for one country may not be for another. Recent work had clarified some of the essential ingredients of these models; wage-setting policies in the urban sector, the nature of rural-urban migration, and the organization of the rural sector, labour, land and credit market.... In any analyses of agricultural policies, the hardest part is to incorporate political economy considerations todecide what are to be taken as political constraints. (Stiglitz 1987: 54)

Development economics in the future will inevitably be concerned with terms such as transaction costs, property rights, externalities, collective action, networks, and the like. These concepts will be treated as endogenous variables in future analyses, and this might help to bring economic theory closer to the real world. Nevertheless, the real world is so complicated that new institutional economics casts only a little light. The most difficult part of the story is about informal institutions that determine the rules of the game in any economy, whether former centrally planned or capitalist market economies. The central point is how to build up good institutions under the prevailing circumstances or how to break down obstructive institutions which may have existed for centuries.

Let's take an example. South Korea implemented import-substitution and then shifted in the 1970s to an export-promoting strategy using export subsidies to help South Korean firms to compete in the world market. Yet in many less developed countries such as Bolivia, Cote d'Ivoire, and Senegal, the same policy failed and became a source of rent seeking (Rodrik 1993: 25). The difference is not easily understood by new neoclassical development economics, possibly because it treats policy tools as neutral. The difference has to be studied through the institutional lens, focusing on the interaction of state and society.

Mainstream development economics is full of diagnoses of the problems of less developed countries, but has failed to provide a concrete policy guide, in particular for the countries of the former Soviet Union and Eastern Europe.

Knowledge was key to the success of the East Asian NIEs. They paid attention to developing human capital and acquiring technology. People worked hard, studied hard, and saved hard. Moses Abramovitz (1989) defined this as social capability. Technology is not only tools, blueprints, and machines but a complex, value-laden social process, embedded in key institutions of each society. The state-society relationship played an important role in forming the technological and industrial culture of East Asian countries with learning by doing and learning by showing, and also in achieving technological autonomy. Latin American and sub-Saharan African countries have lagged behind in this crucial aspect.

In sum, economic theory, in particular mainstream development economics, seems unable to answer the question of where the economic borders of the state should lie, perhaps because economic theory is at best an imperfect corpus of knowledge (Helm 1989: 42). In the end, the answer rests on value judgements.

CHAPTER 7

Growth, Technological Inertia, and a Weak State

A Short Political History

In Thailand as in other traditional societies, from the time of Sukhothai (the first Thai kingdom, circa 1260–1350 AD) to the *coup d'état* of 1932, the king was at the centre of the political structure. The king held extensive power and was responsible for the administrative, judicial, military, religious and cultural life of the country. He also appointed central and provincial officials, issued edicts on a variety of subjects, made decisions on legal issues, oversaw preparations for war, protected the Buddhist faith, and provided generous support for the arts. Many Thai monarchs were leading intellectuals or poets. King Mongkut (r. 1851–67) and King Chulalongkorn (r. 1868–1910) preserved Thailand's independence from the West in an era of colonial expansion. The journey of modern Thailand began when King Chulalongkorn initiated a reform programme which included the introduction of Western-style education and public health systems, railways, and a public security apparatus such as police.

Though the *sakdina* (Thai feudal) regime had survived for centuries, the Thai monarchy was unable to preserve its great power in the twentieth century. By the 1920s, a demand for change in the political system was emerging among military officers, civilian officials, and students who had studied abroad, particularly in France. The coup of 24 June 1932 brought the military to a dominant position in the Thai political structure, and the Provisional Constitution of 27 June 1932 ended the absolute monarchy. On the 2 March 1935 King Prajadhipok abdicated the throne, which remained virtually vacant until King Bhumibol Adulyadej returned to Bangkok in 1950 and became very popular with the Thai people.

The "1932 revolution" also opened Thai politics to a new group of people, mainly bureaucrats, who originated from the great reforms of King Chulalongkorn. The bureaucracy was the major source of employment for educated Thais and became the main source of power in Thai politics for decades. Some observers regard the Thai bureaucracy as a social system with its own values. Between 1932 and early 1973, Thai politics was a matter of competition between bureaucratic cliques for the control of the government. There is no doubt that the most powerful group was the army, which was well organized and well established, and as a result, came out on top of the political competition. Some political writers term this period an era of semi-democracy.

Since 1932, Thailand has had a bicameral parliamentary system with a constitutional monarchy. Although King Bhumibol Adulyadej provided some degree of political continuity, there have been seventeen military coups (the last in 1991) since 1932. A genuine civilian government was installed in 1973, but over the following decades, administrations were always short-lived and unstable (see Table 7.1).

Table 7.1 Changes of Government, 1932–2001

Prime Minister	Dates in Office	Duration (months)	Means of Selection
Manopokon	1/1932–6/1933	12	coup
Phahon	6/1933–9/1938	63	parliament[a]
Phibun	12/1938–8/1944	68	parliament
Khuang[b]	8/1944–8/1945	12+2+4	parliament
Thawi	8/1945–8/1945	0.5	interim
Seni	9/1945–1/1946	4	interim
Pridi	3/1946–8/1946	4	parliament
Thawan	8/1946–11/1947	15	parliament
Phibun (2)	4/1948–9/1957	114	coup
Phot	9/1957–12/1957	3	interim
Sarit[c]	2/1959–12/1963	58	coup
Thanom	12/1963–10/1973	10+118	succession
Sanya	10/1973–2/1975	16	interim
Kukrit[d]	3/1975–1/1976	10	parliament
Seni (2)	4/1976–10/1976	7	parliament
Thanin	10/1976–10/1977	12	coup
Kriangsak	11/1977–2/1980	28	coup
Prem	3/1980–8/1988	100	parliament
Chatchai	8/1988–2/1991	30	parliament

continued overleaf

Table 7.1 continued

Prime Minister	Dates in Office	Duration (months)	Means of Selection
Anand	2/1991–2/1992	12	interim
Suchinda	3/1992–5/1992	2	coup[c]
Anand	6/1992–9/1992	3	interim
Chuan	9/1992–6/1995	33	parliament
Banharn	7/1995–11/1996	16	parliament
Chavalit	11/1996–11/1997	12	parliament
Chuan (2)	11/1997–2/2001	39	parliament

Notes: a. Parliament was restored after another coup.

             b. Khuang was again prime minister from January to March 1946 and from November 1947 to April 1948.

             c. Thanom was prime minister for 10 months while Sarit was being treated for cirrhosis in the United States.

             d. Seni was prime minister for about 20 days before Kukrit.

             e. Suchinda was chosen by Parliament but his selection was the result of a coup.

Sources: Ockey (1996: 345–60) and my observations since the Banharn era.

A critical change occurred in January 2001, when the newly formed Thai Rak Thai (TRT, Thai loves Thai) party under the leadership of a former policeman and telecommunication tycoon, Thaksin Shinawatra, won a resounding victory in a general election. In 2005, the Thaksin government became the first administration to complete a four-year term. Furthermore, in the 2005 elections, the Thai Rak Thai party won an unprecedented second term, and could form a single-party government. Over prior decades, coalition governments had prevailed, but the Thai Rak Thai Party won 377 seats in the lower house, enabling it to govern alone. This represents a new era of Thai politics to the extent that the parliament is controlled by a dominant political force (see Table 7.2).

Table 7.2 House of Representatives, February 2005 Elections

Political Party	Total	Constituency	Party List
Thai Rak Thai	377	310	67
Democrat Party	96	70	26
Chart Thai	25	18	7
Mahachon	2	2	0

Note: The party list MPs were selected by proportional representation.
Source: Election Commission of Thailand.

Politics in Thailand became chaotic again in early 2006, when Thaksin sold his telecom company, Shin Corp, to Singapore's state-owned Temasek Holdings for a tax-free US$ 1.9 billion. The deal, structured to avoid paying tax on capital gains, made a large number of people angry and disappointed. Anti-government protests emerged rapidly, leading to many big demonstrations by middle class and professional people in Bangkok. Opponents of the billionaire leader accused him of abusing the country's system of checks and balances and bending government policy to benefit his family's business. Instead of using parliament to respond to the opposition's demand, Thaksin dissolved the parliament and called a snap general election, which was boycotted by all main opposition parties. Although the Thai Rak Thai Party was returned to power, the no votes (abstentions) were substantial, in particular in Bangkok and in the south. This poll has tainted Thaksin's legitimacy. To defuse the political crisis, Thaksin handed over the premiership to his deputy. What role Thaksin plays in the future remains to be seen.

Economic Progress and Structural Change

Economic Growth, 1855 to 1950

The Thai economy stagnated for at least a hundred years (1855–1949). The growth rate of per capita income over this period averaged just 0.2 per cent per year (Manarungsan 1989). Why did the Thai economy stagnate for such a long period? Some attribute this to the unequal relationships with the colonial powers. For example, Ingram (1971) and Feeny (1982) suggest that Thailand remained *de jure* independent, but the economy was *de facto* similar to a colonial economy. The unequal Bowring treaty that the British imposed on Thailand in 1855 turned the Thai economy into a colonial economy. The treaty set a maximum of 3 per cent for duties on imports and exports, prohibiting high import duties which might have sheltered domestic industries. Cheap imports easily replaced local industrial products, while the country was severely weakened by the limitation on government raising revenue from taxing trade. Feeny (1982) goes further by arguing that the Thai elites chose to use all scarce resources to invest in railways instead of putting money into irrigation projects, which would have improved productivity in the agricultural sector, especially in rice production.

A second explanation for stagnation lies in the fact that Thai *sakdina* did not nurture an entrepreneurial class. Most entrepreneurs working in

Thailand at that time came from Europe and China. Chinese merchants were very active in the Thai economy in all aspects of life. Chinese traders and unskilled workers migrated to Thailand to earn money for sending back to mainland China. According to Ingram (1971), the amount of such money sent back to China was quite substantial, and rendered the Thai economy stagnant in terms of capital accumulation.

The Thai Miracle Since 1950

The Thai economy turned a corner in the 1950s, and grew by 6.2 per cent annually between 1950 and 2003 (Table 7.3). During the decade (1987–96), prior to the crisis, the economy was growing at 9.2 per cent per annum. The economy contracted by –6.1 per cent during 1997–98. It managed to come out of the crisis quickly and the economy has been growing by over 6 per cent. The average inflation rate remained moderate throughout these years (Table 7.4).

Table 7.3 Rates of Growth of GDP and GDP per capita, 1951–2003

Period	Real GDP Growth	Real GDP Growth per capita
1951–86 (Phase I), pre-boom	6.5	3.9
1987–96 (Phase II), boom	9.2	8.0
1997–8 (Phase III), crisis	–6.1	–7.1
1999–2003 (Phase IV), post-crisis	4.0	3.3
Whole period 1951–2003	6.2	4.2

Sources: Warr (2005), based on Bank of Thailand data for 1951 to 1980; and NESDB data from 1987.

Table 7.4 Main Economic Indicators, 1950–99

	1950–59	1960–69	1970–79	1980–89	1990–96	1997–99
Growth rate real GDP	5.4	8.0	7.1	7.3	8.5	–2.4
Savings/GDP ratio	11.5	20.6	21.8	25.1	34.1	31.0
Investment/ GDP ratio	13.6	20.8	23.8	28.6	40.7	24.3
Inflation rate	5.1	2.2	8.0	5.8	5.1	4.7

Sources: Ingram (1971: 222), and data from NESDB and Bank of Thailand.

It is quite surprising that frequent military coups have not had the same pernicious effect on growth as they did in some Latin American countries. As pointed out rightly by Feng (2003), political instability did not translate into economic uncertainty largely because both the over-thrown governments and the coup leaders shared the same commitment to a market economy, and left the difficult job of managing the economy in the hands of technocrats from the Ministry of Finance and Bank of Thailand (Christensen and Siamwalla 1993). Additionally, the monarchy in Thailand as a traditional institution keeps national conflicts at a low level. Thus, a country with many coups was still capable of managing growth quite well. Fundamental principles of macroeconomic stability were maintained.

Sources of Growth

Table 7.5 summarizes the findings of growth-accounting studies for Thailand. Thailand ranks second among East Asian economies with respect to the contribution made by Total Factor Productivity (TFP) growth per worker over the period 1970–85.[1] However, rapid accumulation of

Table 7.5   Growth Accounting

Study	Period	Growth Concept	Growth Rate	Capital Accumu-lation	Labour Input	Quality of Labour	TFP Growth
Young (1995)	1970–85	Output per worker	3.7		1.8		1.9
Collins and Bosworth	1960–94	Output per worker	5.0	2.7		0.4	1.8
Sarel (1997)	1979–96	Output per capita	5.24	2.13	1.09	–	2.03
Tinakorn and Sussangkarn (1996)	1978–90	Output	7.6	2.9	2.0	1.5	1.2
Tinakorn and Sussangkarn (1998)	1981–95	Output	8.12	5.04	0.96	0.84	1.27

Source: Jansen (2004).

---

[1] According to the much cited studies of Young (1995), the contribution of TFP to growth in East Asia over the period 1960–85 varied from 2.5 per cent in Hong Kong to 0.1 per cent in Singapore. Sarel (1997) puts this range from 2.23 per cent for Singapore to –0.78 per cent for the Philippines.

capital made the highest contribution. This is quite evident from the sharp increase in the investment ratio from a very low level in the 1950s to very high levels in the late 1980s and 1990s (Table 7.4). The saving ratio jumped from 11.5 in the 1950s to 34.1 during 1990–96. Capital accumulation was largely domestically financed until the mid-1980s, with household savings playing a major role. Since the mid-1980s, however, corporate and foreign savings have assumed a significant role.

Table 7.6 shows that the contribution from labour quality increased rapidly. The quality adjusted contribution of labour input increased from 4.4 per cent (25.1 less 20.7 per cent) during 1980–85, to 12.1 per cent (21.4 less 9.3 per cent) during 1986–95. What is striking is that the quality adjusted contribution of TFP was 31.3 over 1986–90, but almost negligible in 1991–95, just prior to the crisis of 1997.

Table 7.6 Sources of Growth by Sectors, 1981–95 (percentages)

	Land	Capital	Labour, unadjusted	Labour, quality adjusted	TFP, unadjusted	TFP, quality adjusted
1981–85	2.9	62.2	20.7	25.1	14.1	9.7
Agriculture	4.0	11.7	21.6	41.8	62.7	42.5
Industry		86.2	28.0	42.7	−14.2	−28.9
Manufacturing		68.3	31.9	57.1	−0.2	−25.5
Services		74.9	34.0	52.3	−8.8	−27.2
1986–95	−0.3	61.6	9.3	21.4	29.4	17.3
Agriculture	−0.9	90.6	−7.1	−4.2	17.4	14.5
Industry		64.1	27.3	36.5	8.6	−0.5
Manufacturing		59.4	28.1	37.1	12.5	3.5
Services		65.7	24.6	33.0	9.7	1.3
Of which: 1986–90	−0.2	47.6	13.1	21.3	39.6	31.3
Agriculture	−0.9	59.3	23.3	35.6	18.3	6.0
Industry		49.0	24.3	26.6	26.7	24.4
Manufacturing		47.6	27.0	26.0	25.4	26.4
Services		52.1	18.9	32.6	29.0	15.3
Of which: 1991–95	−0.5	78.6	4.8	21.5	17.1	0.4
Agriculture	−0.8	117.3	−33.2	−38.3	16.7	21.8
Industry		84.5	31.5	49.9	−15.9	−34.4
Manufacturing		75.6	29.7	52.4	−5.3	−28.0
Services		82.3	31.7	33.5	−14.0	−15.8

Sources: Jitsuchon (2002), drawn from Tinnakorn and Sussangkarn (1998, tables 8, 13, 14, 15, 16).

One empirical study (Jansen 1991) identified sources of growth on the demand side under three categories, namely domestic demand, import-substitution and export demand. Between 1960 and 1970, domestic demand contributed 89.1 per cent to economic growth, export demand contributed 11.4 per cent, and the remainder of –0.6 per cent came from import-substitution. During 1985–88, the contribution of export demand rose to 45.3 per cent, while the contribution of import-substitution was sharply negative (–23.4 per cent), and the contribution of domestic demand remained high at 78.1 per cent. Thus, in the late 1980s the Thai economy was still largely domestic demand driven.

Structural Change

The Thai economy has undergone rapid transformation during the past three decades. The role of the agricultural sector, which was the main contributor to GDP, has steadily declined. Between 1970 and 1990, the growth rate in agriculture was about 4 per cent per annum. It dropped over 1986–90 and became unexpectedly negative in 1987 and 1990. Thailand did not participate in the Green Revolution by adopting high-yielding rice varieties such as IR-8, but achieved growth in agriculture by expanding the cultivated area. An abundance of land allowed the Thai farmer to expand land frontiers instead of improving productivity. Land productivity has been very low and stable, while labour productivity (output per farmer) has increased significantly (Timmer 1991).

The growth of the manufacturing sector has been more impressive. By 1980, manufacturing in both import-substituting and local manufacturing sectors had become the largest contributor to the economy. The transformation since the Second World War can be attributed to heavy taxation of the staple primary crop, rice, through a tax on exports, known as the "rice premium". This taxation substantially affected Thai farmers over a long period (Siamwalla 1975; Thanapornpun 1985). It was negative protection for Thai farmers who provided cheap food and labour for the manufacturing sector in Bangkok. Rice is a "wage good" in the sense that workers spend most of their wage income on rice.[2] The heavy rice

---

[2] The price of rice was kept below the border price or world market price through an export tax on rice and other quantitative restrictions such as export bans and quotas. The rice premium was not only a major source of government revenue, but also prevented Thai farmers from gaining business. Additionally, as rice was the main wage good, the policy helped the government to maintain a low wage rate policy (Siamwalla 1975).

taxation was first imposed when Great Britain demanded that Thailand pay a war indemnity in rice. The Thai Rice Office was established to fulfil this obligation. Later, the Thai government's intention to collect an extra profit from a multiple exchange rate led to the rice premium becoming an important source of government revenue from 1955 to the early 1960s (Ingram 1971).

Table 7.7 Sectoral Growth and Shares (per cent)

Period	1957–73	1974–85	1980–96	1997–2001	2002–3
Sectoral Growth					
Agriculture	5.0	3.7	3.1	2.1	4.9
Non-agriculture	9.6	7.4	11.8	0.7	7.6
Industry	9.7	7.1	12.3	2.0	8.6
Service	8.3	3.7	8.3	–1.7	4.4
Total	7.8	4.7	9.2	–0.1	6.1
Sectoral Share					
Agriculture	24.5	17.7	12.3	10.1	10.1
Non-agriculture	25.3	33.8	45.5	51.0	53.2
Industry	14.7	22.0	29.6	35.2	37.3
Service	50.2	48.5	42.2	38.9	36.7
Total	100.0	100.0	100.0	100.0	100.0

Source: NESDB.

As can be seen from Table 7.7, the share of agriculture in GDP declined from 24.5 per cent during 1957–73 to only 17.7 per cent during 1974–85. With impressive growth rates, the manufacturing sector experienced rapid structural changes over two decades from 1960 to 1980. Import-substituting industries in food processing (food, beverages, tobacco) expanded in the early 1960s to 1970s, but food processing as a single major contributor to manufacturing value added declined from 34.6 per cent in 1960 to 20.1 per cent in 1978. Several new manufactured products emerged, for instance, tapioca processing, canned food, animal feed, dairy products, textiles, paper and paper products, rubber products, and chemical products.

The structure of the manufacturing sector had changed by 1985 when food products no longer dominated the sector. By 1985, the shares of food products, textiles, wearing apparel, beverages, transport equipment, tobacco, non-metallic mineral products and petroleum products were 15.4 per cent, 14.9 per cent, 11.4 per cent, 8.1 per cent, 7.4 per cent, 5.6 per cent, 6.0 per cent, and 4.1 per cent, respectively.

Macroeconomic Performance

Inflation

Price stability in Thailand over the last 50 years has been remarkable. Only in 1973–74 and 1980–81 did the inflation rate exceed 10 per cent. Rice is the main staple food, and its price has been insulated from the world market price by using various policies since the Second World War. The price of this wage good has been kept low and stable over the last fifty years, contributing significantly to sustained price stability (Christensen and Siamwalla 1993; Siamwalla and Setboonsarng 1989).

Government Budget and External Debt

After 1950, the Thai government regularly ran a budget deficit. However, this was not financed by borrowing from the central bank, but by public external debt (Ingram 1971; Warr and Nidhiprabha 1996). Although this mode of financing deficits was non-inflationary, it created another problem. The total external debt jumped from 16.6 per cent of GNP to 51.3 per cent in 2004. The total debt service ratio reached the high level of 27.4 per cent in 1985, levelled off after 1987, jumped above 20 per cent in 1998 after the economic crisis, and declined again to a manageable level at 8.4 per cent in 2004.

Compared to other developing countries, the budget deficit in Thailand was not so desperate given the rate of economic growth. After 2002, when the budget deficit was reeled in to −1.4 per cent, economic growth was 5 to 6 per cent per annum over 2002 to 2004, indicating a return to normalcy. However, it is very difficult to be sure that the current recovery has been due to expansionary fiscal policies, as the recovery has been aided by the external environment, as in other Asian countries.

Economists in Thailand are concerned about the Thaksin government's non-budgetary expenditures, which are not subject to parliamentary scrutiny, and may be susceptible to corruption and political pork barrelling. In 2004, the non-budget deficit was 3,900 million baht, and there is a tendency for this deficit to grow with neo-populist policies (Table 7.8).[3]

---

[3] A non-budget policy refers to expenditure proposals that do not need to be scrutinized by parliament. They can be implemented directly by the incumbent government.

Table 7.8 Deficit in Non-budgetary Balance

	1997	1998	1999	2000	2001	2002	2003	2004
Deficit in non-budgetary balance	13.0	−4.2	−34.4	−1.8	9.8	1.8	7.6	−3.9

Source: Bank of Thailand.

Most of the time the current account deficit was within a moderate level of less than 4 per cent of GDP. However, it jumped to −7.9 per cent of GDP in 1995–96, perhaps indicating that the rapid growth prior to the crisis was not sustainable. After 1990, Thailand's terms of trade deteriorated, which may also have contributed to the rise in current account deficits. This deterioration of Thailand's external position might have led to the speculative attack on the Thai baht in early 1997.

Trade and Balance of Payments

In the 1950s, no less than 50 per cent of the total value of exports was attributed to rice, while four major products — rice, rubber, tin and teak — comprised 83.1 per cent. Exports of manufactured goods were negligible (Falkus 1991; Ingram 1971).

Over the 1960s and 1970s, the structure of international trade changed considerably. Diversification began dramatically in the early 1970s, both within the agricultural sector, into a wide range of crops, and beyond, into manufactures. This was partly due to problems associated with the oil shocks and the realization of the limits on import-substituting industrialization. The share of manufactures in exports rose dramatically from 2.4 per cent in 1961 to 10 per cent in 1971 and 35.8 per cent in 1981. In the mid-1980s, manufactured exports, for the first time, surpassed traditional agricultural products (rice, rubber, maize, sugarcane, and tapioca) in value. Manufactured exports grew at 35.7 per cent per annum on average between 1985 and 1990. The principal items were textiles, garments, canned foods, canned fish, gems, jewellery, and integrated circuits.

Although Thailand has had a high growth rate of manufactured exports since the mid-1980s, the growth rate of imports was still higher in terms of value. Major items of imports included raw materials (including petroleum), capital goods (machinery), and chemical goods. This suggests that Thailand might have tried to exploit import-substitute-then-export (ISTE) strategies in manufacturing.

The current account deficit increased from 7.9 per cent of GDP in 1989 to 12.4 per cent in 1990.[4] The prolonged deficit on the current account was caused by rapidly rising imports of capital goods, intermediate goods, and raw materials. This indicates that import dependence did not decline despite decades of import-substituting industrialization (ISI). Although international trade has played a vital role in the Thai industrialization process since the 1980s, the legacy of ISI could still be noticed in some industries, such as iron and steel and automobiles.

Persistent current account deficits and rapidly increasing foreign debt had become major problems by the early 1980s. Thailand had to go to the International Monetary Fund and World Bank for balance of payments support and adjustment assistance in 1984. The unfavourable terms of trade led to the largest trade deficit that the country had experienced since the Second World War. The deficit rose from 5.8 per cent of GDP in 1978 to 9.8 per cent in 1983. Prices of rice and other traditional crops were in decline, while the Thai government and public enterprises were heavily burdened with debts accumulated in the 1970s.

The rising value of the US dollar in 1981, and the deterioration in Thailand's balance of payments inevitably encouraged speculation that the Thai baht would be devalued. Finally on 15 July 1981, the baht was devalued by 8.7 per cent, and the daily fixing method was abolished. The Thai government had to devalue again on 2 November 1984, setting a new rate at 27 baht per dollar.[5] The value of the baht had increased with the dollar value since 1981, which in turn made the baht overvalued compared with other important currencies such as the British pound and German mark, hindering any strategy of export promotion (Meesook *et al.* 1988). The overvalued exchange rate was biased against export producers, especially primary commodity producers such as rice farmers, and harmful to the export-promoting trade strategy. Before May 1981, the Bank of Thailand had been reluctant to devalue the baht, despite a significant appreciation of the real exchange rate, because devaluation

---

[4] The current account deficit was 5.2 billion baht in 1970 (3.5 per cent of GDP), and 42.4 billions in 1980 (6.4 per cent of GDP).

[5] The rate was set at 21 baht per dollar from 1955 to 12 May 1981 when the Bank of Thailand devalued the baht by 1.1 per cent. After 15 July 1981, the rate was 23 baht per dollar.

was considered politically sensitive, something to be avoided if there was a choice.

Trade and Industrialization Policies

Like most other developing countries, Thailand began industrialization with import-substitution. During the import-substitution period, the Thai government was strongly biased against the agricultural sector, while providing many incentives for industrial firms (mostly big foreign firms in Bangkok). Export tax was imposed on agricultural products such as rice, rubber, and timber[6] while manufactures were not subject to taxes but highly protected by quantitative restrictions. In addition, the Board of Investment granted tax concessions on imported machinery, equipment, raw materials, and other intermediate inputs.[7] The heavy tax on the agricultural sector encouraged farmers to expand by exploiting the comparative advantage of abundant resources, especially land, rather than intensifying cultivation.[8]

By the early 1970s, Thai policy makers began to realize the adverse effects of an import-substitution strategy that relied heavily on imported inputs, especially of capital goods. The subsidies for cheap machinery and intermediate goods encouraged promoted firms to prefer more capital-intensive technologies. Furthermore, quantitative allocation systems administered by state bureaucrats encouraged rent-seeking activities and corruption. As a consequence, the import-substitution strategy failed to achieve the government's objectives, and did not conform to the country's factor endowment, namely cheap labour. The import-substitution strategy also failed to create forward and backward linkages among industrial sectors.

In the early 1970s, technocrats (mostly in the National Economic and Social Development Board, NESDB) introduced a strategy to promote manufactured exports as the key industrial strategy of the Third National Economic and Social Development Plan (1972–76).[9] In 1972,

---

[6] The export tax on rice was removed in 1986 because of the sluggish price of rice in the world market.

[7] The prime minister is chairman of the BOI and vice chairman of the Ministry of Industry.

[8] This partly explains why Thai farmers preferred extending cultivated land instead of intensifying their cultivation methods.

[9] The stated objectives of this plan were to correct the balance of payments problems and to increase overall employment through policy measures to promote exports and adjust the import structure.

the investment promotion law was replaced by the National Executive Council Announcement No. 227, intended to give greater incentives for export industries. These included exemption from export duties and business taxes for export products of promoted firms. In addition, imported material inputs and imported products destined for re-export were exempt from import duties and business taxes when the income was derived from export activities. Promoted firms were permitted a 2 per cent deduction on the increases of income over the previous year for income tax purposes. The 1972 investment law and the 1977 revision of the Industrial Promotion Act empowered the BOI to grant and provide privileges to promoted firms. The BOI had considerable discretionary authority to determine the list of activities and the list of firms eligible for promotional privileges.

Although the government tried to promote exports of manufactured goods by revising the investment promotion law in 1972, and again in 1977, the structure of incentives still favoured import-substitution industry, and remained biased against the agricultural sector.

The Fifth National Plan (1983–86) and the Sixth National Plan (1987–91) were probably responsible for the impressive export-led growth. The former initiated the restructuring of local industries to encourage competitiveness in production, emphasized export production and industrial rationalization, and highlighted the strategic importance of machinery and agro-industries. The serious push for export-oriented industrialization was partly encouraged by the success of the export-led development of newly industrializing economies (NIEs), such as Singapore, Taiwan, and South Korea. It was also pushed by the International Monetary Fund and the World Bank as part of their structural adjustment programmes to help Thailand overcome its balance of payment crises in the late 1970s and early 1980s.

Export-oriented industrialization took off from the mid-1980s, in accordance with major changes in the world economic environment. After the Plaza Accord of September 1985, the currencies of the Asian NIEs, except that of Hong Kong, appreciated against the US dollar and other currencies such as the Deutschmark. As the Thai baht was closely tied to the dollar, it was devalued against these other currencies, especially the yen, immensely benefiting the export strategy. The year 1985 was a turning point for the Thai economy. The external environment also improved with declines in interest rates and oil prices, while the prices of traditional commodity exports began to recover. Demand for Thai exports had begun to pick up after the two devaluations in 1981 and 1984.

The annual increase in export value jumped to 20.7 per cent in 1986, 28.8 per cent in 1987, and 33.9 per cent in 1988. After the currency realignment in 1985, Japanese manufacturers began to relocate their production bases to Thailand.

By the late 1980s, Thailand had become an attractive investment location in Southeast Asia as a result of both economic and non-economic factors. The country had high economic growth without high inflation, unstable exchange rates, or political turmoil (Mackie 1988). Furthermore, the private-enterprise economy, positive attitude towards foreigners, and increasingly export-oriented strategy induced foreign investors to relocate industrial plants in Thailand. In particular, Thailand was an attractive country for Japanese firms because of abundant, cheap, and hard-working labour.

Foreign direct investment increased by 67 per cent in 1986, 360 per cent in 1987, and 140 per cent in 1988. In 1987, Japanese investment approved by the BOI exceeded the cumulative investment in Thailand since the 1960s. Japanese foreign firms invested in both natural resource-based and labour-intensive industries, including electrical appliances, electronics, transportation equipment, metal products, textile, agricultural and fishery products. Taiwan was the next biggest foreign investor with concentration on labour-intensive light manufacturing such as sports goods, toys, shoes, bags, plastics, and some agro-industries such as frozen shrimp.

Some Critical Observations About the Thai Miracle

Environmental Consequences

The growth rate of Thai exports has far exceeded that of world exports since 1984. It is often claimed that the economy of Thailand demonstrates a pattern of export-driven economic growth like the first generation of East Asian NIEs. However, unlike the East Asian NIEs, Thai manufactured exports are mainly resource-based. Thailand's export-oriented industrialization relies very much on labour abundance and natural resources. There has been very little technological breakthrough, or human capital formation (Dahlman and Brimble 1990; UNIDO 1992). Furthermore, the contribution of exports to growth declined from 28.8 per cent in 1989 to only 11 per cent in 1990 (Santikarn Kaosa-ard 1992). Thai manufactured exports have not matured.

An obvious casualty of high economic growth is the environment. There has been severe deforestation and environmental degradation such as pollution (Brander 1992; see Chapter 3). One recent study by the Thailand Development Research Institute (TDRI) indicates that the quantity of hazardous waste rose from 1.1 million tons in 1986 to 6 million tons by 2001. Most of this waste is generated by the manufacturing sector. Furthermore, a high number of serious accidents indicate that Thai bureaucrats are not competent enough to cope with problems emerging from rapid industrialization.

Ninety million *rai* of forest were cleared between 1960 and 1990 at the average of 3 million *rai* per year. Thailand has seen one of the most rapid rates of deforestation in the world in the post-war period, with forest cover declining from 50 per cent of land area in the early 1960s to approximately 20 per cent in the mid-1980s, or as low as 15 per cent in 1986 according to unofficial estimates. Deforestation proceeded so rapidly that by 1968 Thailand became a net importer of wood.

One factor that contributed to deforestation in Thailand is the state of property rights in the land. Although illegal logging by people with political connections is often seen as the main culprit, the expansion of titled land has been more significant. Landless and small farmers clear land illegally in the expectation that they will eventually receive title (Siamwalla 1991). The Thai state appears to be too weak to enforce the law of the land and secure property rights, which can only be done by political and judicial organizations that effectively and impartially enforce contracts across space and time. Land property rights in Thailand have been very insecure and chaotic.

Urban Bias and Lopsided Development

The Thai development strategy displayed an urban bias. Various levies on agricultural produce, especially the rice tax, and an overvalued exchange rate, disadvantaged the agricultural sector. Thailand was probably the only country in Asia where cultivated land per agricultural worker actually increased until 1977 (Siamwalla 1991). Agriculture was able to absorb a large amount of labour, especially seasonal labour. Thailand still has a larger proportion of its labour force in agriculture than other Asian countries with a similar income level. The expansion of cultivated areas without a corresponding increase in productivity is irrational to say the least. The agricultural sector, employing almost 64 per cent of the labour force, produced less than 13 per cent of GDP in 1990. There is a very low level of productivity in the agricultural sector (Ezaki 1990).

Table 7.9 Labour Force, 2000–4 (million)

	2000	2001	2002	2003	2004
Employed	31.29	32.10	33.06	33.84	34.73
agricultural	13.83	13.61	14.04	13.88	13.63
non-agricultural	17.46	18.49	19.02	19.96	21.09
Unemployed	1.19	1.12	0.82	0.75	0.74
Seasonally inactive	0.74	0.59	0.38	0.31	0.25
Total labour force	33.22	33.81	34.26	34.90	35.72
Unemployment rate	3.6	3.3	2.4	2.2	2.1

Notes: 2004 figures are preliminary. The employment rate is percentage of labour force.
Source: Bank of Thailand.

The employment share of manufacturing industry did not follow its production share. In 1990, manufacturing contributed 26 per cent to GDP but employed only 10 per cent of the labour force. This weak capacity for labour absorption has become a serious obstacle to agricultural modernization and has swollen the ranks of urban poor who migrate from rural areas in search of jobs in Bangkok. With no skills these migrant labourers seek employment in the informal sector at very low wages. Low productivity and low wages in the urban informal sector in Bangkok push down the real wage. Rural-urban migration in Thailand is crucial for many farmers who seek jobs in the slack season. This source of earning has become more significant over time. Migration has increased because the Thai government has failed to insulate domestic markets from international price fluctuations. The price of agricultural products has been declining since the 1980s.

In sum, as Sussangkarn (1992) rightly points out, such an uneven development between agricultural and industrial sectors is a crucial cause of worsening income distribution. Neither import-substitution nor outward orientation has performed well in the condition of labour abundance between the 1950s and 1980s.

Lagging Human Capital Development

Thailand lags behind other countries in the region with the worst secondary education enrolment ratios in Asia (Sussangkarn 1992). TDRI found that in 2000, 70 per cent of Thailand's work force had only primary education or less (6 years). This means Thailand can have a comparative advantage only in unskilled labour. As industrialization proceeds, the unskilled and low-skilled labour force should become smaller compared to high-skilled labour, including managers, professionals, and white-collar workers. This enhances a country's capacity to acquire and make use of advanced technology which, in turn, brings about productivity growth. Over the last half century, Thailand has failed to adequately develop this social capacity. The level of technical competence remains low (Dahlman and Brimble 1990; UNIDO 1992). This can be attributed to the absence of a targeted industrial policy linked closely to technical education in the secondary and vocational training schools.

Inadequate Infrastructure and Legal System

The spurt in economic growth created a demand for infrastructure. However, the Thai government severely cut its public infrastructure investment in the 1980s in order to meet its structural adjustment obligations with the IMF. This resulted in serious bottlenecks when economic growth began to accelerate in the early 1990s, as manifested by rising current account deficits and inflation. Perhaps the root cause of speculative attacks on the baht in 1997 can be found here (Chowdhury 1999).

The private sector did not come forward to fill the gap created by the decline in public infrastructure investment. This was mostly due to the failings of the legal system and the difficulty of enforcing contracts. The state can enforce the law and maintain political stability, but is too weak to protect private property rights, or even public property. The laws are manipulated by political entrepreneurs and state bureaucrats. The application of Thai administrative law lacks transparency and allows state officials to have excessive discretionary power. In particular, departmental regulations vest wide discretionary powers in bureaucrats (Sathirathai 1987). Many young Thai lawyers observe that Thailand's administrative law code insulates the bureaucracy from legal challenges. However, since 1997, a new constitution has paved the way for an administrative court which will play a vital role in controlling the abuse of government power. The accountability of power is still limited (Treerat 2004).

Corruption

The weakness of the state and law encourages corruption among state officials. An unholy alliance between the bureaucracy and political entrepreneurs compounds the problem. Political entrepreneurs, including elected politicians, endeavour to gain influence over productive sectors, such as through controlling the allocation of export quotas for textiles or cassava products. Vote buying is pervasive (Parnwell and Rigg 1993; Samudavanija 1989, 1992; Tamada 1991).

As a result of the country being long under an authoritarian regime from 1947, the Thai parliament has played an insignificant role in scrutinizing the activities of the bureaucracy (Thanapornpun 1990). Although it is widely believed that corruption and rent seeking are rampant, only two politicians have been found guilty and sent to prison by the Criminal Court for Political Office Holders founded under the 1997 constitution (Treerat 2004).

Income Inequality

Although absolute poverty declined with rapid growth (see Table 7.10), Thai society has become more unequal. The Gini coefficient rose from 0.41 in 1965 to 0.50 in 2004 (see Table 7.11). While rural poverty declined significantly, it still remains four times the urban poverty rate.

Table 7.10 Poverty Incidence, 1962–2002 (headcount measure, per cent of total population)

	Total	*Rural*	*Urban*
1962	88.3	96.4	78.5
1975	48.6	57.2	25.8
1981	35.5	43.1	15.5
1986	44.9	56.3	12.1
1990	27.2	33.8	1.6
1996	11.4	14.9	3.0
2002	9.8	12.6	3.0

Sources: Development Evaluation Division, NESDB (2000); and Krongkaew (1993).

Although national plans have touted slogans such as eradicating poverty, declared the year of the farmer in the early 1980s, and espoused land reform in the early 1990s, the effectiveness of these policies in alleviating poverty was still very limited. Thai governments have been inclined to subsidize urban workers by providing food subsidies via a cheap rice policy.

Social Progress

Life expectancy improved substantially after the Second World War, reaching 66 years at birth in 1985, and gradually increasing to 69 years

Table 7.11 Income Distribution, 1975/76–2004

	1975/76	1981	1986	1988	1990	1992	1994	1996	1998	2000	2002	2004
Share of income												
Quintile 1	6.05	5.45	4.47	4.53	4.23	3.98	4.16	4.27	3.89	3.89	4.10	4.20
Quintile 2	9.72	9.26	7.85	7.98	7.43	6.93	7.52	7.69	7.19	7.19	7.80	7.80
Quintile 3	14.02	13.69	12.30	12.38	11.58	10.96	11.78	11.91	11.39	11.39	12.30	12.30
Quintile 4	20.97	21.08	20.43	20.71	19.49	18.80	19.88	19.74	19.70	19.70	20.50	20.30
Quintile 5	49.24	50.52	54.98	54.40	57.26	59.43	56.66	56.39	57.77	57.77	55.20	55.20
Gini coefficient	0.426	0.442	0.496	0.489	0.515	0.536	0.516	0.509	0.525	0.525	0.501	0.499
Q5/Q1	8.1	9.3	12.3	12.0	13.5	14.9	13.6	13.2	14.9	14.9	13.5	13.1

Sources: Tinakorn (2002) for 1975/76 to 2000; National Statistical Office, for 2002, 2004.

at birth in 2002. The infant mortality rate per 1,000 live at births has also fallen from 40 in 1985 to 24 in 2002. The adult illiteracy rate (among people aged 15+) declined from 10 per cent in 1985 to 4 per cent in 2002.

On the Human Development Index (HDI), published by the United Nations Development Programme, Thailand's ranking has fluctuated over the last fifteen years, partly due to the impact of periodic crises, such as in 1997 (see Table 7.12).

Table 7.12 Human Development Index and Human Poverty Index, 1990, 1999, and 2003

	1990	*1999*	*2003*
HDI Value	0.783	0.757	0.778
HDI Rank	78	66	73
PPP GDP ranking-HDI ranking	23	−3	−7
HPI Value	n.a.	n.a.	12.8
HPI Rank	n.a.	n.a	28

Notes: HDI is Human Development Index, and HPI is Human Poverty Index.
         In line 3, a positive figure indicates that Thailand ranks higher on the Human Develop-
         ment Index than in the country rankings for PPP GDP.
Sources: UNDP, *Human Development Reports 1990, 2001, 2003.*

In 1990, Thailand came higher in the country rankings for human development than in the rankings for GDP (calculated at purchasing power parity), suggesting that its social progress was above that of countries of similar income level. But in subsequent years, Thailand's ranking on human development has fallen below the ranking on GDP, suggesting the country is now failing to achieve social progress expected at its level of economic progress.

Another important index, first introduced in 1997, is the Human Poverty Index (HPI), a composite index measuring deprivations in three basic dimensions also captured in the Human Development Index — a long and healthy life, knowledge, and a decent standard of living. The first dimension is measured by the percentage of people who expect to survive to age 40. The second is the adult illiteracy rate. The third is the percentage of people without access to safe water, health care services and underweight children under five.

Concluding Remarks

Thailand began its industrialization process with import-substitution and later shifted to an export-oriented strategy. The main problems are worsening inequality in income distribution, an imbalanced structure of employment and production, damage to the environment, concentration of manufacturing in Bangkok, and a low level of enrolment in secondary schools. The trends seem to have worsened.

Export-oriented strategy is merely a trade policy, and it is not the equivalent of development strategy as such. The most serious problem lies in the role of the Thai state, which follows a laissez-faire philosophy. The Thai state wishes that the magic of the market will lower income inequality and maintain high economic growth. In fact, manufactured exports reap profits with the help of the Thai state through the BOI and other protective institutions, while the agricultural sector bears the burden of industrialization. Foreign investment helps to hasten economic growth and induce the rural poor to migrate to the city. Thailand appears to enjoy high growth compared to other developing countries in Asia, but lags behind in the real meaning of economic development.

The historical process of economic development is strongly influenced by the initial conditions, which in Thailand's case included an abundance of land. Thai elites tapped natural resources to such an extent that resources have dwindled to a critical level. There is a need for new technologies that will raise the agricultural and industrial sectors to a higher level of efficiency in order to sustain economic growth. A benevolent state is needed to create key institutions to bring about economic growth and equity. However, the historical and institutional contexts appear to have hindered rather than promoted any positive change in the last 50 years.

Thailand needs to be more proactive in improving skill and upgrading technology as it faces competition from other labour-surplus countries in the region. This requires investment in higher and technical education and research and development. For well known reasons, the market fails to provide education and R&D so the state needs to be active in these areas.

Since 2001, the political market has become more stable under the Thai Rak Thai Party of Thaksin Shinawatra, a billionaire telecommunications magnate. The new party won strong support among Thai voters, in particular rural voters, and gained a large majority in the parliamentary elections of February 2005, resulting in the new phenomenon of a single-party government. In its first term, the Thaksin administration pursued a range of neo-populist policies, dubbed Thaksinomics, including the One Tambon (village) One Product project, a moratorium on farmers' debts, establishment of a peoples' bank, a universal medical scheme at 30 baht per visit, and several measures supporting small enterprises. Furthermore, the Thaksin administration has been very active in following the ideology of the Washington Consensus on trade liberalization, negotiating and signing bilateral free trade agreements with developing and developed countries. However, the negotiation of a free trade agreement between Thailand and the USA become controversial and was not completed.

The agenda for his second term includes large infrastructure projects and pro-poor polices. These will require substantial government expenditures. The Thaksin administration has already used non-budgetary methods to finance its neo-populist projects which might result in a debt crisis were economic growth to slow because of subdued export performance. Moreover, under the Thaksin government, the role of the press has been restrained, raising fears about the administration's credentials for controlling rampant rent seeking and corruption. Thaksin's family has become embroiled in corruption scandals over the sale of its telecom business, sparking widespread political unrest.

ORIGINAL PUBLICATION DETAILS

1. In *Cooperation East and West — Continued: Ten Years with the Programme for East and Southeast Asian Studies*, ed. Gun Lauritzson (Lund: Lund University Programme for East and Southeast Asian Studies, 1994), pp. 70–82.

2. *Warasan Setthasat Thammasat* (Thammasat Economic Journal) 16, no. 2 (June 1998): 83–138.

3. In *The Village Concept in the Transformation of Rural Southeast Asia: Studies from Indonesia, Malaysia and Thailand*, ed. Mason Hoadley and Christer Gunnarsson (London: Curzon Press for Nordic Institute for Asian Studies-NIAS, 1996), pp. 92–113.

4. In *Social Change in Southeast Asia*, ed. Johannes D. Schmidt, Jacques Hersh, and Niels Fold (London: Longman, 1997), pp. 183–205.

5. *Warasan Setthasat Thammasat* (Thammasat Economic Journal) 15, no. 2 (June 1997): 89–109.

6. From two unpublished papers, "Development Economics and the East Asian Miracle: Lessons for Developing Countries" and "Development Economics and Rent-seeking in the East Asian Miracles: Lessons for Developing Countries".

7. Chapter entitled "Thailand" in *Handbook on the Northeast and Southeast Asian Economies*, ed. Anis Chowdhury and Iyanatul Islam (Cheltenham: Edward Elgar, 2007), pp. 129–48.

ABOUT THE AUTHOR

Somboon Siriprachai was born in Bangkok on 19 March 1956, the second of six siblings. His father and mother ran a small family business selling construction materials.

He received his BA and MA in Economics from Thammasat University in 1980 and 1988 respectively, and a PhD in Economics from the University of Lund in 1998 with a thesis on "Controls and Rent-seeking: The Role of the State in the Thai Cassava Industry", supervised by Professor Christer Gunnarsson and published as a book by Lund University Press in 1998. For his MA and PhD, he received scholarships from Thammasat University, the Ford Foundation, University of Lund, and Kungl Humanistiska Vetenskapssamfundet i Lund.

From the time of his BA degree, he wanted to be a teacher at the Faculty of Economics at Thammasat University, but because he became involved as a leader in the 1976 student uprising, it took him more than the stipulated time period to complete his first degree, and this subsequently became an obstacle to securing a faculty post. So he applied to be a researcher and worked as an assistant manager on the *Thammasat Economic Journal* from 1980 to 1990. Meanwhile he proved himself by writing a large number of quality academic articles. Eventually he was appointed lecturer in 1988, after the completion of his MA. In 2005, he became the editor of the *Thammasat Economic Journal*, one of the most reputable economic journals in the country.

He was an active member of the Faculty and held many administrative posts including member of the Faculty Research Committee, PhD Programme, and Textbook Project, and chairperson of the Seminar Series and the Seminar and Dissemination Committee. He was deputy dean for student affairs between 2001 and 2002. In November 2008 the University Council approved his promotion as Professor.

As a teacher he had a reputation of being very attentive to his students. He prepared his lectures in great detail. He was willing to lend books, articles, and papers to students without thought of whether he would ever get them back. He was also well known for regularly engaging in discussion with his students after class. His honesty and integrity were never in doubt. Even though he had been active in the student movement in the 1970s, he avoided any contact with politics once he became a teacher.

Somboon Siriprachai was a prolific reader, writer, and researcher. The bibliography in this book is testament to his voracious enthusiasm for devouring the latest work in international economics. He published at least 35 articles and research reports in Thai. Of these, two are about rent and rent-seeking, three on rural-urban migration, three on industrial development, five on trade policy, and 18 on miscellaneous issues in economic development. He was active in academic and public debate on current economic policy issues in Thailand and abroad. He participated in the 2005 JSPS NRCT Core University Program Workshop on "Towards a New Model of East Asian Society: Entrepreneurship and the Family" at Kyoto University. He wrote regularly for *Matichon* daily newspaper on economic topics.

At the time of his death on 25 December 2008, Somboon was 52. He is survived by his wife Sompit, a son Chirasin, and daughter Onwanya.

In Somboon's cremation volume, Professor Rangsun Thanapornpan, a colleague and mentor from the Thammasat Faculty of Economics, wrote, "Thailand has lost one of its good citizens. The economic community has lost an economist who still had so much potential to produce academic works. The university has lost a professor who possesses great integrity and honesty as an academician. But all these losses cannot be compared to the loss to his family.... He has gone, but Thai society longs for a person such as Somboon."

BIBLIOGRAPHY

Abramovitz, Moses. 1989. *Thinking About Growth and Other Essays: Economic Growth and Welfare* (Cambridge: Cambridge University Press).

Adams, F. Gerald and Inger Marie Davis. 1994. "The Role of Policy in Economic Development: Comparisons of the East and Southeast Asian and Latin American Experience". *Asian-Pacific Literature* 8, no. 1: 8–47.

Adams, John. 1993. "Institutions and Economic Development: Structure, Process, and Incentive". In *Institutional Economics: Theory, Method, Policy*, ed. Marc R. Tool. (Boston: Kluwer Academic Publishers), pp. 245–69.

Adelman, Irma. 1985. "Beyond Export-Led Growth". *World Development* 12, no. 3: 937–49.

————. 1992. "What is the Evidence on Income Inequality and Development?" In *Equity and Efficiency in Economic Development: Essays in Honour of Benjamin Higgins*, ed. D.J. Savoic and Irving Brecher (Quebec: McGill Queen's University Press).

Akrasanee, Narongchai. 1980. *Industrial Development in Thailand*. Report of the Research and Planning Department (Bangkok: IFCT).

Akrasanee, Narongchai and Atchana Wattananukit. 1990. "Changing Structure and Rising Dynamism in the Thai Economy". In *Southeast Asean Affairs 1990*, ed. Ng Chee Yuen and Chandran Jeshuran (Singapore: Institute of Southeast Asian Studies).

Akrasanee, Narongchai and Juanjai Atjanant. 1986. "Thailand: Manufacturing Industry Production Issues and Empirical Studies". In *The Political Economy of Manufacturing Protection: Experiences of ASEAN and Australia*, ed. C. Findlay and R. Garnaut (London: Allen and Unwin).

Akyüz, Yimaz. 2005. *The WTO Negotiations on Industrial Tariffs: What is at Stake for Developing Countries?* Trade Working Papers 22080, East Asian Bureau of Economic Research.

Allen, William R. 1987. "Mercantilism". In *The New Palgrave Dictionary of Economics*, ed. John Eatwell, Murray Milgate, and Peter Newman (London: Macmillan).

Ampoto-Tuffuor, Emmanuel, Charles D. Delorme, Jr., and David R. Kamaerschen. 1991. "The Nature, Significant, and Cost of Rent Seeking in Ghana". *Kyklos* 44: 527–59.

Amsden, Alice. 1989. *Asia's Next Giant: South Korea and Late Industrialization* (New York: Oxford University Press).

————. 1990. "Third World Industrialization: Global Fordism or a New Model?". *New Left Review* 182: 14–5.

Anderson, Benedict. 1990. "Murder and Progress in Modern Siam". *New Left Review* 181: 33–48.

Anderson, Kym and Yujiro Hayami. 1986. *The Political Economy of Agricultural Protection* (Sydney: Allen and Unwin).

Anderson, Kym, ed. 1992. *New Silk Roads: East Asia and World Textiles Markets* (Cambridge: Cambridge University Press).

Arkadie, Brian Van. 1989. "The Role of Institutions in Development". Paper presented at Proceedings of the World Bank Annual Conference on Development Economics (Washington, D.C.: World Bank).

Arnold, Fred and Supani Boonpratuang. 1976. *1970 Population and Housing Census: Migration* (Bangkok: National Statistical Office).

Auty, Richard M. 1994. "Industrial Policy Reform in Six Large Newly Industrializing Countries: The Resource Curse". *World Development* 22, no. 1: 11–26.

Balassa, Bela A. 1980. *The Process of Industrial Development and Alternative Development Strategies* (Princeton: Princeton University Press).

Bardhan, Pranab. 1989. "Alternative Approaches to the Theory of Institutions in Economic Development". In *The Economic Theory of Agrarian Institutions*, ed. Pranab Bardhan (Oxford: Oxford University Press).

Bauer, Peter T. 1971. *Dissent on Development* (Cambridge, Mass.: Harvard University Press).

Beitzel, George B. 1959. "Expanding Private Investment for Thailand's Economic Growth". Bangkok, USOM, mimeograph (November).

Berend, Iván T. and György Ránki. 1982. *The European Periphery & Industrialisation 1780–1914* (Cambridge: Cambridge University Press).

Bhagwati, Jagdish N. 1988a. "Export-Promoting Trade Strategy: Issues and Evidence". *The World Bank Research Observer* 3, no. 1.

————. 1988b. *Protectionism* (Cambridge, Mass.: The MIT Press).

Blaug, Mark, ed. 1991. *The Early Mercantilists* (Aldershot: Edward Elgar).

Boonmi, Thirayuth. 1988. "Thailand: A Political Figuration of the Traditionalistic Controlled Bourgeois Representation". *Social Science and Humanities Journal* 15, no. 2: 46–67.

Brander, James A. 1992. "Comparative Economic Growth: Evidence and Interpretation". *Canadian Journal of Economics* 25, no. 4: 792–818.

Brooks, Michael A. and Ben J. Heijdra 1988. "In Search of Rent Seeking". In *The Political Economy of Rent Seeking*, ed. C.K. Rowley, R.D. Tollison and G. Tullock. (Boston: Kluwer Academic Publishers).

————. 1989. "An Exploration of Rent-Seeking". *The Economic Record* 65: 32–50.

Brown, Lester R. 1963. "Agricultural Diversification and Economic Development in Thailand: A Case Study". *Foreign Agricultural Economic Reports no. 8*,

United States Department of Agriculture, Economic Research Service, Washington, D.C. (March).

Brunner, Karl. 1987. "The Perception of Man and the Conception of Society: Two Approaches to Understanding Society". *Economic Inquiry* 25: 367–88.

Brunner, Karl and Willaim H. Meckling. 1977. "The Perception of Man and the Conception of Government". *Journal of Money, Credit and Banking* 9, no. 1: 70–85.

Buchanan, James M. 1978. "From Private Preferences to Public Philosophy: The Development of Public Choice". In *The Economics of Politics* (London: Institute of Economic Affairs).

―――. 1980. "Rent-Seeking and Patron-Seeking". In *Toward a Theory of the Rent-Seeking Society*, ed. James M. Buchanan, Robert Tollison, and Gordon Tullock. (College Station: Texas A&M University Press).

Chaloemtiarana, Thak. 1979. *Thailand: The Politics of Despotic Paternalism* (Bangkok: Thammasat University Press).

Chamarik, Saneh. 1981. "Problems of Development in Thai Political Setting". Paper presented at the First International Conference on Thai Studies, New Delhi, 25–27 February 1981.

Chang, Ha-Joon. 1993. "The Political Economy of Industrial Policy in Korea". *Cambridge Journal of Economics* 17: 131–57.

―――. 1994. *The Political Economy of Industrial Policy* (London: St. Martin's Press).

―――. 1995. "Explaining 'Flexible Rigidities' in East Asia". In *The Flexible Economy: Causes and Consequences of the Adaptability of National Economies*, ed. Tony Killick (London: Routledge), pp. 197–221.

―――. 2002. *Kicking Away the Ladder: Development Strategy in Historical Perspective*. London: Anthem.

Chen, Edward K.Y. 1989. "Trade Policy in Asia". In *Lessons in Development: A Comparative Study of Asia and Latin America*, ed. Seiji Naja, Miguel Urrutia, Shelley Mark and Alfredo Fuentes (San Francisco: ICS Press).

Chichilnisky, Graciela and Geoffrey Heal. 1986. *The Evolving International Economy* (Cambridge: Cambridge University Press).

Chowdhury, Anis and Iyanatul Islam. 1993. *The Newly Industrialising Economies of East Asia* (London: Routledge).

Chowdhury, Anis. 1999. "Villain of the Asian Crisis–Thailand or the IMF?". *ASEAN Economic Bulletin* 16, no. 2: 168–77

Christensen, Scott and Ammar Siamwalla. 1993. "Beyond Patronage: Tasks for the Thai State". The 1993 TDRI Year-End Conference "Who Gets What and How?: Challenges for the Future", Pattaya, Thailand, December.

―――. 1994. "Muddling Towards an Economic Miracle". *Bangkok Post*, 23 June, p. 18.

Clark, Cal and Steve Chan. 1994. "The Developmental Roles of the State: Moving Beyond the Developmental State in Conceptualizing Asian Political Economies". *Governance* 7, no. 4: 332–59.

Coase, Ronald H. 1960. "The Problems of Social Cost". *Journal of Law and Economics* 3: 1–44.

Colander, D.C., ed. 1984. *Neoclassical Political Economy: The Analysis of Rent-Seeking Society and DUPs Activities* (Cambridge, Mass.: Ballinger Publishing Co.).

Collins, S.M. and B.P. Bosworth. 1996. "Economic Growth in East Asia: Accumulation versus Assimilation". *Brookings Papers on Economic Activity* 2: 135–203.

Corden, W. Max. 1971. *The Theory of Protection* (Oxford: Oxford University Press).

Corsel, R.R. 1986. "Labour Input and Pattern of Growth in Thai Agriculture, 1950–1983, by Region". MA Thesis, Faculty of Economics, University of Groningen, The Netherlands.

Cotton, James. 1994. "The State in the Asian NICs". *Asian Perspective* 18 (Spring/Summer): 39–56.

Cunningham, William. 1882, reprint 1907. *The Growth of English Industry and Commerce* (Cambridge: Cambridge University Press).

Dahlman, Carl J. and Peter Brimble. 1990. *Technology Strategy and Policy for Industrial Competitiveness: A Case Study of Thailand* (Washington, D.C.: World Bank).

Dasgupta, Partha. 1991. "Poverty, Resources, and Fertility: The Household as a Reproductive Partnership". Paper presented at *Holger Crafoords Ekonomidagar* at Lund University, Sweden.

Datta-Chaudhuri, Mrinal. 1990. "Market Failure and Government Failure". *Journal of Economic Perspectives* 4: 25–39.

De Jasay, A. 1985. *The State* (Oxford: Basil Blackwell).

De Soto, Hernando. 1989. *The Other Path: The Invisible Revolution in the Third World* (London: Touris Publishers).

Donges, J. 1976. "A Comparative Study of Industrialisation Policies in Fifteen Semi-Industrial Countries". *Weltwirtschaftliches Archiv* 112, no. 4: 626–59.

Doner, Richard F. 2009. *The Politics of Uneven Development: Thailand's Economic Growth in Comparative Perspective* (Cambridge: Cambridge University Press).

———. 2010. Contribution to a discussion of "Economic Strategy and the Roots of Thai Political Turmoil", initiated by Peter Warr, on New Mandala, 25 April, at <http://asiapacific.anu.edu.au/newmandala/2010/04/page/2/>.

Dore, Ronald. 1986. *Flexible Rigidities, Industrial Policy and Structural Adjustment in the Japanese Economy, 1970–1980* (London: Athlone).

Dutt, Amitava Krishna. 1992. "Two Issues in the State of Development Economics". In *New Directions in Development Economics*, ed. Amitava Krishna Dutt and Kenneth P. Jameson (Aldershot: Edward Elgar).

Eggertsson, Thràinn. 1990. *Economic Behavior and Institutions* (Cambridge: Cambridge University Press).

Ekelund, Robert B. and Robert D. Tollison. 1981. *Mercantilism as a Rent-Seeking Society: Economic Regulation in Historical Perspective* (College Station: Texas A&M University Press).

Elkan, Walter. 1988. "Entrepreneurs and Entrepreneurship in Africa". *The World Bank Research Observer* 3, no. 2: 171–88.

Eoseewong, Nidhi. 1993. "On the Future Road". Paper presented at the 1993 TDRI Year-End Conference, "Who Gets What and How?: Challenges for the Future", 10–11 December, Thailand (in Thai).

———. n.d. "The Social Foundation of the Thai Elite and Non-Elite Culture". unpublished.

Evans, David H. 1990. "Outward Orientation: An Assessment". In *Export Promotion Strategies: Theory and Evidence from Developing Countries*, ed. Milner, C. (New York: Harvester Press).

———. 1991. "Visible and Invisible Hands in Trade Policy Reform". In *States or Markets? Neo-liberalism and the Development Policy Debate*, ed. Christopher Colclough and James Manor (Oxford: Clarendon Press), pp. 48–77.

———. 1992. "Import Controls and the Sequencing of Trade Policy Reform with Special Reference to Africa". In *Foreign Trade Reforms and Development Strategy*, ed. Jean-Marc Fontaine (London: Routledge), pp. 79–92.

Evans, P.B., D. Rueschmeyer, and T. Skocpol, ed. 1989. *Bringing the State Back In* (Cambridge: Cambridge University Press).

Evans, Peter. 1989. "Predatory, Developmental and Other Apparatus: A Comparative Political Economy Perspective on the Third World State". *Sociological Forum* 4, no. 4 (Dec.): 561–87.

———. 1992. "The State as Problem and Solution: Predation, Embedded Autonomy, and Structural Change". In *The Politics of Economic Adjustment*, ed. Stephen Haggard and Robert R. Kaufman (Princeton: Princeton University Press).

———. 1995. *Embedded Autonomy: States and Industrial Transformation* (Princeton: Princeton University Press).

Ezaki, Mitsio. 1990. "ASEAN Prospects Towards NICs". Paper presented at the Second Conference of East Asian Economic Association, at Bandung, Indonesia (August).

Falkus, Malcolm. 1991. "The Economic History of Thailand". *Australian Economic History Review* 30, no. 1 (March): 53–70.

———. 1992. "Thailand Industrialisation: An Overview". Paper presented at the Conference on the Thai Making of a Fifth Tiger? Thailand's Industrialisation and Its Consequences, held at the Australian National University, 7–9 December.

Feder, Gershon and Tongroj Onchan. 1986. "Land Ownership Security and Capital Formarion in Rural Thailand". Discussion Paper, *Report no. ARU 50*, World Bank.

————. 1987. "Land Ownership Security and Farm Investment in Thailand". *American Journal of Agricultural Economics* 69: 311–20.

Feeny, David. 1979a. "Paddy, Princes and Productivity: Irrigation and Thai Agricultural Development, 1900–1940". *Explorations in Economic History* 16: 132–50.

————. 1979b. "Competing Hypotheses of Underdevelopment: A Thai Case Study". *Journal of Economic History* 39: 113–27.

————. 1982. *The Political Economy of Productivity: Thai Agricultural Development, 1880–1975* (Vancouver: University of British Columbia).

Felix, David. 1994. "Industrial Development in East Asia: What Are the Lessons for Latin America?" UNCTAD Discussion Papers, no. 84.

Feng, Yi. 2003. *Democracy, Governance and Economic Performance: Theory and Evidence* (Cambridge, Mass.: The MIT Press).

Findlay, Ronald. 1989a. "Is the New Political Economy Relevant to Developing Countries?" World Bank Working Papers, WPS 292 (November).

————. 1989b. "Trade, Development, and the State". In *The State of Development Economics: Progress and Perspectives*, ed. Gustav Ranis and T. Paul Schultz (Oxford: Basil Blackwell), pp. 78–95.

Fishlow, Albert. 1989. "Latin American Failure against the Backdrop of Asian Success". *Annals of the American Academy of Political and Social Science*, no. 505: 117–28.

————. 1994. "Economic Development in the 1990s". *World Development* 22, no. 12: 1825–32.

Fitzpatrick, Ellen T. 1989. "Agricultural Policy, Trade, Economic Growth, and Development". USDA, *Staff Report no. AGES 89-19* (May).

Fuller, Theodore D., Peerasit Kamnuansilpa, and Paul Lightfoot. 1990. "Urban Ties of Rural Thais". *International Migration Review* 24, no. 3: 534–62.

General Agreement on Tariffs and Trade (GATT). 1991. *Trade Policy Review: Thailand* (Geneva: GATT).

Ghose, Ajit K. 1993. "Global Changes, Agriculture and Economic Growth in the 1980s: A Study of Four Asian Countries". In *Economic Crisis and Third World Agriculture*, ed. Ajit Singh and Mamid Tabatabai (Cambridge: Cambridge University Press).

Girling, John. 1986. "Is Small-holder Cultivation Viable? A Question of Political Economy with Reference to Thailand". *Pacific Affairs* 59, no. 2: 189–213.

Goldin, Ian and L. Alan Winters. 1992. *Open Economies: Structural Adjustment and Agriculture* (Cambridge: Cambridge University Press).

Goldstein, S. and A. Goldstein. 1986. *Migration in Thailand: A Twenty-five Year Review*. Papers of the East-West Population Institute, no. 53, Honolulu: East-West Center.

Grabowski, Richard. 1994a. "The Successful Developmental State: Where Does it Come From?" *World Development* 22: 413–22.

————. 1994b. "Import Substitution, Export Promotion, and the State in Economic Development". *Journal of Developing Areas* 28: 535–54.

Greenaway, David and Oliver Morrissey. 1993. "Structural Adjustment and Liberalisation in Developing Countries: What Lessons Have We Learned?" *Kyklos* 46: 241–61.

Gregory, Paul R. 1994. *Before Command: An Economic History of Russia from Emancipation to the First Five-Year Plan* (Princeton: Princeton University Press).

Griffin, Keith. 1989. *Alternative Strategies for Economic Development* (London: Macmillan).

Grindle, Merilee and John W. Thomas. 1991. *Public Choices and Policy Change: The Political Economy of Reform in Developing Countries* (Baltimore: Johns Hopkins University Press).

Gunnarsson, Christer. 1985. "Agricultural Demand-Led or Export-Led Growth in East and Southeast Asia?" In *Rural Transformation in Southeast Asia*, ed. C. Gunnarsson, M.C. Hoadley, and Peter Wad (Lund: NASEAS).

————. 1991. "Dirigisme or Undistorted Free-Trade Regimes?: An Historical and Institutional Interpretation of the Taiwanese Success". Paper presented at the Arne Ryde Conference on International Trade and Economic Development. Elsinore, Denmark, June.

————. 1993. "Mercantilism Old and New: A Transaction Cost Theory of Developmental States in Europe and East Asia". Paper presented at the Conference on Public Choice Theories and Third World Experiences, London School of Economics and Political Science, 17–19 September.

Gunnarsson, Christer and Mats Lundahl. 1994. "The Good, the Bad and the Wobbly: State Forms and Third World Economic Performance". Paper presented at International Colloquium on New Directions in Development Economics, held by SAREC at Hässelby Slott, Stockholm, Sweden, March.

Haggard, Stephen. 1990. *Pathways from the Periphery: The Politics of Growth in the Newly Industrializing Countries* (Ithaca: Cornell University Press).

————. 1994. "Politics and Institutions in the World Bank's Asia". In *Miracle or Design? Lessons From the East Asian Experience*, ed. Albert Fishlow *et al.* (Washington, D.C.: Overseas Development Council), pp. 81–110.

Haggard, Stephen and Moon Chung-In. 1983. "The South Korean State on the International Economy". In *The Anatomies of Independence*, ed. John G. Ruggie (New York: Columbia University Press).

Haggard, Stephen and Steven B. Webb. 1993. "What Do We Know About The Political Economy of Economic Policy Reform". *The World Bank Research Observer* 8, no. 2: 143–68.

Harper, Lawrence A. 1942. "Mercantilism and the American Revolution". *Canadian Historical Review* 23, no. 1: 1–15.

Hayami, Yujiro and Keijiro Otsuka. 1993. *The Economics of Contract Choice: An Agrarian Perspective* (Oxford: Clarendon Press).

Hayami, Yujiro and Masao Kikuchi. 1982. *Asian Village Economy at the Crossroads: An Economic Approach to Institutional Change* (Baltimore: Johns Hopkins University Press).

Heaton, Robert. 1937. "Heckscher on Mercantilism". *Journal of Political Economy* 45: 370–93.

Heckscher, Eli. 1933. "Mercantilism". In the *Encyclopedia of the Social Science* (New York: Macmillan).

———. 1935. *Mercantilism* (London: Macmillan).

Helm, Dieter, ed. 1989. *The Economic Borders of the State* (Oxford: Oxford University Press).

Hettne, Björn. 1993. "Neo-Mercantilism: What's in a Word?" In *New Institutional Economics and Development Theory*, ed. John Martinussen. Occasional Papers, Roskilde University.

Hirsch, Philip. 1987. "Deforestation and Development in Thailand". *Singapore Journal of Tropical Geography* 8, no. 2: 4–10.

Hirschman, Albert O. 1958. *The Strategy of Economic Development* (New Haven: Yale University Press).

———. 1970. *Exit, Voice and Loyalty* (Cambridge, Mass.: Harvard University Press).

———. 1981. "The Rise and Decline of Development Economics". In Albert Hirschman, *Essays in Trespassing: Economics to Politics and Beyond* (Cambridge: Cambridge University Press).

Hughes, Alan and Ajit Singh. 1991. "The World Economy Slowdown and the Asian and Latin American Economies: A Comparative Analysis of Economic Structure, Policy, and Performance". In *Economic Liberalization: No Panacea: The Experiences of Latin America and Asia*, ed. Tariq Banuri (Oxford: Clarendon Press), pp. 57–99.

Hughes, Helen, ed. 1988. *Achieving Industrialization in East Asia* (Cambridge: Cambridge University Press).

Hutaserani, Sukanya and James Roumasset. 1991. "Institutional Change and the Democraphic Transition in Rural Thailand". *Economic Development and Cultural Change* 39, no. 5: 75–100.

Hutaserani, Sukanya and Somchai Jitsuchon. 1988. "Thailand's Income Distribution and Poverty Profile and Their Current Situation". Paper presented at TDRI Year End Conference, Pattaya, 17–18 December.

Ichikawa, Nobuko, Michael A. Cusumano, and Karen R. Polenske. 1991. "Japanese Investment and Influence in Thai Development". *Technology in Society* 13: 447–69.

Ingram, James C. 1971. *Economic Change in Thailand, 1980–1970* (Stanford: Stanford University Press).

Irfan ul Haque. 2007. *Rethinking Industrial Policy*. UNCTAD Discussion papers, no. 183, April.

Islam, Iyanatul. 1992. "Political Economy and East Asian Economic Development". *Asian-Pacific Economic Literature* 6, no. 2: 69–101.

James, William, Seiji Naya, and Gerald M. Meier. 1989. *Asian Development: Economic Success and Policy Lessons* (Madison: University of Wisconsin Press).

Jansen, Karel. 1991 "Thailand: The Next NIC?" *Journal of Contemporary Asia* 21: 13–31.

————. 2004 "Thailand: The Making of a Miracle?" *Development and Change* 32: 343–70.

Jenkins, Rhys. 1991. "The Political Economy of Industrialization: A Comparison of Latin America and East Asian NICs". *Development and Change* 22: 197–231.

Jitsuchon, Somchai. 2002. "Thailand's Economic Growth: A Fifty-Years Perspective (1950–2000)". Mimeograph, Thailand Development Research Institute.

Johnson, Chalmers. 1982. *MITI and the Japanese Miracle: The Growth of Industrial Policy, 1925–1975* (Stanford: Stanford University Press).

Johnson, D. Gale. 1991. *World Agriculture in Disarray* (London: Macmillan).

Jomo, K.S. 2003. "Reforming East Asia for Sustainable Development". *Asian Business and Management* 2: 7–38.

Jörberg, Lennart. 1965. "Structural Change and Economic Growth: Sweden in the 19th Century". *Economy and History* 8: 3–46.

————. 1972. "Some Notes on Education in Sweden in the 19th century". *Annales Cisalpines d'Historie Sociale* 2.

————. 1991. "The Diffusion of Technology and Industrial Change in Sweden during the 19th Century". In *Technology Transfer and Scandinavian Economic Growth*, ed. Kristina Bruland (New York: Berg), pp. 185–99.

Judges, A.V. 1939. "A Mercantile State". *Transactions of the Royal Historical Society* 21.

Kamnuansilpa, Peerasit, Aphichat Chamratrithirong, and John Knodel. 1982. "Thailand's Reproductive Revolution: An Update". *International Family Planning Perspectives* 8, no. 2: 51–66.

————. 1988. *Contraceptive Use and Fertility in Thailand: Results from the 1984 Contraceptive Prevalence Survey*. National Family Planning Program, Ministry of Public Health.

Killick, Tony. 1993. "Markets and Governments in Agricultural and Industrial Adjustment". In *The Adaptive Economy: Adjustment Policies in Small Low-Income Countries*, ed. Tony Killick (London: Overseas Development Institute), pp. 177–249.

————. 1994. "East Asian Miracles and Development Ideology". *Development Policy Review* 12: 69–79.

Kim, Hyung Kook. 1994. "Between State and Market: Development Dynamics in East Asian Capitalism". *Asian Perspective* 18, no. 1: 57–88.

Kimenyi, Mwangi and John M. Mbaku. 1993. "Rent-Seeking and Institutional Stability in Developing Countries". *Public Choice* 77: 383–405.

Klausner, William J. 1989. "Thai Society's Legal Barriers". *Solidarity* 121: 57–64.

Knodel, John E. 1977. "Family Limitation and the Fertility Transition: Evidence from the Age Patterns of Fertility in Europe and Asia". *Population Studies* 31, no. 2: 219–49.

Knodel, John, Napaporn Havanon, and Anthony Pramualratana. 1984. "Fertility Transition in Thailand: A Qualitative Analysis". *Population and Development Review* 10, no. 2: 297–328.

Kohli, Atul. 1994. "Where Do High Growth Political Economies Come From? The Japanese Lineage of Korea's 'Developmental State". *World Development* 22, no. 9: 1269–93.

Krongkaew, Medhi. 1993. "Poverty and Income Distribution". In *The Thai Economy in Transition*, ed. Peter Warr (Cambridge: Cambridge University Press).

Krueger, Anne O. 1974. "The Political Economy of the Rent-Seeking Society". *American Economic Review* 64, no. 3: 291–303.

――――. 1990a. "Government Failures in Development". *Journal of Economic Perspectives* 4: 9–23.

――――. 1990b. "Economists' Changing Perceptions of Government". *Welwirtschaftliches Archiv*, Band 126, Heft 3, pp. 417–31.

――――. 1993a. "Some Policy Perspectives". In *The Bias Against Agriculture: Trade and Macroeconomic Policies in Developing Countries*, ed. Romeo M. Bautista and Alberto Valdes (San Francisco: ICS).

――――. 1993b. *Political Economy of Policy Reform in Developing Countries* (Cambridge, Mass.: The MIT Press).

Lal, Deepak. 1983. *The Poverty of 'Development Economics'* (London: Institute of Economic Affairs).

Lall, Sanjaya. 1993a. "Policies for Building Technological Capabilities: Lessons from Asian Experience". *Asian Development Review* 11, no. 2: 72–103.

――――. 1993b. "Technological Capabilities and Industrialization". *World Development* 20, no. 2: 165–86.

――――. 1993c. "Understanding Technology Development". *Development and Change* 24: 719–53.

――――. 1994. "Industrial Policy: The Role of Government in Promoting Industrial and Technological Development". *UNCTAD Review*, pp. 65–89.

Lam, Danny and Cal Clark. 1994. "Beyond the Developmental State: The Cultural Roots of 'Guerrilla Capitalism' in Taiwan". *Governnance* 7, no. 4: 412–30.

Landes, David S. 1969. *The Unbound Prometheus, Technological Change and Industrial Development in Western Europe from 1750 to the Present* (Cambridge: Cambridge University Press).

Laothamatas, Anek. 1988. "Business and Politics in Thailand: New Patterns of Influence". *Asian Survey* 8: 451–70.

――――. 1992. *Business Associations and the New Political Economy of Thailand: From Bureaucratic Polity to Liberal Corporatism* (Boulder: Westview).

Lauridsen, Laurids S. 1991. "From Newly Exporting Countries (NECs) to Newly Industrializing Countries (NICs): The Developmental Role of the State in Taiwan and Thailand". In *Asian Societies in Comparative Perspective, Nordic Proceedings in Asian Studies*, no.2, NIAS/NASEAS.

Lee, Keun. 1993. *New East Asian Economic Development: Interacting Capitalism and Socialism* (New York: M.E. Sharpe).

Leftwich, Adrian. 1994. "Governance, the State and the Politics of Development". *Development and Change* 25, no. 2: 363–86.

————. 1995. "Bringing Politics Back In: Towards a Model of the Developmental State". *Journal of Development Studies* 31, no. 3: 400–27.

Lewis, Arthur W. 1954. "Economic Development with Unlimited Supplies of Labour". *Manchester School of Economics and Social Studies* 22: 139–91.

Little, I.M.D., T. Scitovsky, and M.F.G. Scott. 1970. *Industry and Trade in Some Developing Countries* (London: Oxford University Press).

Lucas, R.E. Jr. 1988. "On the Mechanics of Development". *Journal of Monetary Economics* 22: 3–42.

Mackie, J.A.C. 1988. "Economic Growth in the ASEAN Region: The Political Underpinnings". In *Trade and Development Achieving Industrialization in East Asia*, ed. Helen Hughes (Cambridge: Cambridge University Press).

Magee, Stephen P. 1984. "Endogenous Tariff Policy: A Survey". In *Neoclassical Political Economy*, ed. David C. Colander (Cambridge, Mass.: Ballinger Press), pp. 41–54.

Magnusson, Lars. 1995. *Mercantilism: The Shaping of An Economic Language* (London: Routledge).

Manarungsan, Sompop. 1978. "The History of Fertilizer Policies in Thailand: An Economic Study, 1969–1975". MA Thesis, Faculty of Economics, Thammasat University.

————. 1989. *Economic Development of Thailand, 1850–1950: Response to the Change of the World Economy* (Bangkok: Institute of Asian Studies, Chulalongkorn University).

Marzouk, G.A. 1972. *Economic Development and Policies: Case Study of Thailand* (Rotterdam: Rotterdam University Press).

McGuire, James W. 1994. "Development Policy and Its Determinants in East Asia and Latin America". *Journal of Public Policy* 14, no. 2: 205–42.

McVey, Ruth, ed. 1992a. *Southeast Asian Capitalists* (Ithaca: Cornell University Press).

————. 1992b. "The Materialization of the Southeast Asian Entrepreneur". In *Southeast Asian Capitalists*, ed. Ruth McVey (Ithaca: Cornell University Press).

Meesook, Oey Astra, Pranee Tinakorn, and Chayan Vaddhanaphuti. 1988. *The Political Economy of Thailand's Development: Poverty, Equity and Growth, 1850–1985* (Washington, D.C.: World Bank).

Meier, Gerald M. 1991. "Policy Lessons and Policy Formation". In *Politics and Policy Making in Developing Countries: Perspectives on the New Political Economy*, ed. G.M. Meier (San Francisco: ICS Press).

Michaely, Michael, Demitris Papageorgiou, and Armeane M. Choksi. 1991. *Lesson of Experience in the Developing World* 7 (Oxford: Oxford University Press).

Milner, Chris. 1990. "The Role of Import Liberalisation in Export Promotion". In *Export Promotion Strategies: Theory and Evidence from Developing Countries*, ed. C. Milner (New York: Harvester Press).

Minchinton, Walter E. 1969. *Mercantilism: System or Expediency?* (Lexington, Mass.: D.C. Health and Company).

Mohammad, Sharif and John Whalley. 1984. "Rent-Seeking in India: Its Cost and Policy Significance". *Kyklos* 37: 387–413.

Moon, C.I. and R. Prasad. 1994. "Beyond the Developmental State: Networks, Politics and Institutions". *Governance* 7: 360–86.

Mueller, Dennis. 1989. *Public Choice II: A Revised Edition of Public Choice* (Cambridge: Cambridge University Press).

Mun, Thomas. 1928. *England's Treasure by Foreign Trade*. Reprint of the first edition of 1664 (Oxford: Oxford University Press).

Muscat, Robert. 1993. *The Fifth Tiger: A Study of Thai Development Policy* (New York: M. E. Sharpe).

Myhrman, Johan. 1989. "The New Institutional Economics and the Process of Economic Development". *Journal of Institutional and Theoretical Economics* 145: 38–59.

Myrdal, Gunnar. 1957. *Economic Theory and Underdeveloped Regions* (New York: Harper Torchbooks).

_____. 1968. *Asian Drama* (New York: Twentieth Century Fund).

NESDB (National Economic and Social Development Board). 2000. "Poverty and Income Distribution in 1999". In *Indicators of Well-Being and Policy Analysis Newsletter* 4, no. 1.

Noland, Marcus. 1990. *Pacific Basin Developing Countries: Prospects for the Future* (Washington, D.C.: Institute for International Economics).

North, Douglass C. 1990. *Institutions, Institutional Change and Economic Performance* (Cambridge: Cambridge University Press).

_____. 1993. "The New Institutional Economics and Development". Paper presented at the Conference on Public Choice and Development: The New Institutional Economics and Third World Development, held by London School of Economics, September.

North, Douglass C. and Robert P. Thomas. 1973. *The Rise of the Western World: A New Economic History* (Cambridge: Cambridge University Press).

Nurkse, Ragnar. 1967. *Problems of Capital Formation in Underdeveloped Countries and Patterns of Trade and Development* (Oxford: Oxford University Press).

O' Brien, P.K., ed. 1994. *The Industrial Revolution in Europe I* (Oxford: Blackwell).

Ockey, James. 1996. "Thai Society and Patterns of Political Leadership". *Asian Survey* 36: 345–60.

OECF. 1991. "Macroeconomic Survey of Thailand". OECF Country Economic Papers, no. 7, Tokyo, Japan.

Ohlin, Goran. 1991. "The Population Concern". Paper presented at *Holger Crafoords Ekonomidagar* at Lund University, Sweden (October).

Olson, Mancur. 1965. *The Logic of Collective Action* (Cambridge, Mass.: Harvard University Press).

Oshima, Harry T. 1987. *Economic Growth in Monsoon Asia: A Comparative Survey* (Tokyo: University of Tokyo Press).

————. 1993. *Strategic Processes in Monsoon Asia's Economic Development* (Baltimore: Johns Hopkins University Press).

Panayotou, Theodore and Chartchai Parasuk. 1990. "Land and Forest: Projecting Demand and Managing Encroachment". *Thailand Development Research Institute Year-End Conference*, Research Report no. 1, 8–9 December, Pattaya, Thailand.

Panayotou, Theodore and Somthawin Sungsuwan. 1989. "An Econometric Study of the Causes of Tropical Deforestation: the Case of Northeast Thailand". Harvard Institute for International Development, Development Discussion Paper, no. 284, Harvard University (March).

Papanek, Gustav F. 1987. "Capitalist Development and Income Distribution". In *Modern Capitalism, Vol. II: Capitalism and Equity in the Third World*, ed. Peter L. Berger (Lanham: Hamilton Press), pp. 248–99.

Parnwell, Michael and Jonathan Rigg. 1993. "The People of Isan: Missing Out on the Economic Boom?" In *Ethnodevelopment: Concepts and Case Studies*, ed. Dennis Dwyer and David Drakakis-Smith (London: Longman).

Patamasiriwat, Direk. 1993. "Tax Reform". Paper presented at the 16th Annual Symposium on Fiscal Revolution for Economic Policy Reform in Thailand, held by Faculty of Economics, Thammasat University, Bangkok (in Thai).

Pecorino, Paul. 1992. "Rent Seeking and Growth: The Case of Growth through Human Capital Accumulation". *Canadian Journal of Economics* 35, no. 4.

Pejaranonda, Chintana, *et al.* 1984. *Migration, 1980 Population and Housing Census* (Bangkok: National Statistical Office).

Pollard, Sidney. 1990. *Typology of Industrialization Processes in the Nineteenth Century* (Chur: Harwood Academic Publishers).

Pomfret, Richard. 1991. *International Trade: An Introduction to Theory and Policy* (Oxford: Basil Blackwell).

Prasith-rathsing, Suchart, ed. 1987. *Thailand's National Development: Policy Issues and Challenges* (Bangkok: Thailand University Research Association, CIDA).

Prothero, R. and M. Chapman. 1985. *Circulation in Third World Countries* (London: Routledge).

Ranis, Gustav. 1991. "The Political Economy of Development Policy Change". In *Politics and Policy Making in Developing Countries: Perspectives on the New Political Economy*, ed. Gerald M. Meier (San Francisco: ICS Press).

Ranis, Gustav and S.A. Mahmood. 1992. *The Political Economy of Development Policy Change* (Oxford: Basil Blackwell).

Resnick, Stephen. 1970. "The Decline of Rural Industry under Export Expansion: A Comparison among Burma, Philippines and Thailand, 1870–1938". *Journal of Economic History* 30: 51–73.

Richter, H.V. and C.T. Edwards. 1993. "Recent Economic Development in Thailand". In *Studies of Contemporary Thailand*, ed. R. Ho and E.C. Chapman (Canberra: Australian University Press).

Richupan, Somchai. 1990. "Tax Policy and Economic Development in Thailand". Paper presented at the Conference on Tax Policy and Economic Development among Pacific Asian Countries, Taipei (January).

Rigg, Jonathan. 1987. "Forces and Influences Behind the Development of Upland Cash Cropping in Northeast Thailand". *The Geographical Journal* 153: 370–82.

Riggs, Fred W. 1966. *Thailand: The Modernization of a Bureaucratic Polity* (Honolulu: East-West Center Press).

———. 1993. "Bureau Power in Southeast Asia". *Asian Journal of Political Science* 1: 3–28.

Robinson, David, Yangho Byeon, and Ranjit Teja 1991. *Thailand: Adjustment to Success Current Policy Issues*, Occasional Paper 85 (Washington, D.C.: IMF).

Rodrik, Dani. 1992a. "The Rush to Free Trade in the Developing World: Why So Late? Why Now? Will It Last?" National Bureau of Economic Research, Working Paper no. 3947 (January).

———. 1992b. "Conceptual Issues in the Design of Trade Policy for Industrialization". *World Development* 20, no. 3: 309–20.

———. 1992c. "Political Economy and Development Policy". *European Economic Review* 36: 329–36.

———. 1993. "Trade and Industrial Policy Reform in Developing Countries: A Review of Recent Theory and Evidence". National Bureau of Economic Research, Working Paper no. 4417 (August).

———. 1994. "King Kong Meets Godzilla: The World Bank and the East Asian Miracle". In *Miracle or Design? Lessons From the East Asian Experience*, ed. Albert Fishlow (Washington, D.C.: Overseas Development Council), pp. 13–53.

———. 1995. "Getting Intervention Right: How South Korea and Taiwan Grew Rich". *Economic Policy* 20: 55–97.

———. 2004. "Industrial Policy in the Twenty-first Century". Paper prepared for UNIDO, available at <www.ksg.harvard.edu/rodrik/>.

———. 2010. "The Return of Industrial Policy". *Project Syndicate*, 12 April, <http://www.project-syndicate.org/commentary/rodrik42/English>.

Roll, Eric. 1953. *A History of Economic Thought* (London: Faber).

Rosenberg, Nathan. 1976. *Perspectives on Technology* (Cambridge: Cambridge University Press).

Rosenberg, Nathan and L.E. Birdzell. 1986. *How the West Grew Rich* (New York: Basic Books).

Rosenbers, Hans. 1958. *Bureaucracy, Aristocracy and Autocracy: The Prussian Experience, 1660–1815* (Cambridge, Mass.: Harvard University Press).

Rosenstein-Rodan, Paul. 1943. "Problems of Industrialization of Eastern and South-Eastern Europe". *Economic Journal* 53: 202–11.

Rowley, Charles, K. and R.D. Tollison. 1986. "Rent-Seeking and Trade Protection". *Swiss Journal of International Relations* 41: 141–66.

Rowley, Charles, K., R.D. Tollison, and Gordon Tullock, ed. 1988. *The Political Economy of Rent-Seeking* (Boston: Kluwer Academic Publishers).

Samudavanija, Chai-anan. 1989. "Thailand: A Stable Semi-Democracy". In *Democracy in Developing Countries Vol. 3*, ed. Larry Diamond, Juan J. Ling, and Seymour Martin Lipset (Boulder: Lynne Rienner).

———. 1992. "Industrialisation and Democracy in Thailand". Paper presented at the Conference on the Making of A Fifth Tiger? Thailand's Industrialization and Its Consequences, December, Australian National University, 7–9 December.

Santikarn Kaosa-ard, Mingsarn. 1992. "Manufacturing Growth: A Blessing for All?" The 1992-TDRI Year End Conference on Thailand's Economic Structure: Towards Balanced Development, Synthesis Report, Vol. 1 (December).

Santikarn Kaosa-ard, Mingsarn and Adis Israngkura. 1988. "Industrial Policies of Thailand". In *Economic Development Policy in Thailand: A Historical Review*, ed. Warin Wonghanchao and Yukio Ikemoto (Tokyo: Institute of Developing Economies).

Sarel, M. 1997. "Growth and Productivity in Asian Countries". *IMF Working Papers* no. 97.

Sathirathai, Surakiart. 1987. *Laws and Regulations Concerning Natural Resources, Financial Institutions, and Export: Their Effects on Economic and Social Development* (Bangkok: Thailand Development Research Institute).

Schmidt, Johannes D. 1993 "Increasing Exports in a Decreasing World Market: The Role of Developmental States in ASEAN-4". Paper presented at the 10th Nordic Association for Southeast Asian Studies (NASEAS) Conference on How Free are the Southeast Asian Markets, Turku Åbo, Finland, 10–12 September.

Schmoller, Gustav. 1884, reprint 1967. *The Mercantile System and Its Historical Significance* (New York: Augustus M. Kelly).

Screpanti, Ernesto and Stefano Zamagni. 1993. *An Outline of the History of Economic Thought* (Oxford: Clarendon Press).

Senghaas, Dieter. 1982. *The European Experience: A Historical Critique of Development Theory* (Leamington Spa: Berg).

Setboonsarng, Suthad and Robert E. Svenson. 1991. "Technology, Infrastructure, Output Supply, and Factor Demand in Thai Agriculture". In *Research and*

Productivity in Asian Agriculture, ed. Robert E. Svenson and Carl E. Pray (Ithaca: Cornell University Press).

Shinohara, M. 1989. "High Yen, Overseas Direct Investment, and the Industrial Adjustments in Asia-Pacific Area". In *Trends of Economic Development in East Asia: Essays in Honour of Willy Kraus*, ed. Wolfgang Klenner (Berlin: Springer-Verlag).

Shleifer, Andrei and Robert W. Vishny. 1993. "Corruption". *Quarterly Journal of Economics* 108, no. 3: 599–617.

Siamwalla, Ammar. 1975. "A History of Rice Policies in Thailand". *Food Research Institute Studies* 19, no. 3: 233–49.

―――. 1986. "Rent Dissipation in Quota Allocations for Cassava in Thailand". Mimeographed, TDRI.

―――. 1989. "Land-Abundant Agricultural Growth and Some of Its Consequences: the Case of Thailand". TDRI, unpublished paper.

―――. 1991. "Why Do Voters Elect Corrupt Politicians? Towards a Theory of Representative Kleptocracy". TDRI, unpublished paper, version 2.0 (November).

―――. 1993. "Four Episodes of Economic Reform in Thailand". TDRI, unpublished paper, July.

Siamwalla, Ammar and Suthad Setboonsarng. 1987. *Agricultural Pricing Policies in Thailand, 1960–1985*. Report submitted to the World Bank (October).

―――. 1989. *Trade Exchange Rate, and Agricultural Pricing Policies in Thailand* (Washington, D.C.: World Bank).

―――. 1991. "Thailand". In *The Political Economy of Agricultural Policy: Asia*, ed. Anne O. Krueger, Maurice Schiff, and Alberto Valdes (Baltimore: Johns Hopkins University Press).

Silcock, T.H. 1970. *The Economic Development of Thai Agriculture* (Ithaca: Cornell University Press).

Singh, Ajit. 1992. "The Actual Crisis of Economic Development in the 1980s: An Alternative Policy Perspective for the Future". In *New Directions in Development Economics*, ed. A.K. Dutt and K.P. Jameson (Aldershot: Edward Elgar).

―――. 1994a. "Growing Independently of the World Economy: Asian Economic Development since 1980". *UNCTAD Review*, pp. 91–105.

―――. 1994b. "Openness and the Market Friendly Approach to Development: Learning the Right Lessons from Development Experience". *World Development* 22, no. 12: 1811–24.

―――. 2002. "Competition and Competition Policy in Emerging Markets: International and Developmental Dimensions". G-24 Discussion paper Series no.18. UNCTAD, Geneva, September.

Siriprachai, Somboon. 1985a. "A Preliminary Note of International Technology Transfer to Thailand". Thai Khadi Research Institute, Thammasat University, mimeo (in Thai).

———. 1985b. "Migrants from Rural to Bangkok Metropolitan: A Survey of Knowledge". Research report submitted to Thai Khadi Research Institute, Thammasat University, September (in Thai).

———. 1988. "VER and Thai Government Policy Implementation: A Special Case of Cassava Trade between the European Community and Thailand, 1982–1987". MA Thesis, Faculty of Economics, Thammasat University (in Thai).

———. 1990. "Thai Law and International Trade Sectors: A Case Study of Rice and Cassava Exports". Research Report submitted to Faculty of Economics, Thammasat University (in Thai)

———. 1993a. *Rent-Seeking Activities: A Survey of Recent Issues.* Lund Papers in Economic History, no. 28, Department of Economic History, Lund University, Sweden.

———. 1993b. "Can Southeast Asian States Emulate East Asian Developmental States?" *NONESA* (*Newsletter of the Nordic Association for Southeast Asian Studies*), no. 8: 9–16.

Skinner, G.W. 1957. *Chinese Society in Thailand: An Analytical History* (Ithaca: Cornell University Press).

Soon, Cho. 1994. "Government and Market in Economic Development". *Asian Development Review* 12, no. 2: 144–65.

Srinivasan, T.N. 1994. "Development Economics, Then and Now". Economic Center Paper no. 482, Yale University.

Stein, Howard. 1992. "Deindustrialization, Adjustment, the World Bank and the IMF in Africa". *World Development* 20, no. 1: 83–95.

———. 1994a. "The World Bank and the Application of Asian Industrial Policy to Africa: Theoretical Considerations". *Journal of International Development* 6: 287–305.

———. 1994b. "Theories of Institutions and Economic Reform in Africa". *World Development* 22, no. 2: 1833–50.

Stern, Nicholas. 1991. "Public Policy and the Economics of Development". *European Economic Review* 35: 241–71.

Stiglitz, Joseph E. 1987. "Some Theoretical Aspects of Development". *The World Bank Research Observer* 2: 43–60.

———. 1992. "Alternative Tactics and Strategies for Economic Development". In *New Directions in Development Economics*, ed. A.K. Dutt and K.P. Jameson (Aldershot: Edward Elgar).

Suphachalasai, Suphat. 1992. "Thailand's Growth in Textile and Clothing Exports". In *New Silk Roads: East Asia and World Textile Markets*, ed. Kym Anderson (Cambridge: Cambridge University Press).

Suphachalasai, Suphat and Direk Patamasiriwat. 1991. "Poverty and Government Policy in Thailand". *Working Paper, no. 91/12*, National Centre for Development Studies, Australian National University.

Sussangkarn, Chalongphob. 1987. "The Thai Labour Market: A Study of Seasona-lity and Segmentation". Paper Presented at the International Conference on Thai Studies, Australian National University, Canberra (July).

———. 1990. "Thailand". In *Human Resource Policy and Economic Development: Selected Country Studies* (Manila: Asian Development Bank).

———. 1992. "Towards Balanced Development: Sectoral, Spatial and Other Dimensions". In The 1992 TDRI Year-end Conference Thailand's Economic Structure: Towards Balanced Development?, 12–13 December.

Tamada, Yoshifumi. 1991. "Ittiphon and Amnat: An Informal Aspects of Thai Politics". *Southeast Asian Studies* 28: 455–66.

Tambunlertchai, Somsak. 1987. "Development of the Manufacturing Sector in Thailand". Paper Presented at The International Conference on Thai Studies, Australian National University, Canberra (December).

Tanzi, Vito and Parthasarathi Shome. 1992. "The Role of Taxation in the Develop-ment of East Asian Economies". In *The Political Economy of Tax Reform*, ed. Takatoshi Ito and Anne O. Krueger (Chicago: University of Chicago Press).

Taylor, Lance. 1993. "Stabilization, Adjustment, and Reform". In *The Rocky Road to Reform: Adjustment, Income Distribution, and Growth in the Developing World*, ed. Lance Taylor (Cambridge, Mass.: MIT Press), pp. 39–94.

Thailand Development Research Institute (TDRI). 1986. *Final Report: Land Policy Study* (Bangkok: TDRI).

Thanapornpun, Rangsun. 1980. "The Role of Farmers' Aid Fund". Research Report Series in Agricultural Pricing and Merketing, submitted to NESDB (in Thai).

———. 1985. "The Economics of Rice Premium: Limits of Knowledge". Report submitted to Thai Khadi Research Institute, Thammasat University, June (in Thai).

———. 1990. *The Process of Economic Policy Making in Thailand: Historical Analysis of Political Economy, 1932–1987* (Bangkok: Social Science Association) (in Thai).

Thomas, Vinod, *et al.* 1991. *Best Practices in Trade Policy Reform* (Oxford: Oxford University Press published for the World Bank).

Timmer, C. Peter. 1992. "Agriculture and Economic Development Revisited". *Agricultural Systems* 40: 22–58.

Timmer, C. Peter, ed. 1991. *Agriculture and the State: Growth, Employment and Poverty in Developing Countries* (Ithaca: Cornell University Press).

Tinakorn, Pranee. 1992. "Industrialization and Welfare: How Poverty and Income Distribution Are Affected". Paper presented at the Conference on the Making of a Fifth Tiger? Thailand's Industrialization and Its Consequences, Australian National University, December.

———. 2002. "Income Inequality over the Last Four Decades, 1961–2001". Paper Presented at the Faculty of Economics Conference on Five Decades under

National Social and Economic Development Plan, Thammasat University, 12 June (in Thai).

Tinakorn, Pranee, and Chalongphob Sussangkarn. 1996. *Productivity Growth in Thailand*. TDRI Research Monograph, no.15.

———. 1998. *Total Factor Productivity Growth in Thailand; 1980–1995* (Bangkok: Thailand Research Development Institute).

Tinbergen, Jan. 1958. *The Design of Development* (Baltimore: Johns Hopkins University Press).

Treerat, Nualnoi. 2004. "Controlling Corruption in Thailand: Transforming the Problems and Paradoxes". In *Challenging Corruption in Asia*, ed. Bhargava, Ninay and Bemil Bolongaita (Washington D.C.: The World Bank).

Tullock, Gordon. 1967. "The Welfare Costs of Tariffs, Monopolies and Theft". *Western Economic Journal* 5: 73–9.

Turton, Andrew. 1989. "Local Powers and Rural Differentation". In *Agrarian Transformations: Local Processes and the State in the Southeast Asia*, ed. Gillian Hart, Andrew Turton, and Benjamin White (Berkeley, CA: University of California Press).

UNIDO. 1992. *Thailand: Coping with the Strains of Success* (Oxford: Basil Blackwell).

Vestal, James E. 1993. *Planning for Change: Industrial Policy and Japanese Economic Development, 1945–1990* (Oxford: Clarendon Press).

Viner, Jacob. 1937. *Studies in the Theory of International Trade* (London: Harper and Brother).

———. 1948–49. "Power versus Plenty as Objectives of Foreign Policy in the Seventeenth and Eighteenth Centuries". *World Politics* 1: 10–20.

———. 1968. "Mercantilist Thought". In *International Encyclopedia of the Social Science* (New York: Macmillan).

Vogel, Ezra F. 1991. *The Four Little Dragons: The Spread of Industrialization in East Asia* (Cambridge, MA: Harvard University Press).

Wade, Robert. 1990. *Governing the Market: Economic Theory and the Role of Government in East Asian Industrialization* (Princeton: Princeton University Press).

———. 1993. "Taiwan and South Korea as Challenges to Economics and Politics and Political Science". *Comparative Politics* 25, no. 2: 147–67.

———. 1994. "Is The East Asian Miracle Right?" In *Miracle or Design? Lessons From the East Asian Experience*, ed. Albert Fishlow *et al.* (Washington, D.C.: Overseas Development Council), pp. 57–80.

Warr, P. and B. Nidhiprabha 1996. *Thailand's Macroeconomic Miracle* (Washington D.C.: World Bank).

Warr, Peter, ed. 1993. *The Thai Economy in Transition* (Cambridge: Cambridge University Press).

———. 2005. *Thailand: Beyond the Crisis* (London: Routledge).

Watanabe, Toshiro. 1992. *Asia: Its Growth and Agony* (Honolulu: East-West Center).

White, Gordon, ed. 1988 *Developmental States in East Asia* (London: Macmillan).

Wilson, Charles. 1959. "The Other Face of Mercantilism". *Transaction of the Royal Historical Society* 9: 81–101.

Woo, J.H. 1990. "Education and Economic Growth in Taiwan: A Case of Successful Planning". *World Development* 19: 1029–44.

World Bank. 1984. *World Development Report 1984* (New York: Oxford University Press).

_____. 1988. *Thailand: Country Economic Memorandum: Building on the Recent Success. A Policy Framework* (Washington, D.C.: World Bank).

_____. 1993. *The East Asian Economies: Economic Growth and Public Policy* (Oxford: Oxford University Press for the World Bank).

Yoshida, Mikimasa. 1990. "Foreign Direct Investment in Thailand". In *Thai Economy in the Changing Decade and Industrial Promotion Policy*, ed. Samart Chisakul and Mikimasa Yoshida (Tokyo: Institute of Developing Economies).

Yoshihara, Kunio. 1988. *The Rise of Ersatz Capitalism in South-East Asia* (Singapore: Oxford University Press).

_____. 1995. *The Nation and Economic Growth: The Philippines and Thailand* (Kuala Lumpur: Oxford University Press).

Young, Alwyn. 1995. "The Tyranny of Numbers: Confronting the Statistical Realities of the East Asian Growth Experience". *Quarterly Journal of Economics* 110, no. 3: 641–80.

Yuen, Ng Chee, Sueo Sudo, and Donald Crone. 1992. "The Strategic Dimension of the East Asian Development States". *ASEAN Economic Bulletin* 9, no. 2: 219–33.

INDEX

Abramovitz, Moses, 45, 133
Africa, 5, 102, 105, 107, 114–5, 117–8, 121, 128, 133
agricultural expansion, 8, 11, 14, 27, 39, 49, 62, 68
Akyuz, Yilmaz, 4
Amin, Samir, 111
Ammar Siamwalla, 22, 31, 39, 50, 77
Anand Panyarachun, 86
Argentina, 120
Arnold, Fred, 57
ASEAN Free Trade Area (AFTA), 19, 87

Balassa, Bela, 115, 118
Bangkok, 8, 19–20, 33, 40, 49, 53, 67, 89, 134, 137, 150
Bank of Thailand, 14, 16, 35, 78, 138–9, 145
Bardhan, Pranab, 58
Beitzel Report, 13
Bhagwati, Jagdish, 115, 118
Bhumibol Adulyadej, King (Rama IX), 134–5
Big Push, 2, 29, 33–4, 110, 112–3
Board of Investment (BOI), 13, 24, 31–3, 36, 50, 75–80, 82, 86–7, 146–8, 155
Bolivia, 133
Bowring Treaty, 11, 137
Brazil, 48, 120
Britain, 4, 11, 26, 71, 95, 98–9, 101, 110, 122, 142

Buchanan, J.M., 118, 125
Buddhism, 58

Cardoso, Fernando, 111
cassava, 18, 39, 47, 63, 83, 86, 91, 152
Chang, Ha-Joon, 4, 42
China, 30, 43, 138
Chinese, 12, 16, 53–5, 73, 75, 79, 138
Chulalongkorn, King (Rama V), 72, 134
Colbert, Jean-Baptiste, 97, 101–2
Cold War, 4, 43, 59, 123
Confucianism, 3, 46, 101, 110, 121–2, 127
Corden, Max, 115
corruption, 10, 12, 18, 20–1, 31, 44, 46, 48, 83, 90–1, 143, 151–2, 156
Cote d'Ivoire, 133
Cunningham, William, 93–5

De Soto, Hernando, 97
deforestation, 39, 62–4, 66–7, 148–9
democratic politics, 8, 18, 19, 49, 72, 88, 135–7
devaluation, 17, 35, 82, 109, 145
developmental state, 2–4, 6, 9, 41–3, 71, 73, 82, 89, 96, 99, 126, 128–31
Dilok Nabarath, Prince, 7

Dobb, Maurice, 98
Dos Santos, Theotonio, 111

East India Company, 98–9, 102
East Indies Company, 98
Eastern Seaboard, 33
education, 21, 45–6, 69, 90
Egypt, 30
Emmanuel, A., 111
employment, 40, 63, 86, 150
England, 93, 99

Falkus, Malcolm, 52
Feeny, David, 137
fertilizer, 33, 41, 68
Fifth Plan, 34, 56, 147
Findlay, Ronald, 121
foreign direct investment, 8, 36–7, 53, 74, 80
Fourth Plan, 16, 33, 80
France, 93, 97, 102, 134

General Agreement on Tariffs and Trade (GATT), 17, 22, 82
Germany, 3, 24, 112
Gerschenkron, Alexander, 72, 113
Gini coefficient, 48, 152–3
Green Revolution, 27, 68, 141
growth accounting, 37, 140
Gunder Frank, André, 111
Gunnarsson, Christer, 22, 70, 98, 105

Haggard, Stephen, 121
Hamilton, Alexander, 112
Heckscher, Eli, 92, 94–6, 98–100, 102
Hindu, 46, 107
Hirschman, Albert, 30, 110, 114
Holland, 93
Hong Kong, 35, 71, 105–6, 129, 147
Human Development Index, 154

income inequality, 1, 4, 6–7, 10, 18–9, 23–4, 40, 47–50, 65, 74, 85, 91, 114, 122, 152–5
India, 30, 56, 98–9, 102
Indonesia, 2, 72, 129–30
Industrial Promotion Act, 12, 33, 147
infant industry argument, 68, 78, 81, 87, 112
Ingram, J.C., 137–8, 143
institutional economics, 59, 120–2, 126, 132–3
insurgency, 8, 20, 89
International Monetary Fund (IMF), 11, 18–9, 23, 32, 34, 81, 106, 112–5, 145, 147, 151
Investment Promotion Law, 15, 79
Irfan ul Haque, 4
Islamic, 46, 107, 110, 127
Israel, 30
Italy, 93

Japan, 3–4, 23, 28, 36, 42–3, 96, 101, 105
Johnson, 41, 43–4, 101, 109, 124–5
Jomo Sundaram, 4

Keynesianism, 106, 108
Killick, Tony, 124
Kohli, Atul, 128
Korea, *see* South Korea
Krueger, Anne, 31, 115, 117–8, 125, 128
Kuznets, Simon, 40, 122

land reform, 4, 6–7, 18, 41, 44, 47–9, 71, 85, 100, 122–3, 152
Landes, David, 101
Laothamatas, Anek, 63, 88
Latin America, 5, 25, 30, 34, 48, 102, 105, 107, 111–2, 114–5, 117–23, 125–6, 128, 133, 139

Lauridsen, L., 2, 130
Lewis, Arthur, 24, 30, 109–10, 123–4
List, Friedrich, 93, 100, 112
Little, Ian, 115

Malaysia, 2, 129–30
Malynes, Gerald de, 96
Marshall Plan, 113
Marzouk, G.A., 78
Meiji period, 3–4, 43
mercantilism, 3, 92–104
Mexico, 48, 120
migration, 40, 54–6, 64–7, 69–70, 97,
    103, 132, 150
Misselden, Edward, 96
Mongkut, King (Rama IV), 11, 134
Mun, Thomas, 96, 98–9
Myrdal, Gunnar, 39, 109, 112

National Economic and Social
    Development Board (NESDB),
    15, 31–3, 79, 85, 138, 142, 146,
    152
North, Douglass C., 43, 65, 67, 132
Nurkse, Ragnar, 109, 112

O'Brien, P.K., 50
October 1973 student uprising, 16, 79
oil crises, 15, 25, 34, 80, 120

Pakistan, 30
Pareto, Vilfredo, 109
Phibun Songkhram, 12, 20, 89, 135
Philippines, 25, 29, 36, 131
Phuket, 85
Plaza Accord, 35, 147
pollution, 24, 37, 46, 149
population growth, 7, 38, 41, 50,
    53–8, 62–3, 69

poverty, 20, 47, 53, 85, 152
Prajadhipok, King (Rama VII), 134
Prebisch, Raul, 109, 111
Pridi Banomyong, 7
property rights, 39, 46, 66, 73
Protestant, 110, 128

Rama IV, *see* Mongkut
Rama V, *see* Chulalongkorn
rent seeking, 3–6, 31–2, 42–6, 82–8,
    91, 96, 102, 106, 117–8, 120–1,
    125, 131, 133, 152, 156
Ricardo, David, 42
rice premium, 14, 26, 38, 89, 141–2
Rodrik, Dani, 4, 125, 128, 130
Rosenberg, Nathan, 101
Rosenstein-Rodan, Paul, 109, 112
Rostow, Walt, 112

sakdina, 53, 66, 68, 72, 134, 137
Sarit Thanarat, 12–4, 42, 75, 136
Schmidt, Johannes D., 70, 128
Schmoller, Gustav, 93–5
Scitovsky, Tibor, 115
Scott, Maurice, 115
Seers, Dudley, 112
Senegal, 133
Shin Corp, 137
Singapore, 105–6, 129
Singer, Hans, 109
Sixth Plan, 34, 147
skilled labour, 23–4, 45, 68, 74, 81,
    84, 102, 127, 150–1
Smith, Adam, 92–5, 97, 102
South Korea, 2–4, 7, 24, 42–3, 89,
    95, 100, 116, 118, 121–3, 125–9,
    133
Soviet Union, 106, 109, 113, 133
Spain, 93, 95, 97
Stalin, Josef, 113–4
Stern, Nicholas, 115, 117

Stiglitz, Joseph, 4, 132
Structural Adjustment Loan, 18, 81, 84
Sunkel, O., 111
Sweden, 45, 93

Taiwan, 2–4, 7, 24, 36, 43–4, 72, 78,
    96, 100, 105–6, 116, 118, 121–9,
    147–8
tax structure, 18, 86–7
Temasek Holdings, 137
textiles, 18, 23, 27–8, 36, 47, 83, 151
Thai Rak Thai Party, 136–7, 155
Thailand Development Research
    Institute (TDRI), 25, 37, 45, 55,
    65–6, 69, 150
Thaksin Shinawatra, 9, 136–7, 143,
    155–6
Third Plan, 33
Tinbergen, Jan, 108, 116
total factor productivity (TFP), 38,
    139–40
Tullock, Gordon, 118, 125

USAID, 56

Viner, Jacob, 94–6, 102

Wade, Robert, 121
Washington Consensus, 5, 118, 156
Weber, Max, 127
White, Gordon, 121
Wilson, Charles, 94, 103
World Bank, 1, 11–2, 15, 18, 20,
    22–3, 28, 32, 34, 38, 44, 56, 58,
    69–70, 78, 81, 90, 100, 105–6,
    112–5, 127, 131, 145, 147
World Trade Organization (WTO),
    4–5

Yoshihara, 25, 29, 36, 130–1